D0991155

AUG 1 0 2010

ON THE TRAIL
OF THE D.C.
SNIPER

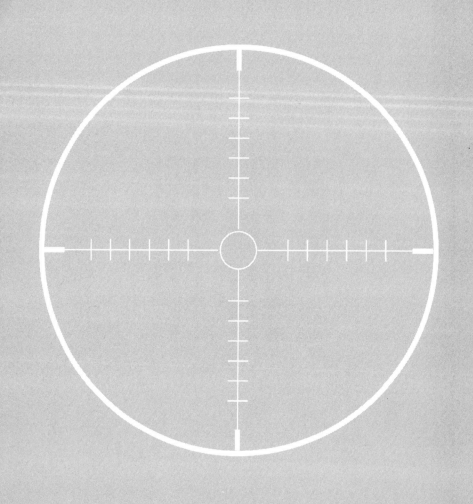

# ON THE TRAIL OF THE D.C. SNIPER

## *Fear and the Media*

JACK R. CENSER   *with the assistance of William Miller*

UNIVERSITY OF VIRGINIA PRESS — Charlottesville and London

University of Virginia Press
© 2010 by the Rector and Visitors of the University of Virginia
All rights reserved
Printed in the United States of America on acid-free paper

*First published 2010*

9 8 7 6 5 4 3 2 1


Library of Congress Cataloging-in-Publication Data
Censer, Jack Richard.
   On the trail of the D.C. Sniper : fear and the media / Jack R. Censer ; with the
assistance of William Miller.
        p.      cm.
   Includes bibliographical references and index.
   ISBN 978-0-8139-2894-4 (cloth: alk. paper) – ISBN 978-0-8139-2899-9
(e-book)
   1. Serial murder investigation–Washington Metropolitan Area. 2. Criminal
snipers–Washington Metropolitan Area. 3. Crime and the press–Washington
Metropolitan Area. I. Miller, William, 1951- II. Title.
   HV6534.W18C46 2010
   364.152′320975–dc22

                                                              2009035833

*To my wonderful children*
*Marjorie and Joel*

# Contents

# Acknowledgments

Following the reporting of the Washington D.C. area sniper, first as a resident and then as a scholar, has been as engrossing as any of my other scholarly projects. The event, which occurred in October 2002, rattled the region and set off reverberations far beyond it. This drew me to the story, but I wanted to tell it as scrupulously and fairly as possible. While I hope this work contributes to important scholarly debates in its framing and conclusion, the narrative forms the emotional core of the book.

My first thanks must go to my colleagues and students at George Mason University. Although I have heretofore published in the area of the French Revolution, I have taught the history of the press to history and communications students for many years. This book was written at the intersection of the two disciplines, and I hold an appointment in both. The opportunity to work with creative scholars, to teach demanding students, and to read the engaging communications scholarship about the press has enabled me to write this book. However, it is important to add that on the base level–both theoretically and for scholarly example–I am deeply indebted to historians.

Michael Schudson and Robert Snyder, the readers of my manuscript for the University of Virginia Press, responded with interesting and challenging questions that forced me to think harder about what I wanted the book to accomplish. Lenard Berlanstein, J. William Harris, and Peter Stearns also assisted me by reading the manuscript and providing useful feedback. Likewise, Frank Sesno, Peter Slevin, and Lenny Steinhorn gave very useful advice. I thank them and others too numerous to name for their invaluable assistance. I appreciate the kindness and generosity of the Shadow TV staff who helped me gain access to local and national television coverage as well.

Many respondents both in the schools and in the media gave freely of their time in the many interviews conducted for this study. In particular, I want to thank a few who not only spoke with me but also facilitated connections to others and/or who took repeated questions. They include Jeremy Redmon, Tom Kapsedelis, Tom Bettag, Gail Pennybacker, Sari Horwitz, Michael Ruane, Peter Slevin, and Mike McMearty. Jerry Weast and Brian Porter of the Montgomery County Public Schools gave generously of their time and provided access to the excellent records of the central administration during the sniper incident. No one spent more time with me than journalist Jamie Stockwell, then of the *Washington Post,* who assiduously guided me through her three weeks with the sniper case.

Writing a book while serving as an administrator provided a much different experience. The constraints on my time required me to rely upon others much more than before. Most important, Professor William Miller, the Director of Mason's Creative Writing Program, wrote drafts of the chronological narrative in the introduction and provided significant copyediting to a late draft of the work. I am deeply grateful for his conscientious, thoughtful, and capable assistance in all matters. I enjoyed the assistance of three research assistants: Ben Huggins, Tom Cogliano, and Lynn Price, all of whom were critical to this project. Additional thanks go to Lynn Price who authored the footnoted biographies of journalists and other actors in this book. Kathleen Curtis provided considerable assistance in the closing stages of work. Marjorie Censer did excellent work locating on-line many of the media sources I used here. Her organizing skills were invaluable. Katie Clare, my administrative assistant over the last several years, put much energy into the project–some during work and some outside of it. It would be hard to overestimate how much she helped, not only in the support of the project, but also as a friend and colleague.

Finally, my family forms the base of what I am able to do as a professional. Joel and Marjorie have lived through many of my projects, but they were older, more interested, and more informed for this one. It has been a joy to talk with them about the book and hear their ideas. Even more important than their direct assistance, however, are the love and pleasure that they bring into my life, which underpin productivity of every kind. My greatest debt goes to Jane Turner Censer, fellow historian, who has discussed the project with me and read drafts at every stage. Her good sense and emotional support have provided the platform for this and most everything else I try to do.

# Introduction

The murder of James D. Martin in the late afternoon of October 2, 2002, at a grocery story parking lot in Montgomery County, Maryland, and an errant shot through the window of a neighboring store minutes earlier, went largely unremarked in the media. However, the gunning down nearby of four more people the following morning soon attracted attention. By the time a fifth person was shot on October 3, near the border between Maryland and the District of Columbia, police resources had been focused—an effort that only increased during the next twenty-one days, before the capture of the culprits less than fifty miles northwest of the original shooting.

• • •

When the snipers assailed Washington, the events made a story that was told all over the globe, although with more intensity by the media outlets between Baltimore, Maryland, and Richmond, Virginia. A number of reasons suggest the importance of studying the press during this particular time, not the least of which is the understanding that can be gained through a carefully focused case study that allows a very detailed understanding of the press in action.

Most scholars of the recent press have opted for a more thematic approach that covers a wider territory than will this present study.[1] And even though library shelves already groan with historical case studies of the media, highly focused endeavors to comprehend the press's very recent history have been mainly limited to scholars who gained access

---

1. See, e.g., Stuart Taylor and K. C. Johnson, *Until Proven Innocent: Political Correctness and the Shameful Injustices of the Duke Lacrosse Rape Case* (New York: St. Martins, 2007).

for specific periods of time and then reported their observations.[2] Although this approach allows the scholar the ability to gather information, ask pointed questions, and avoid the dimming of memory with the passage of time, such studies depend on the events that occur within the selected time period, whether those events are coincidental or major. This study, however, examines a critical period when the press intensified its usual efforts, methodologies, patterns, and practices, and, at least in some ways, the effects of its work. Further, this exploration depicts the press after the events of September 11, 2001, at a time when the American public had grown enormously fearful. To be certain, there have been many other periods when American citizens have been fearful, whether such anxieties have been justified or not. But there can be little doubt that following the buoyant years at the end of the Cold War and accompanying the economic growth that characterized the last decade of the millennium, the attacks on the Pentagon in Washington and on New York's World Trade Center towers shocked most every American. Further, a spate of anthrax poisonings, focused in the Washington area several months before the sniper incident, had served to greatly re-arouse the jitters of area residents, if not a larger segment of the American populace. Thus, a study of the press in the Washington area during October 2002, can help us to understand America's anxieties in the early twenty-first century, and to examine the relationships between those heightened anxieties, public events, and the news media's coverage of those events.[3]

While the fearful politics of the particular period in question have resonance deep in the American past, as well as more recently,[4] the situation of Washington, D.C., in 2002, was less deeply rooted. At the time of the shootings, the capital region was very far away from its situation as a relatively small population and media center. In the half-century since World War II, Washington had come to rival New York as a base for news reporters. These circumstances meant that while a

2. For an extraordinary example that has influenced others, see Herbert J. Gans, *Deciding What's News* (New York: Pantheon, 1979). Any study of the recent press must also begin with Michael Schudson's *The Sociology of News* (New York: W. W. Norton, 2003). See also Phyllis Kaniss, *The Media and the Mayor's Race: The Failure of Urban Political Reporting* (Bloomington: Indiana University Press, 1995).

3. See Peter N. Stearns, *American Fear: The Causes and Consequences of High Anxiety* (New York: Roultedge, 2006).

4. See Richard Hofstadter, *The Paranoid Style in American Politics* (New York: Vintage Books, 1967). For the origins of the term terror, see Robert R. Palmer, *Twelve Who Ruled* (Princeton, N.J.: Princeton University Press, 1981).

relatively similar shooting in Ohio might go ignored by most national reporters and be carried by their news outlets in a national wrap-up, the story of the Washington snipers was carefully watched in the District and broadcast across the world.

Technologically, the period also proved quite distinct. Radio and television had challenged print media for many years, but the preceding decade had seen evolve three full-fledged, cable-based, twenty-four-hour news networks–CNN, FOX News, and MSNBC–as well as a business network, CNBC. For our purposes, this produced two very significant changes: the news cycle accelerated greatly as these cable networks showed their insatiable appetite for new information, and the press relied increasingly on images instead of words.

Together, these changes vastly altered the situation that had prevailed just a few years before, at the close of the twentieth century. The use of images put a premium on emotion that words would find hard to match. Secondly, cable news, to keep its viewers, had to make its fare constantly newsworthy. This encouraged more scoops, as people in the news business call the situation when one reporter or news outlet has a story before others do. But the situation also led to more hyping of the available news when what legitimately might be called a scoop was not available. Together, these tendencies raised the tempo and tenor of reporting. Yet even this situation would not remain stable in the period after 2002, as Internet-distributed news became independent of the established print and electronic news outlets. In 2002, blogging was still in its infancy and most news reported live on the Internet was simply an accelerated version of material already or soon to be in print or on television. The opinions of ordinary individuals were not regarded as news. Within two years, even what constituted "the media" had evolved to include an unfettered, vast element of Web-based self-expression, much of which was not at all vetted by editors and publishers. Even the outpouring by self-appointed purveyors of information and opinion was coming to be considered news. Though keyed much more to the word than to the image, this new world allowed a wider array of publications, both creative and histrionic. And even though back in October 2002, these changes still were somewhere in the future, it nevertheless was the case that the media world of that date was more emotional and competitive than it had been before, and the effect was to discourage restraint much more so than when print and television networks dominated news delivery.

• • •

While analysts from many disciplines and backgrounds have examined the press for its political bias (as detailed extensively in the bibliographical essay of this book), many media scholars in the academy have systematically broadened the discussion by mapping a broad network of assumptions that have shaped the press, and have developed the notion of "framing" stories. In this version of bias, "framing" is not deliberate but rather results from other tendencies, like reporters' growing professionalism, an event orientation that characterizes most news reports, a reliance by reporters on official sources for the bulk of their information, and much more.[5] Thus, media experts veer away from seeing political bias as a primary motivation for the workaday members of the press. Furthermore, while the experts admit that framing can yield a political point of view, or slant, they see it as a values inclination rather than the partisan content that so many in the public sphere despise—a perhaps subtle but nevertheless real difference, since one has to do with effects and the other with motivations. Thus, neither the motivations of the press nor its contents can generally be reduced to an expression of "politics" in the narrow, partisan sense of the term.

This study attempts to go beyond the usual scholarly efforts to comprehend journalistic framing by examining the coverage of an event that produced very little evidence of conscious politics as an influence on reporting. In fact, there was universal condemnation across the spectrum of these acts. A few commentators who wished to interpret these attacks as Muslim-inspired inserted a political coloration, but no one suggested that the media was sympathetic to these shootings. Thus, the efforts going into this study will deepen our understanding of the nonpolitical assumptions that operate to produce the reporting that exists. Nevertheless, despite this study's looking at the media in this apolitical atmosphere, a frame does emerge. Do the values here still produce, however unintended, a partisan edge? Even if not, the frame will contribute to our understanding of politics, as this coverage took place little more than a year after the cataclysmic political change ushered in by the bombings in New York and Washington. Inevitably, it mixes into political developments.

But why look for an apolitical set of assumptions at all? It seems worth pointing out a few of the characteristics that do grace the many memoirs produced by journalists. Such self-descriptions include many

5. See Schudson, *Sociology of News*, 33–63.

apolitical motivations. Journalists want to know what is happening and why, and what someone is going to do about it. Most reporters report that they are pumped up by having their curiosities satisfied. Further, they hope what they're curious about lands their words on page one or at the top of the broadcast.

Memoirs show that when chasing a big story, reporters fall back on a mix of the routine and the abnormal to do their work. The routine is just that—it's the routine, the series of things a reporter does when there isn't a story working and he or she is just nosing for news. Such things as visiting the police station one more time to leaf through the offense reports when there hasn't been anything there the previous six times he or she has looked. So in times like these, the reporter will go back and leaf through the offense reports to see if there is anything there that the police or authorities themselves might have missed, such as someone's seeing a car or a white van sitting outside a certain building, arousing suspicions, when later, someone else was shot at that same building and the police who checked out the car reported that it didn't seem like anything—but the reporter, piecing together some other fragmentary bit of information, hopes to find out that it was something after all.

Aside from being curious, journalists describe themselves as competitive, and that they're in the news business. Reporters want to be the first to report a story, to get the scoop on everyone else, because it puts them on the front page or at least the local section front, and that means they've done well—for today, anyway. Tomorrow is a different day. Their editors want them to get the scoop because they know they will have a better issue of the paper that day, which means they've done well that day, too. And the publishers of the paper want a better paper every day because it means they have done well—yes, they can sell more ads at good rates because circulation is good, but in the larger sense, the community's general interest in what's in the paper every day is running solid and strong, and that makes everyone at the paper feel he or she has done well.

Recollections of news gathering contest the dominant and opposite view of political bias and do encourage study of journalists' potential for apolitical reporting and attitudes. As the following chapters make clear, this study investigates the reporting and assumptions of the journalistic community in a case study, important and interesting in its own right, but also in a circumstance in which the apolitical views of this commu-

nity might come to the fore. Moreover, this study endeavors to go beyond political bias to see other interests at work; as will become quite
clear, even apolitical does not mean a lack of viewpoint.

In sum, this book seeks its niche and its value by providing a closely
defined case study of the recent past, a critical period because in part we
still live within its politics. Understanding the media and how they
worked during such a critical period can allow contemporaries to grasp
the present and perhaps improve the future at a time when the United
States is conflicted about its own direction. Ironically, choosing a non-
political topic in these politicized times gives even greater insights into
the fundamental assumptions of the press. Eliminating political motives leaves, I assert, a layer of uncontested frames of thinking that
underlie all reporting.

To evaluate the material in the media assumes that the media are
not simply a mirror of events. Despite the oft-stated and yet abstract
goal of journalism to record simply the facts, such is patently impossible
given that a news story must be extracted from and yet constructed with
the multitude of facts available. But this study delves deeper to inquire
about patterns of information that the press was able to extract from the
events.[6]

Here the issue becomes thorny. Customarily, what historians have
done is to examine the press coverage of a particular event, or series of
events, and compare it to a "true" narrative that has been constructed
with the benefit of hindsight. Thus, scholars may designate the press as
accurate or sensationalistic, or they may deliver some similar assessment. The problem here is that an objective account is impossible.
While it is always a problem to divine the most accurate account, this
case was particularly difficult because the press could ascertain little or
no accurate information. With no evidence about the shooters, the
press had little choice but to speculate or rely on others who speculated
about the possibilities. And the other aspect of the story, the public reaction, cannot provide a measurable baseline because historians'
main access to the wide public is through the press itself. Thus, it
becomes very difficult to characterize reporting using the traditional

6. Determining the meanings of the content of the media, grouped or individually, requires attention and assessment. However, the media itself provides cues:
placement of the story, headlines and banners, labeling or placement of clear editorials, among many others. In trying to comprehend the messages communicated,
I included these indicators in my general understanding of the story and its importance in shaping the ideas that emanated.

approach, even if that approach might be meaningful in other circumstances. To avoid the role of a critic operating from his own assumptions, I turned to the collective response of another social organization, the elementary and secondary schools, and compared their views with those that emerged in the press. In this way, a comparison to a contemporary group whose knowledge roughly equaled that shown in the press, allows some evaluation of the media.

As we shall see, the main variable in the press coverage was the degree of fear portrayed—from pandemonium to indifference. Few occupied the latter ground, while there were varying degrees of the former. Although a rich literature exists in many fields on the subject of fear, historians and students of communication have generally approached it in a pragmatic manner, even eschewing the rather impressionistic categories like those employed here.[7] Following the sources—that is, the media—proves difficult to do otherwise. Sorting the evidence into theoretical descriptions of psychological prototypes proved rather difficult, so I have developed working definitions of two intermediate groups of reactions that I have used throughout this volume.[8] Less complacent than those articles that were indifferent to danger or found the odds of catastrophe very low were those that evinced the view that while perils were present, with precautions, life could continue much as

7. Two of the best studies do not define any states of fear, but rather use the term "fear" in various circumstances as needed (see Joel Best, *Random Violence: How We Talk about New Crimes and New Victims* [Berkeley: University of California Press, 1999]; and Stearns, *American Fear*). This lacuna may result from the fact that such scholars are more interested in the context that produces fear than in the emotion itself.

8. Certainly, psychologists have spent a lot of time discussing fear, but their focus generally is on interiority of the experience and often concerns the rather specific psychological phenomena that produce dread. Even when they use more general categories, the focus on mental state means that these categories are not that helpful in assessing how the media project fear as they do through descriptions of individual, societal, and political responses. The categories developed here help add up different reported behaviors much more than the successive mental states that process them and constitute the main focus of psychology. For two compilations of studies of fear by psychologists, see Paul L. Gower, ed., *Psychology of Fear* (Hauppage, N.Y.: Nova Science Publishers, 2004); and Paul L. Gower, ed., *New Research on the Psychology of Fear* (New York: Nova Science Publishers, 2005). Other useful studies by psychologists include Isaac M. Marks, *Living with Fear: Understanding and Coping with Anxiety* (New York: McGraw-Hill, 1978); Shlomo Breznitz, *Cry Wolf: The Psychology of False Alarms* (Hillsdale, N.J.: Lawrence Erlbaum Associates, 1984); and Michael Lewis and Leonard A. Rosenblum, eds., *The Origins of Fear* (New York: Wiley, 1974).

usual. On the more anxious side were those articles that, while emphasizing fear, suggested the necessity of living life even as doom threatened. Still, these generated less anxiety than did accounts of those who
hunkered down at home or who took precautions so severe as to magnify
the threat far more than the ability to cope.

Evidently, these are loose, pragmatic descriptions. I have used
them to underpin my analysis, but I did not let these ideational devices
rigidly limit the sources. Clearly, at times the sources straddled categories, or even combined disparate ones. But these working definitions
allowed a somewhat systematic approach to the news.

• • •

Chapters 1 through 3 analyze the press and reveal the way that a high
level of fear dominated the press. Short of pandemonium, the press
most often combined coping and doom in its reporting. Because the
*Washington Post* put far more resources into covering this event than
did any other outlet, and thus led the others in coverage, the paper
deserves to be treated first and by itself, in chapter 1. The *Post* published hundreds of thousands of words in the twenty-three days of the
event and developed a richly textured view of the fear permeating the
region. At times, the *Post*'s articles conjured a commentary about social cohesion to resist the panic gripping the area, but more often than
not, the coverage treated the snipers as pure evil and as capable of
inflicting great harm. Overall, readers would have been little reassured.

Yet another medium that informed many people about this event
was the continuous television coverage to which local channels and
cable networks frequently resorted. Chapter 2 takes up a selection of
this coverage. This chapter breaks new ground because of the general
difficulty that scholars have found in obtaining access to this sort of
television. As far as I am aware, this is the first study of this kind of
treatment, often called "wall-to-wall" coverage. Most important for the
substantive argument developed here, this non-stop reporting had little reserve and, though not deliberately, greatly deepened the *Post*'s
emphasis on fear. Ominous in tone at every minute, these broadcasts
spread fear widely.

More news reporters than police were assigned to the sniper case.
Because the journalists from many, many outlets were already stationed
in Washington, original reporting turned up all over the world. Chapter
3 samples this vast landscape of news articles, ranging from the local
press that itself ranged from Baltimore to Richmond and included television, radio, and newspapers, to the national press, including news-

papers, evening television news, and cable talk shows. A sample of foreign newspapers was also consulted. Only a representative group of this vast outpouring could be read. Interestingly, these papers added little that differed from the coverage of the *Post,* except that they omitted any sense of community, leaving only fear–ranging from high to enormous anxiety–to dominate. Contrary to this general approach were some notable exceptions, which the chapter considers. Some periodicals even saw an internal battle over how to treat this event.

Chapter 4 contextualizes this reporting by providing a narrative of the journalistic response, from the first shooting in the area to the capture of the two suspects. Thanks to the cooperation of numerous journalists, this section of the book permits insights into the drama as well as the boredom felt by the reporters. Also, the book shows how representatives of the press extracted information from authorities. Furthermore, the false leads, the chase, and the fear felt by the journalists themselves all play a role in this chapter, as they played a role in coverage of the events at the time.

Chapter 5 takes us to how another important social organization– the schools–also had to deal with the snipers. Three school districts– Prince George's and Montgomery counties in Maryland, and Fairfax County in Virginia–provide the focus. These locales were selected because of their enormous size, collectively. They include over 500,000 students and employees, and they encircle the city of Washington. Each was the scene of at least one shooting, and the focus on the sniper began after five shootings in Montgomery County. In deciding whether to remain open, how to provide security, and whether to hold scheduled athletic contests, these county systems also produced, at least implicitly, their own depictions of the danger posed by the sniper. In this way, the schools provide a reference point to evaluate a wider range of perspectives on the sniper. Interestingly, in contrast to the press, they all generally agreed, in part because their leaders regularly communicated with each other, but also because they all concluded that the best place for students during these trying situations was in school. I maintain that the schools constructed an image of a less-threatening sniper than was constructed for the general public by news accounts.

Perhaps the most controversial part of this study is the decision to use the school districts as a point of comparison instead of simply evaluating the press coverage. The majority of people who lived through these events still strongly believe that fear was justified and completely understandable, given the circumstances and the timing.

Furthermore, seconding this view has been the subsequent testimony at the trials, particularly that of Malvo, who described plots for more outlandish crimes than those the snipers actually committed.[9] But the media did not know the information that would be disclosed at the trials. In fact, no one could reasonably assess the threat the snipers actually posed. Consequently, this study requires using some contemporaneous marker, rather than interposing my individual standards. Unfortunately, no efforts were taken at the time of the events to gauge scientifically the views of the population. Reliance on another measure is absolutely necessary, then, in order to evaluate press coverage along some sort of reasonable spectrum. Evidently, the schools and the press diverged. How they did and why they did are key for this book.

The conclusion pulls together all the materials in order to speculate about why the press covered the sniper event as it did. The testimony and actions of the reporters prove significant, as does the comparison with the schools. Finally, a discussion on the state of the press and the possibilities for its reform and improvement concludes this volume. Though this study emerges from the notion of "framing" largely to fill a gap in the study of political events, still other elements of the historical and communications literature can aid in our understanding of the press actions in October 2002. Although the historical study of fear still leaves many gaps, the few studies available can cast light on this incident. And from this discussion can emerge comments on broader issues, including the power of the press as well as the politics of the Bush and subsequent administrations.

9. See the *Washington Post* editions for May 22 and May 26, 2006.

# PROLOGUE

It was Wednesday, October 2, 2002, just after 6 p.m., and James D. Martin was on his way home from his job with the federal government. He worked as a program analyst at the National Oceanic and Atmospheric Administration headquarters in Silver Spring, Maryland, and lived in Wheaton, places located about ten miles apart in the closer-in suburbs of Washington, D.C. Five miles from home, Martin stopped at a Shoppers Food Warehouse in Glenmont to pick up a few things. His wife, Billie, and eleven-year-old son, Ben, waited for him at their house.[1]

Martin parked his 1990 Mazda pickup in a slot a few spaces from the store entrance—he waited for another vehicle to move first. The truck bore an American flag on its antenna, and it had a camper shell closing off its back. Martin himself was fifty-five, balding, and dressed in a suit and tie. He was a churchgoing man, and he worked with the youth group there. He was stopping to pick up items for his family's dinner that night, as well as some bargain-priced supplies for the church group. He had the list in his coat pocket. He had chosen this particular store for its prices; there were other stores he could have gone to.

Those who watched Martin make his way toward the store entrance would have seen only the bespectacled man and would not have known that Martin had served in the military during Vietnam and then worked his way through college. Would not have known that, having lived in

1. The following account is drawn primarily from Sari Horwitz and Michael E. Ruane, *Sniper: Inside the Hunt for the Killers Who Terrorized the Nation,* rev. ed. (New York: Random House, 2004). See also Angie Cannon, *23 Days of Terror: The Compelling True Story of the Hunt and Capture of the Beltway Snipers* (New York: Pocket Books, 2003); and Charles A. Moose and Charles Fleming, *Three Weeks in October: The Manhunt for the Serial Sniper* (New York: Dutton, 2003).

the Washington area for more than thirty years, he had earned his way into a nice suburban house with a rec room he decorated with Civil War memorabilia. Would not have known that he also was into genealogy and mentoring children in an inner-city neighborhood. Only later would these details about Martin's life become widely known, after they had been dug out and relayed by the news media.

As Martin walked toward the door of the grocery, a sound like a muffled rifle shot broke the air and a small-caliber bullet, only .223 inches in diameter, entered through Martin's back, severing his spinal cord and paralyzing him. The bullet went on to cut his aorta and pulmonary artery before tearing an exit wound in his chest that was more than four times larger than the original wound in his back. The sudden loss of blood pressure felled Martin to the concrete and within seconds rendered him unconscious.

The two men who randomly selected James Martin for death fired the shot from not more than about fifty yards away, yet they slipped from the scene entirely unnoticed. No one saw anyone running or acting suspicious, nor were there casings or other physical evidence left on the ground.

Initial news media coverage of the shooting talked about the single-shot, sniper-like nature of it. The next day, the coverage linked Martin's death to four more shootings that had occurred, starting at 7:41 a.m. on the day after his death. Two more men and two women had been killed, all within a 2½-mile radius.

The coverage began immediately to point out that Washington was a terror-conscious region that remained on high alert after the September 11 attacks only one year earlier. The news reports carried word of the massive combined force of law enforcement agencies that had joined in the search for the killer or killers, using both air and ground techniques. There would be word, too, that turned out to be mistaken, about a white box truck that was seen at the shootings. Over the course of events, the police would search aggressively for the white truck, stopping several that fit the general description. All the stops would be futile. They would lead to no clues.

The news coverage often called the shooter or shooters skilled marksmen, and reports said he or they had acted with no apparent motive. Words such as indiscriminate violence were invoked.

Within days, Montgomery County police chief Charles Moose was heading an investigative team that included about a hundred county police, plus fifty agents from the Bureau of Alcohol, Tobacco and

Firearms, and the FBI. So intensely was the public focused on the events that the investigative team received about four thousand calls in the first few days, and Moose said the calls had given them eight hundred credible leads that the team was sifting through. The police thought they were looking for–by type–a terrorist, a serial killer, or a thrill killer.

The police also noted that the shortest road distance between two of the shootings actually led by the building out of which they operated their command center. News reports said the police were stunned at the audacity of the killer or killers to drive right by the command center between two of the shootings. Then there was a shooting in Virginia, widening the search and the apparent confusion: a man who was the subject of a missing-person's report was said to be linked to the shootings, but the next day the police sent out another bulletin and said the missing person was not a suspect in the murders.

There were news stories that said parents were hugging their children a little tighter these days, sometimes keeping them out of school–attendance in Montgomery County was running between 85 and 90 percent, compared to the norm of 96 percent. Grief counselors were sent to schools where students had lost relatives to the shootings.

For twenty-three days, events and millions of news-report words about the events spooled out, until police closed in on a blue Chevy Caprice at a rest stop off the interstate in western Maryland and arrested two men who were asleep in the car–John Muhammad and Lee Boyd Malvo. Their arrests would end the shootings. Their stories would be pieced together, would become known, and to the extent possible, would be understood.

• • •

John Muhammad was born John A. Williams on December 31, 1960, in New Orleans, the son of a railroad porter who was often absent and a mother who developed breast cancer and died when John was three. He then was raised by aunts living near Baton Rouge. With a girlfriend, he produced a son out of wedlock. Later, in 1981, at age twenty-one, he married another woman, with whom he had a second son. Divorced in 1987, he then married his second wife, Mildred, or Millie, in 1988. Over the next seven years, while John served in the U.S. Army, he and Millie had three children. John's time in the military was fraught with challenges. Though accused of setting off a charge in a housing tent that could have killed his comrades, he never faced formal charges and was not prosecuted. After he left the Army, in 1994, the family settled in Tacoma, Washington. He and Millie tried to run a car repair business, but it faltered and Muhammad blamed Millie, who was the business manager. In 1999, Muhammad and Millie separated and she filed for divorce.

In March 2000, Muhammad concocted a story about taking his three children shopping, but instead he spirited them off to Antigua. For the next seventeen months he had unauthorized custody of them, living in a variety of arrangements in Antigua but also returning occasionally by himself to the United States, sometimes legally and sometimes not. He made money by either fixing cars or selling falsified documents and airline tickets to persons wanting to enter the United States.

One of the people that Muhammad helped enter the country was Una James, a Jamaican-born woman who was a single mother and who wanted badly to obtain the opportunity she hoped to find in America. She immigrated in the fall of 2000, leaving her son, Lee Boyd Malvo, in Antigua, with the promise that she would send for him after she had settled in Florida and set herself up. Instead, Malvo fell under the care of Muhammad. At the time, Malvo was fifteen. To Malvo, Muhammad was what he had never had–a father figure. A former military man who talked about being a rifle marksman, Muhammad became someone Malvo looked up to.

Muhammad had legally changed his name from Williams in April 2001, through the county district court in Tacoma during one of his trips back to the States. At the end of May 2001, Muhammad, Malvo, and Muhammad's three children left Antigua, flying to Florida, where Malvo was left with his mother and a new stepfather. Muhammad took his own children to Bellingham, Washington, where he put them into schools and tried to register the family to receive public assistance. At that point, authorities discovered him and the fact that he had the children without legal custody. A county detective took the children from their schools in August. After a court hearing in Tacoma, the children were reunited with their mother.

Upon regaining custody, Millie took the children to the place where she herself had moved–Clinton, Maryland, just southeast of Washington, D.C., not many miles from the site of the first attacks that Muhammad and Malvo would commit in the area.

Malvo left his mother in Florida in October 2001 and rode a bus across the country to join Muhammad in Bellingham. They stayed at a homeless mission. In December, Malvo's mother packed herself up and also took a bus to Bellingham to try to retrieve her son. Events went badly and sank into confusion. Malvo and his mother were put in the custody of the Immigration and Naturalization Service. In late January 2002, after a month in custody, they both were mistakenly released, and not long after, Malvo found his way back to Muhammad.

In February, Muhammad and Malvo together moved in with a friend of Muhammad. The friend, Earl Lee Dancy Jr., later quoted Muhammad as saying that the terrorist attacks of September 11, 2001, were what the country deserved. Dancy described Muhammad as an angry man who had lost custody of his three children and had almost lost Malvo, his young protégé and companion. After their arrests, Malvo also would explain what they had done by saying that Muhammad "hates this country." Speaking in May 2006, during Muhammad's trial for the Maryland killings, Malvo would also declare that Muhammad had made him "a monster." While Malvo initially told authorities after their arrests that *he* had committed all of the Washington-area shootings, he would recant those statements at Muhammad's trial and testify that Muhammad had pulled the trigger ten times and that he had shot only three times.

Although it was the shootings in the Washington area that catapulted the snipers to national attention, they had begun their rampage of violence much earlier, with shootings all over the country in a long arc that stretched from Washington state south through Arizona and to Georgia before it turned north to the nation's capital. Indeed, as we have seen, the precipitating events lay even further away, in Jamaica, where Una James's indifference to her son Lee had sent him in search of a strong father figure, which he found in John Muhammad. Later, in Bellingham, after Muhammad had turned Malvo's trust and dependency into a weapon of destruction, the two would set off on their killing spree.

• • •

On Saturday, October 5, 2002, a group of people who had planned an outdoor festival in Fairfax, Virginia, stood talking about why attendance was so much lower than expected. One organizer, a woman, questioned whether it could have been caused by the reports of a sniper in the area, over in Maryland, just across the Potomac River. Based on their conversation, it was clear that some members of the group were barely aware of the reports of a sniper. Others thought the reports must have made a difference. Consider, they said—an outdoor festival, advertised broadly in the region, bringing together people for all the world to see—or even shoot at; the reports must have made a difference. Yet, a

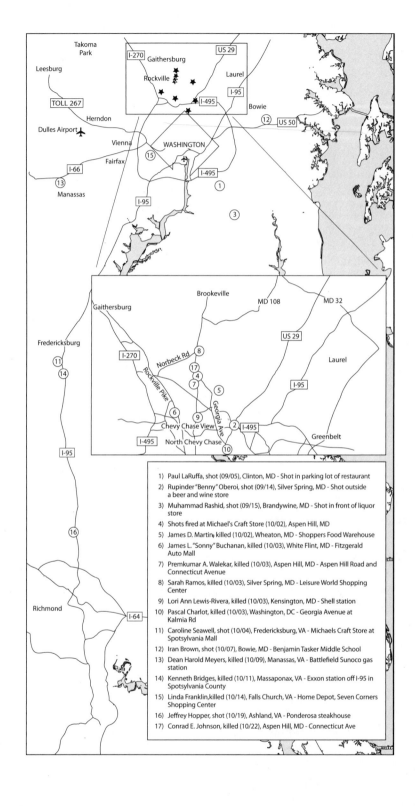

1) Paul LaRuffa, shot (09/05), Clinton, MD - Shot in parking lot of restaurant

2) Rupinder "Benny" Oberoi, shot (09/14), Silver Spring, MD - Shot outside a beer and wine store

3) Muhammad Rashid, shot (09/15), Brandywine, MD - Shot in front of liquor store

4) Shots fired at Michael's Craft Store (10/02), Aspen Hill, MD

5) James D. Martin, killed (10/02), Wheaton, MD - Shoppers Food Warehouse

6) James L. "Sonny" Buchanan, killed (10/03), White Flint, MD - Fitzgerald Auto Mall

7) Premkumar A. Walekar, killed (10/03), Aspen Hill, MD - Aspen Hill Road and Connecticut Avenue

8) Sarah Ramos, killed (10/03), Silver Spring, MD - Leisure World Shopping Center

9) Lori Ann Lewis-Rivera, killed (10/03), Kensington, MD - Shell station

10) Pascal Charlot, killed (10/03), Washington, DC - Georgia Avenue at Kalmia Rd

11) Caroline Seawell, shot (10/04), Fredericksburg, VA - Michaels Craft Store at Spotsylvania Mall

12) Iran Brown, shot (10/07), Bowie, MD - Benjamin Tasker Middle School

13) Dean Harold Meyers, killed (10/09), Manassas, VA - Battlefield Sunoco gas station

14) Kenneth Bridges, killed (10/11), Massaponax, VA - Exxon station off I-95 in Spotsylvania County

15) Linda Franklin, killed (10/14), Falls Church, VA - Home Depot, Seven Corners Shopping Center

16) Jeffrey Hopper, shot (10/19), Ashland, VA - Ponderosa steakhouse

17) Conrad E. Johnson, killed (10/22), Aspen Hill, MD - Connecticut Ave

core sampling of the group members, who had heard nothing about the sniper, remained unfazed.

Over the days and weeks to come, these kinds of discussions would be repeated many times over. For three weeks, between Wednesday, October 2, and Tuesday, October 22, ten people would be killed and three more wounded in random shootings throughout the wider Washington metro area.

News reports of the events suggest they were all "stealth" killings—without witnesses, the killers floating in and out, dispensing death and injury along their way. Yes, some reasoned, other communities had experienced attacks from stranglers or sexual predators; but these attacks seemed different because they were public, they were taking place over a wide part of the Washington metro area, and they had brought injury or death from a long distance by means of a well-placed rifle shot. Thus, in some minds, the shootings were the kinds of events that captured the imagination, and they gave rise to fears that shaped people's choices. After several of the shootings occurred at gas stations, for example, some station owners began to shield their stations by draping them with large tarps, a reaction that often was cited as evidence of the fear that had gripped the region. The existence of the tarps also seemed to justify the fear, becoming a physical manifestation of it.

Could the tarps have indicated something altogether different? Could they simply have represented the logical choice of business people to protect their businesses? Were gas station owners worried that their customers would fuel up elsewhere, at stations whose pumps seemed somehow more protected? Or, as another possibility, did merchants actually erect the tarps to expand their business, using them to indicate the high level of safety that existed at their stations in an effort to lure new customers to fuel up there instead of at their usual stations? The tarps, obviously, are not the most serious aspect of the events that took place in October 2002, and discussing the motives of business people during events such as these may seem cynical.

In fact, there seems little doubt that a high level of fear gripped many, if not most, area residents. To cite but a couple of examples, one construction executive, accustomed from his youth to walking on high steel girders, was sitting in his office when he heard the report of a shooting on the radio. Calculating the distance between the site of the shooting and his own office, the executive discerned a window of safety: if he went to his car just then, he could gas up without fear, and so he did. Likewise, for one well-known business woman whose resolute strength of character was also well known, filling up at the gas station also became a concern. After inserting the nozzle in the gas tank, she proceeded to spend the rest of her time at the station pressed close to the floor of her automobile.

When things seemed random, when the identities of the assailants were not known, there were only questions and huge amounts of uncertainty. People everywhere, but especially those in the capital region, who wondered daily how to react to the ongoing shootings, relied for vital information on the array of journalists who were covering events as they unfolded, when little was known but much was speculated.

•  •  •

Not long after he and Millie had separated, John Muhammad had bought a rifle that assembled and operated similarly to the M16 he had learned to use in the army. It was a Bushmaster XM15, not the actual weapon but the same brand of rifle he and Malvo would later use in the sniper attacks; short of money not long after he bought the first Bushmaster, he was forced to sell that one. The gun that Muhammad and Malvo would use in the sniper attacks was actually stolen from a Tacoma gun shop called Bull's Eye Shooter Supply. Gun shop personnel remembered they had added some extras to the gun, including a stand to stabilize it during shooting, and a holographic sight. The rifle was displayed on a countertop in the shop, propped on the bipod stand. The gun shop personnel did not connect the gun used in the attacks with the one they had had in inventory until after the fact. When they noticed that their gun was missing, they simply thought it had been sold to someone.[2]

Aside from its similarities to the M16, the Bushmaster perhaps was an odd choice for someone who wanted to be a sharpshooting sniper. It is not considered by gun experts to be great for hunting, since it is not heavy enough and fires a relatively small round. But guns of its size and caliber are popular, even within the military, because the rounds are lighter in weight and so are easier to carry, and the gun is relatively easy to learn to use and assemble/disassemble, and is accurate enough to be highly effective in stopping a target. With some practice, and with the ability to stabilize the gun and carefully select a target, a shooter could use the rifle with deadly effect.

2. In September 2004, eight of the sniper victims' families settled suits they had filed against Bushmaster and Bull's Eye Shooter Supply for $2.5 million. Under the terms that were made public at the time, Bushmaster was to pay the family members $550,000, and Bull's Eye Shooter Supply was to pay $2 million.

The way that Muhammad and Malvo used the weapon most often resulted in the death of the victim. The bullet would enter making a hole not much bigger around than a pencil. But oftentimes the bullet broke up or shattered as it traveled through the body, damaging the body's tissues as the fragments tore their way through. If enough of the bullet stayed together to reach the other side, the exit wound would be far larger than the tiny entry wound.

• • •

At the time of the first shooting, that of federal worker James Martin at the Shoppers Food Warehouse, the exit wound the bullet made in Martin's body was so large that for the first few minutes after efforts to save Martin were ended, the investigators miscalculated the direction of the shot, effectively searching for evidence on the wrong side of the parking lot. They quickly corrected the mistake, although they still found nothing. This was but one of many ironies that would plague the three-week-long episode. Less than an hour before Martin was felled, someone had fired a single shot through the window of a Michael's craft store a short distance away. No one was injured, but a man in a nearby car had looked around when he heard the muffled sound of a rifle shot, and he later said he saw a blue sedan driving away. He said two African American men were inside the car, and they were laughing.

Two hours after Martin was slain, a Montgomery County policeman was on stakeout in his patrol car not far from the grocery store parking lot. He had been detailed to watch for stolen cars, a routine assignment unrelated to the shooting, and he spotted a vehicle that caught his notice. An old blue Chevrolet Caprice with darkly tinted windows. He followed it, putting the license plate number into his computer. The inquiry returned nothing that would give the officer cause for a stop, so he let the car go.

Two hours later and four miles away, a security guard at a shopping mall saw the same vehicle. This time, the driver was outside the car. He told the security guard that he was traveling with his son and they were resting before moving on. The guard let them stay, even going so far as to warn the man to leave before the parking lot gates were locked. When the guard returned later, the men and the car were gone.

John Muhammad was the man with whom the guard spoke. The young man asleep in the car was Lee Boyd Malvo, still a teenager.

• • •

When police were able to assemble the chain of events, they would learn that the first person whom Muhammad and Malvo had killed was actually not in the Washington, D.C., region at all. The list of the snipers' victims, it turned out, stretched back to before they had come to the area, to February 2002, to the death of Keenya Cook in Tacoma, Washington. She was the niece of Isa Nichols, a former bookkeeper at the business that Muhammad and his wife had run. Nichols became a friend and supporter of Millie Muhammad after the business faltered and Muhammad and Millie broke up. On February 16, 2002, Keenya Cook was shot at her aunt's house in Tacoma when she went downstairs to answer a knock at the door. Malvo later would say that Muhammad used this shooting to test him—both his loyalty to Muhammad and his willingness to kill.

Muhammad's and Malvo's second victim was Jerry Ray Taylor, who was shot, killed, and robbed while on a golf course near Tucson, Arizona, in March 2002.

Then the pair had made their way to Washington. Their next three victims, all shot in Maryland in the period from early- to mid-September 2002, had not died. But all had lived not far from the Clinton, Maryland, townhouse where Millie Muhammad had moved with her children. The victims of those first three shootings in the D.C. area were Paul LaRuffa, a restaurant manager, gunned down as he closed up the business at the end of the day; Rupinder Oberoi, manager of a beer and wine store, shot as he was closing up his business; and Muhammad Rashid, a liquor store worker, also attacked as he was closing. All three survived, but LaRuffa lost a computer as well as money, which Muhammad had then used to help finance his and Malvo's spree.

After these three suburban Washington attacks, Muhammad and Malvo made a swing south, to Atlanta and then to Montgomery, Alabama. The victims, again, were all at liquor stores—Milton Woldemariam, killed at a store in Atlanta, and Claudine Parfer and Kellie Adams, the former killed and the latter wounded, at a store in Montgomery. Then Hong Im Ballenger was killed in the parking lot of a beauty shop supply business that she ran in Baton Rouge. From there, the two returned to Washington and settled in for the month of October, beginning the violence again by shooting out the window of the Michael's craft store in Aspen Hill and then killing James Martin at the Shoppers Food Warehouse in Wheaton, on October 2.

The snipers then roamed the Washington area and down into Virginia as far as Ashland, which is on Interstate 95 about half an hour's drive north of Richmond, before they were apprehended in late October. Those killed were all just going about the routine tasks of life:

James L. Buchanan, shot while mowing the lawn at an auto dealership in White Flint, Maryland; Premkumar Walekar, shot while pumping gas at a Mobil station in Aspen Hill, Maryland; Sarah Ramos, shot while sitting on a bench in front of a restaurant in Silver Spring, Maryland; Lori Lewis-Rivera, shot while vacuuming her minivan at a Shell station in Kensington, Maryland; Pascal Charlot, shot while waiting to cross a street in Washington, D.C.; Dean Meyers, shot while pumping gas at a station in Manassas, Virginia; Kenneth H. Bridges, shot while pumping gas in Massaponax, Virginia; Linda Franklin, shot while loading goods into her car at a Home Depot in Falls Church, Virginia; Conrad Johnson, a Ride-On bus driver shot while inside his bus in Aspen Hill, Maryland. The dead ranged in age from twenty-five to seventy-two. The wounded, on the other hand, included a thirteen-year-old boy, Iran Brown, who was shot on October 7 while walking toward his school in Bowie, Maryland. The other victims who were wounded by the snipers were Caroline Sewell, shot while loading goods into a car in Fredericksburg, Virginia, on October 4; and Jeffrey Hopper, shot on October 19 in the parking lot of a Ponderosa Steakhouse in Ashland, Virginia, a restaurant in which Muhammad and Malvo had eaten some time before.

In total, twenty-two people fell prey to Muhammad and Malvo, fifteen of them killed. Twenty-one of them had no prior involvement with John Muhammad or Lee Malvo before they were attacked. Only the first victim, Keenya Cook, had a connection, although tenuous. She was simply the niece of a friend and supporter of Muhammad's wife. Malvo later stated that this attack had actually been intended for Millie's friend, Isa Nichols.

Five of the victims–Buchanan, Walekar, Ramos, Lewis-Rivera, Charlot–were all killed on the same day, the day after Martin's killing at the Shoppers. In sixteen hours, five deaths occurred, four of them in a little over two hours. All of them had taken place in the close-in Maryland suburbs, except for the last one, which happened just over the line in the city of Washington. Muhammad and Malvo would not go on such a rampage again. But they had gained the attention of the Washington community, enough to compel the outdoor fall festival planners in Fairfax on Saturday to wonder if the sniper could be the reason for low attendance. That logic was spurred along by another attack, on October 4. In that case, the snipers left Maryland to strike in Fredericksburg, Virginia, wounding Caroline Seawell. Then they went back to Maryland, to Bowie, on October 7, which was followed by four more attacks in Virginia–Manassas on the 9th, Massaponax on the 11th, Falls

Church on the 14th, and Ashland on the 19th. Their final attack took place three days later, back in Aspen Hill, Maryland.

• • •

Muhammad bought the car from which he and Malvo aimed many of their shots the day after they had shot and robbed Paul LaRuffa, the restaurant manager, in the Maryland suburbs. Apparently, Muhammad used LaRuffa's money to buy the car. Prior to that, Muhammad and Malvo had gotten around, even crossed the country, by public conveyance, mostly buses. With LaRuffa's cash, Muhammad could afford to get a car so that he and Malvo no longer had to ride the bus. In Camden, New Jersey, Muhammad telephoned the brother of an acquaintance from his Antigua days. The man took them in for the day and helped them shop for a car. What they bought was a 1990 Chevy Caprice. A former police cruiser from Bordentown, New Jersey, it originally had been white, but the police had painted it blue so that it would be less obtrusive, which later seemed to help Muhammad as well. He bought the car for $250. It was to serve as their getaway vehicle after an attack, and their home and hideout in between, as well as their means of transportation from one attack to the next. But it also became their hunter's stand. By cutting a hole in the trunk, they were able to fire the Bushmaster at their victims without opening the trunk lid or leaving the car and making themselves visible to witnesses. They didn't always attack this way, but they had that option if they chose to use it. Malvo would testify at Muhammad's Maryland trial, in May 2006, that Muhammad had gotten the idea to set up the Caprice as a rolling sniper station from an Irish Republican Army training manual.

In truth, it was not a car that escaped notice. At least nine times police spotted the car and ran the license plate number through their computer system. Because the search always came up clean, or at worst showed only a protective order that Millie Muhammad had taken out against Muhammad, the officers and troopers never stopped the vehicle. Muhammad and Malvo were fairly law-abiding drivers, and the one time the car was stopped for a traffic violation, in the suburbs of Maryland, the officer let Muhammad go because he was sober, polite, and courteous. The officer decided a warning was sufficient. Whenever Muhammad encountered the police during the pair's month-long spree, he always seemed calm, polite, and reasonable—not the image of the sniper that police thought they were looking for. In the wake of the Sarah Ramos shooting, after one witness thought he saw a white box truck speeding away, the car itself, though not that common, became essentially invisible at the crime scenes, since police now focused much of their attention, and that of the public, on looking for the white box truck.

. . .

Motives for a person committing murder are always intriguing, more so when there are multiple victims who were apparently unknown to their killers, which is not usually the case with most homicides. If Muhammad was so calm and polite, why was he doing this? Friends from the period prior to the attacks cited his anger at losing his three children after having spent nearly a year and a half with them (illegally) in Antigua. They also quoted him as saying that the September 11 attacks were deserved. One friend noted that Muhammad and Malvo had lived the life of vagabonds, that they had had nothing during the months after they returned to the States and Muhammad lost the children. During that time, Muhammad had stayed with one friend for a while, and then had traveled to visit with another. Muhammad was obsessed with guns, and he usually visited friends who had guns too. He also frequented shelters for the homeless. He joined the Tacoma YMCA and, as he and Malvo would do during their murderous tour, he several times used the Y's facilities at various stopovers to exercise and then shower and shave.

Muhammad's acquaintances from that period also noted his obsession with trying to make a silencer for a rifle. Gun experts had told him it couldn't be done, and why. At one point, he came up with an invention he wanted to try. He had grooves cut into a steel tube so that it would screw onto the end of a rifle barrel. But when he test-fired the device into a tree trunk in the back yard of his friend Robert Holmes, in Tacoma, the silencer seemed to break down quickly. At the beginning of the shootings, witnesses would comment about the loud bang that accompanied the shots. Whatever else they saw or thought they saw, the explosion itself was a constant.

. . .

Toward the end of the killing spree, as the murderous events spun themselves out, Muhammad and Malvo actually tried to extort money from local authorities. After the shooting of Iran Brown, the thirteen-year-old student who was shot outside of his school in Maryland, the pair left behind a tarot card—the death card—with a message that Muhammad had written on it. He was trying to open a line of communication that he hoped to use to negotiate for ten million dollars. At first the card wasn't found, and when it *was* discovered, word leaked out. The news media, covering a case that had had few new developments in a long time, pounced on this tidbit of news. Events then accelerated in seriocomic fashion. When Muhammad and Malvo tried to telephone authorities, they couldn't get through. When they tried the national tip line that officials had set up, their calls seemed to fall on deaf ears—the people working the phones were dealing with thousands upon thousands of calls, many of them from cranks. When Muhammad and Malvo tried going outside the established system, calling other police officers and even a parish priest, their words were passed along, but without urgency or even understanding. Muhammad and Malvo grew frustrated and angry. They tried a written message again at the scene of their next-to-last shooting, that of Jeffrey Hopper, who was shot as he and his wife left the Ponderosa Steakhouse outside of Ashland, Virginia. This time, they printed their message on several sheets of paper and left it in a plastic baggie, tacked to a tree. Police at the scene found it not long after the shooting. The new message repeated what Muhammad and Malvo had written on the tarot card:

For you mr. Police

"Call me God."

Do not release to the

Press.

It went on to say that earlier attempts to open negotiations had failed, and the message even listed the calls they had made. The snipers said they wanted ten million dollars deposited to the credit card account of a female Greyhound bus driver (they had stolen her credit card when they traveled aboard her bus, before the shootings began). If the authorities did not meet their demands, and tried instead to catch them, Muhammad and Malvo wrote, the two would go on killing people, including children.

At Muhammad's Maryland trial, in May 2006, Malvo testified that Muhammad was driven by two motives. One was to take his children away from Millie and to move with them to Canada. But Malvo also declared that partway through the shootings, he and Muhammad had come close to having a falling out. It was then, Malvo said, that Muhammad had promised him that, after they had received the ten-million-dollar payment from authorities in return for halting the killings, they would take the money and Muhammad's children and move to Canada, where they would train 140 homeless children to sweep down into the United States and attack Americans. Malvo testified that Muhammad "hates this country."

Muhammad's plan was to kill six people a day for a month, according to Malvo's testimony. In a second phase, or wave of attacks, they would target schoolchildren and school buses in particular. That second wave also was to include setting off bombs that would incorporate ball-bearings into the devices.

• • •

As the shootings continued, the national, state, and local authorities amassed one of the largest investigative teams ever assembled and gave it the most extensive resources. Indeed, at times it seemed that the Task Force was too large, too cumbersome to respond nimbly to events. After finding the plastic baggie and note near the Ashland shooting scene, authorities sent it off to an ATF, and then to an FBI, laboratory for analysis. By the time the analysis was complete, early the following morning, the first deadline that Muhammad and Malvo had set in the note had already passed. An even bigger problem was that the phone number at the Ponderosa, at which Muhammad and Malvo had told authorities to call them, was incorrect. In writing it in the note, the pair had transposed two of the numbers.

Still, authorities believed they finally had a motive—extortion—and it was a knowable, even familiar, motive. They also had evidence—handwriting, fingerprints, a bag that could be traced and that, it turned out, had been bought just hours before the shooting at a store that was nearby. Authorities would later discover that Malvo had been caught on the store's security camera. They also had a list of people with whom the killers had communicated, and so could interview the officers, and even the priest, to whom Muhammad and Malvo had spoken. Finally, then, after weeks of nothing, the police had something they could investigate. They had leads.

To an anxious and weary public, things just seemed confused, especially after police swarmed a white van at a Richmond-area gas station, on Sunday, October 21, and arrested two men. Could this be it? Everyone wondered if the shootings might at last be over. But Montgomery County police chief Charles Moose, the head of the investigative team, said on camera at a news conference the following day that they had not found the people they were seeking, and he asked the killers to keep calling, to keep trying to get through.

The police were decoding the messages they had received, both in writing and over the phone, and they were beginning to understand the references that were coming out of the evidence—tie-ins to rock and rap songs, allusions to the culture of Jamaica, plus Malvo's voice patterns on the phone recordings that suggested a Jamaican upbringing.

Muhammad and Malvo themselves were wary of more phone calls. They decided another killing would be the best next step. That was when they shot and killed bus driver Conrad Johnson.

The day of Johnson's shooting, and the next, the public schools in and around Richmond were closed because in their phone calls and written statements Malvo and Muhammad had made references to the fact that children would not be safe from their murderous ways. One day off for the schools became two, in an effort to keep the children safe.

In the chaotic environment of the final days of the sniper shootings, the news media were accused of worsening fears rather than calming them. News reporters frequently cite what they call "the public's right to know" as justification for reporting information that authorities do not wish to make public. The journalists' idea is that, in a relatively free and democratic society, the people have a right to know about events that may affect them. In the waning days and hours of the sniper case, this theory ran into another one: the public's right to be safe.

In their messages to the police, Muhammad and Malvo insisted that the response to their demands should be by way of coded messages delivered through the media. Of course, this required the cooperation of the media, whose members were being fed their information by means of en masse press conferences directed by Montgomery County Police Chief Moose. At the press conferences, reporters badgered officials for confirmation about reports that Muhammad and Malvo were threatening to shoot more schoolchildren. Journalists speculated that this warning was why the schools in and around Richmond had closed. The press wanted to know about rumors that the killers were demanding money. The reporters desperately sought some word that might offer relief from the uncertainty and the fear that prevailed.

The tarot card had been the first effort by the killers at communication, and Chief Moose himself worried about blowing this opportunity to break the case open. The news media would not–did not–play the role he felt he needed them to play, that of silent conduit.

It is axiomatic in the news business that the best reporters are innately curious. They don't think of the questions that have to be asked, the questions just come to them the same way they draw breath. And curious reporters know that fully truthful answers do not flow from the person at the podium. Indeed, experienced reporters know that to trust only the spokesperson is to surrender control over information entirely to the managers of the information, who control the podium.

Moose thought he needed that control–lives were at stake, the possibility of apprehending the murderers was at stake–especially in the waning days of these events. But he could not obtain what he believed he and the public so desperately needed, the cooperation of the media.

The police did start getting breaks, though, in the person of Muhammad's former friend from Tacoma, Robert Holmes. A week after he first tried to tell police of his suspicions that Muhammad was the shooter, the authorities went to see Holmes, who laid out his interpretation of events. Holmes's evidence included Muhammad's obsession with finding a silencer for his rifle and the test shots he had fired into a tree in Holmes's backyard. That led to a noisy operation to remove the tree trunk from the yard so that authorities could search it for bullets that could be matched to those recovered from the crime scenes, and to an extensive search of the backyard for spent casings. The search ended up on television, which was the last thing the police wanted. And that further fed the reporters' desire for information. But it also led, ultimately, to the arrest of the snipers.

Another break came when police ran the fingerprints recovered at one of the shooting scenes and matched them to Malvo, whose prints had been left at the shooting in Alabama. They then discovered from Malvo's mother that he was traveling with Muhammad. So in fairly quick order, the police had the names of two suspects and were then able to match Muhammad to the blue Caprice.

Yet a final irony was necessary before police could effect the capture. Muhammad and Malvo, for all intents and purposes, were living out of the Caprice. They had no television, and they didn't listen to the car radio; or if they did, they missed the broadcasts that identified the car as the subject of a police search. And although they had a computer, they didn't use it to tap into news reports that also might have warned them that the police were closing in. The authorities now knew their identities and the car they were driving. The pair were asleep in the car at a rest stop off of I-70, west of Frederick, Maryland, when Whitney Donahue, a commercial refrigerator repairman, drove through and recognized the car and plate number from information he had heard over his car radio. It was October 23. Before dawn on the 24th, the police would have Muhammad and Malvo in handcuffs, and the series of shootings, deaths, and woundings would reach its end.

Muhammad's ex-wife, Millie, later said that she thought the entire killing spree had been orchestrated by Muhammad so that he could

# Richmond Times-Dispatch

FINAL     RICHMOND, VIRGINIA

*VIRGINIA'S NEWS LEADER*
A MEDIA GENERAL NEWSPAPER

FRIDAY, OCTOBER 25, 2002

50¢

# CAPTURED

## GUN FOUND IN CAR LINKED TO 11 SNIPER ATTACKS

### WAS 17-YEAR-OLD SUSPECT AMONG ONLOOKERS AT ASHLAND SHOOTING?

## Muhammad's life a series of troubles

FROM WIRE AND STAFF REPORTS

WASHINGTON — In a photograph shown on TV news, the man and the teenager both smile broadly for the camera, their arms draped around each other in a sunny portrait of contentment.

But a gravely sinister picture, and a snapshot of the adult's tangled life path, began emerging after the duo's early-morning capture yesterday by police seeking to end a three-week wave of lethal sniper attacks.

John Allen Muhammad, 41, a former Army soldier and veteran of the Persian Gulf War, and John Lee Malvo, 17, a Jamaican citizen, were arrested early yesterday at a Maryland highway rest stop.

They were not immediately charged with murder in the sniper attacks that have killed 10 people and critically wounded three others. But authorities conducting the massive, cross-country investigation labeled them suspects.

Muhammad and Malvo may have been motivated by anti-American views, federal officials told The Seattle Times. Muhammad was discharged in the mid-1990s. The Times quoted federal sources as saying the two had been known to speak sympathetically about the hijackers who attacked the World Trade Center and the Pentagon.

Neither man was believed to be associated with the al-Qaida terrorist network or any other organized group. "It appears that they are and have acted on their own," Bellingham, Wash., Police Chief Randy Carroll said.

Muhammad was born and raised in Baton Rouge, La., where family members describe him as a normal boy who married his high school sweetheart. His mother died when he was little, and his dad was not around, so he was raised by his grandfather and his aunt, a cousin said.

He converted to Islam 17 years ago and changed his name from John Allen Williams a year ago. He also divorced twice.

*SEE SUSPECTS, PAGE A7 ▶*

John Lee Malvo, 17, and John Allen Muhammad, 41, in a recent family photo provided by a former sister-in-law in Baton Rouge, La.

THE ASSOCIATED PRESS

## Arrests cap three weeks of terror, death

BY PAUL BRADLEY, FRANK GREEN AND BILL McKELWAY
*Times-Dispatch Staff Writers*

ROCKVILLE, Md. — Three weeks of murder and fear came to a stunningly swift conclusion yesterday as police arrested an Army veteran and a teenager thought to be responsible for a bloody sniping rampage that left 10 people dead.

John Allen Muhammad, 41, and 17-year-old John Lee Malvo were arrested by a team of federal, state and local police who crept up with guns pointed and swooped in on the pair as they napped in a highway rest stop off Interstate 70, 11 miles west of Frederick.

"People in the Washington, D.C., area are breathing a collective sigh of relief," Douglas Duncan, county executive of Montgomery County, Md., said last night.

Special Agent Michael Bouchard of the Bureau of Alcohol, Tobacco and Firearms said that ballistic tests of a weapon found in Muhammad's car match it to the bullets that killed eight people and wounded three others in the attacks.

Montgomery County Police Chief Charles A. Moose hinted that the two men are the principal figures behind the killing spree.

But he said the investigation is continuing and that a regional task force is far from "pucking boxes and going home."

The arrest came at 3:19 a.m., just hours after police issued an all-points bulletin for two men traveling in a 1990 Chevrolet Caprice with New Jersey plates.

Ron Lantz, a Cincinnati trucker idling in the rest area, spotted the car, dialed 911 and helped block the rest area exit ramp as he waited for police to arrive.

The call was the tip police had been awaiting for three weeks, and they arrived at the picturesque visitor center in force.

A gun-toting tactical squad surrounded the car, smashed out its windows and whisked the two

*SEE CAPTURED, PAGE A6 ▶*

---

## While suspects were in Ashland . . .

### Malvo may have mingled in crowd

BY CHRIS DOVI, MEREDITH FISCHER AND MARK HOLMBERG
*Times-Dispatch Staff Writers*

Authorities are investigating "a strong possibility" that at least one of the two suspects captured in connection with the deadly sniper shootings milled around after Saturday's attack at an Ashland restaurant, sources told The Times-Dispatch.

At least one officer at the scene recalled seeing the younger suspect, John Lee Malvo, 17, mingling with the throng of reporters and onlookers while police investigated the shooting in the Ponderosa Steak House parking lot, a police source said.

"Why wouldn't they have come back?" the source said of the suspect. "Arsonists like to come back to the scene to see their work. It happens all the time."

Malvo was arrested at a Frederick County, Md., rest stop along with another man, John Allen Muhammad, 41. The two

*SEE ASHLAND, PAGE A8 ▶*

### Police say sniper called local priest

BY CHRIS DOVI
*Times-Dispatch Staff Writer*

The night before a shooting at an area steakhouse, a man police believe was the sniper made a telephone call to Monsignor William V. Sullivan, the pastor of St. Ann Catholic Church in Ashland.

"I'm told that he told Father Sullivan that 'I am God,' " said the Most Rev. Walter F. Sullivan, bishop of the Catholic Diocese of Richmond. "It was all kind of strange . . . and very muffled."

Monsignor Sullivan was out of town yesterday and was unavailable for comment.

The call to Monsignor Sullivan was not the only phone call of that type made to a priest last Friday. The New York Times reported in today's editions that a call was made to Assumption Catholic Church in Bellingham, Wash., about 5 p.m. Pacific Coast time. The caller, a male, demanded to talk to a priest but grew angry and slammed down the phone when he was told a priest was not available, the

*SEE PRIEST, PAGE A12 ▶*

---

## EIGHT PAGES OF COVERAGE

- **The investigation**
  What may have been a boastful phone call from the sniper helped close the case. Page A7.

- **A sense of relief**
  In Ashland, residents breathe a sigh of relief and commend work of police. Page A9.

- **A return to normalcy**
  Recess, sports practices and other extracurricular activities to resume today at area schools. Page A13.

- **Prep delay proposed**
  Central Region officials recommend moving this week's football games to Nov. 15-16. Page D1.

- **A starring role**
  Electronic media were at center of sniper investigation. Page C1.

---

## FRIDAY

ONLINE http://www.timesdispatch.com

**Today's weather**
Showers. High: 58. Low: 53. **B16**

Copyright © 2002, 152nd Year, No. 298

**Crowd still held in theater**
The hostage situation in Moscow drags on and Russians increasingly wonder about the war in Chechnya.

**A Giant win**
San Francisco slams Anaheim to take a 3-2 lead in World Series.
Sports **/D1**

**Strike ends**
Teamsters call off 3-year-old strike against Overnite Transportation

**TKO**
"Punch-Drunk Love" falls short.

**COMING**
TOMORROW

**Near the mountaintop**
Dallas Cowboys running back Emmitt Smith is on the cusp of becoming the NFL's all-time leading rusher
Sports

---

Initial photograph of the snipers in the *Richmond Times-Dispatch.*

kill her and get away with it. Had Muhammad remained unknown and therefore invisible to police, such a plan might well have succeeded, whether he originally intended it or not.

As a result of the trials that have been held in both Maryland and Virginia, Muhammad was sentenced to death in Virginia for the killing of Dean Myers and to six life terms in prison without parole in the cases for which he was tried in Maryland. Malvo, a juvenile at the time of the attacks, was sentenced in Virginia to life without parole for the shooting of Linda Franklin and also received six life terms in connection with the Maryland cases.

In October 2006, police from Tucson, Arizona, interviewed Malvo regarding the golf course shooting death of Jerry Taylor in March 2002. Malvo was persuaded to agree to be interviewed by a letter from Taylor's daughter pleading with him to help clear up the unsolved death of her father by telling police what, if anything, he knew. Malvo told the police that he and Muhammad had committed the murder. Even though this and other cases have yet to be resolved, all further legal action seems to have ended with the execution of John Muhammad on November 10, 2009.

Thus the cases seem to have ended, but not the damage inflicted on the lives affected by the crimes.

# *The* Washington Post *and the Sniper*

On October 25, 2002, on the day after the arrests of John Muhammad and Lee Boyd Malvo, *Washington Post* columnist Marjorie Williams[1] began her op-ed piece with these words: "Now that two solid suspects are in custody for the killings that have dominated the region for the past three weeks, we may hope to recapture our everyday sense of safety. It is less obvious whether we can retrieve our dignity so fast." Noting that she did not fault "any of those who took precautions to protect themselves or their loved ones," Williams charged: "Over the past week, our public reactions to the killings–the media coverage, the poses of the authorities charged with ensuring our safety, the language in which we talked about the mystery man or men who held us in suspense–crossed an invisible but palpable line into social hysteria."

During the weeks between the initial killings and recognition of the existence of a sniper, and the capture of the two suspects, a quarter of a million words were published by the *Post* about the events. Williams's column, one of the last in this remarkable string of reporting, acknowledged rational concern but also cautioned against overreaction. She

1. Marjorie Williams attended Harvard University for two years, subsequently relocating to New York to start a career in publishing. She soon moved to journalism, becoming an editor for the *Washington Post* in 1986. A year later, she began to make a name for herself in the Style section of the paper, and then in *Vanity Fair,* for her insightful portraits of Washington's political elite. She also penned a weekly op-ed column in the *Post* from 2000 to November 2004. Diagnosed with liver cancer in 2001, she died shortly after writing her last column on January 16, 2005, at forty-seven years of age. Her work has since been published in book form and has received numerous awards. (Sources: *Washington Post,* January 17, 2005, http://www.washingtonpost.com/wp-dyn/articles/A14297-2005Jan16.html; Wikipedia: The Free Encyclopedia, http://en.wikipedia.org/wiki/Marjorie_Williams.)

primarily questioned whether parents had not gone too far in their zeal
to protect their children:

> When they wrote this threat ("Your children are not safe any-
> where at any time") at the end of a letter left at the scene of Satur-
> day's shooting, we reacted with a dreadful lack of perspective. In
> fact, we already knew that the mysterious killer was willing to gun
> down a child; and in truth, we had shown ourselves pretty well
> able to protect most of our children in most places most of the
> time, precisely because they spend their days inside structures
> well regulated by public authorities. They are not the people who
> need to pump gas and drive buses and vacuum out minivans.
>
> It seemed obvious that the snipers' threat against children was
> mostly an ominous afterthought (after all, it was contained in a
> "P.S."), thrown in to reinforce the fear that we had so vividly
> shown them they had the power to induce.

At the time they first appeared, these passages seemed more an indict-
ment of the media's hyperbolic role in the events, but in actuality they
slid toward a similar view of the public at large, in which Williams
included herself, by writing in the first-person plural. And in pointing
out that children had not been particularly vulnerable, Williams was
arguing that the community's anxiety had encouraged the sniper. Communicating the threat to children, she showed, actually increased society's sense of its own victimization.

Williams then concluded with her solution. While she conceded
that, given the snipers' capture, her words assumed an aspect of omni-
scient hindsight, she also asserted that her readers should examine
their reactions, labeling them self-pity that had overwhelmed fact:
"Better to have dealt with and acted on our fears as the individual
emotions they were, while at least trying to maintain a public attitude of
greater stoicism." And she made a passionate plea generally for courage, instead of fear, in the face of adversity, referencing the events of
September 11, 2001:

> We all need to understand these reactions to the extent they are
> forces in our own lives. But at some point it serves us very ill as a
> culture to dwell so fondly on our emotional injuries, which are
> not at all the same as the actual injuries of those who died or lost
> loved ones on that day, or as the public injury we suffered in
> being the target of sudden attack.

Williams's words invite a number of different interpretations. Did
the citizens of the Washington, D.C., area respond poorly to the sniper

threat? Or, as she allowed, did this line of thinking become possible only after Malvo and Muhammad were safely behind bars? Many readers would react angrily to her challenge, while others would agree with her. Whether Williams was correct is not the focus of this chapter, however. Rather, my focus here is an examination of how the press—and, specifically, the *Post*—covered the sniper-related events, and of how the newspaper wrote about the thoughts, moods, and actions spurred by those events, up until the arrests of Malvo and Muhammad. In other words, I ask how the press reacted to the varying circumstances of this situation, and what this coverage suggests about the media in general.

The *Washington Post* is one of America's largest and most significant newspapers, and without a doubt was the dominant newspaper in the coverage of the sniper. As the analysis will indicate, fear soon became the predominant sentiment characterizing this coverage, even though the *Post*'s coverage lacked some of the emotional impact and hyperbole of the electronic press. Indeed, even the continuation of the crisis, which created anxiety in some elements of the electronic media, was less apparent than was the development of themes. In fact, fear was more a constant, as is evident in the following descriptions of the content of the *Post*'s coverage. To be fair, the *Post* also articulated the opposite emotion in its coverage; while not negating the prodigious amount of fear, the paper did at times call upon its readers for courage. However, most often, in providing a different direction in its coverage, the *Post* promoted cooperation and a strong sense of community. Even the portrayals of the snipers, which oftentimes demonized them, had the effect of strengthening community. By treating these men as monsters, the *Post* left the rest of the community purified.

In contrast to coverage by electronic news outlets, which emphasized primarily the narrative of the police investigation and the search for the sniper or snipers, the *Post*'s coverage was considerably more intense and varied and, as we shall see, thematic. The *Post* published a large number of articles every day, even when the investigation itself produced little to cover, or when there were few mainstream events about which to write. Even in the issues that appeared immediately after another shooting by the sniper, the paper endeavored to cover many aspects other than police activities. According to Paul Duggan and Jo-Ann Armao, two editors at the paper, this occurred in large part because the paper believed in "flooding the zone," or covering everything that might relate to a subject. To the *Post*, the sniper events became the most important news story in Washington since the break-in at the Watergate by Richard Nixon's operatives, and the *Post*'s staff members intended to make it their own.

By extending well beyond the police investigation in its overall coverage, the *Post* actually minimized the chronological power of its account. While police activities sometimes created a narrative by systematically relating past efforts to future plans, other stories tended much more toward depicting slices of reality. And the emphasis on community reaction in various articles rotated the focus from place to place.

One other structural factor may have lessened the narrative strength of the *Post*'s reporting. Committed to providing "news," each daily issue of the paper tends to found anew the relevant world. This creates "big" stories, but not a timeline. Moreover, while, in general, stories about running events bring readers up to date each time on previous developments in the chain, for this subject the *Post* seemed rightfully to assume that readers already knew the chain's general framework, and so minimized the retelling from past days.[2] Readers, not the newspaper, supplied the chronological stream.

In addition, even though the paper appeared daily, it could not communicate the minute-by-minute anxiety and exhilaration that were available electronically. Furthermore, the press generally took advantage of its ex post facto publishing schedule to view the story retrospectively. It seldom laid out a detailed chronology, and even when such details were given, the paper's perspective created a level of omniscience unavailable to those providing immediate coverage. Such knowledge tended to foreshorten the entire event coverage, eliminating elements that over time seemed less significant.

Although the *Post*'s approach minimized the most salient aspects of television's continuous coverage, it did produce some chronology. Overall, a reader of the paper could be excused if the articles produced the semblance of an investigation that, even on the same day, alternated between frustration and hope. Exceptions to this pattern include the extreme uncertainty shown in the first days of the shootings, the optimism about an eyewitness after the Home Depot shooting, and a flurry of attention that followed the Ponderosa shooting, lasting until the capture of Muhammad and Malvo. Yet even these emphases never recaptured the narrative focus of electronic coverage.

In such circumstances, where chronology does not provide such a powerful frame, themes did emerge. As noted in the prologue, the

2. See, e.g., the reporting on October 15, 2002.

discussion of fear permeated both the press and the expectations of the public. This preeminent issue can serve as an organizing principle and, as will become apparent, can reveal much about specific topics, including the activity of the police and the competence of the investigation. Consequently, here and in chapter 3, we will use the portrayal of levels of anxiety and concern to provide organization to our analysis.

Clearly, if Williams's column in itself typified the slant of the reporting, she could not have been correct that the media participated in the escalation of fear. But, as will become apparent, her viewpoint was uncommon, compared to the onslaught of news from an opposite perspective.

In one of two lead stories on page 1 for Friday, October 4, at the beginning of the episode, the *Post* gave a full chronology of the initial shootings – seventeen hours that began on Wednesday evening and concluded on Thursday morning with three men and two women dead. (Another died late Thursday night, too late for the *Post* story.) The account noted the suddenness and unexpectedness of this explosion of violence. Much uncertainty was apparent in the details, except that all the murders were "single-shot, sniper-like." Interestingly, the police applied the label of "sniper" right away, according to the *Post*'s articles.[3] Few witnesses could report anything, but the search for a "slightly damaged white truck" began immediately.

Then the story turned to public reaction. Having been away in Chicago, Montgomery County (Md.) Executive Douglas Duncan[4] rushed home. According to the *Post,* many people in that state were staying inside, and some "streets and public places appeared deserted." The newspaper quoted a shaken bystander who had happened upon one of the first slayings: "They're shooting all around!" The paper continued by describing the succession of murders whose horror so contrasted with the normality of a typical fall morning and the "bustle" of the workday.

3. This account and those that follow are all taken from articles that appeared in various editions of the *Washington Post* in October 2002.

4. Douglas M. Duncan had earned his bachelor's degree in psychology and political science from Columbia University. He began his career on the Rockville, Md., city council in 1982 and served on that body until 1987, when he was named mayor of Rockville, a post he held until 1993. Duncan was elected Montgomery County Executive in 1994, and served until 2006. That year, he ran for the Democratic nomination for governor of Maryland, dropping out of the race before its conclusion. He was Vice President of Administrative Affairs at the University of Maryland, College Park, until his resignation in 2008. (Source: Wikipedia: The Free Encyclopedia, http://en.wikipedia.org/wiki/Doug_Duncan.)

**Weather**

**Today:** Rain, drizzle.
High 64, Low 60.
**Saturday:** Mostly cloudy.
High 68, Low 60.
Details, Page 88

# The Washington Post

**FINAL**

*Inside: Weekend*
*Today's Crossword on Page A2*
NEWSSTAND 35¢
HOME DELIVERY 30¢

125TH YEAR No. 310    M2    DM   VA

FRIDAY, OCTOBER 11, 2002

# Congress Passes Iraq Resolution

**Analysis**

## A Muscular First Step

*Bush Gains Freedom, Negotiating Power*

By GLENN KESSLER
Washington Post Staff Writer

In almost the reverse of his father's path to battle nearly 12 years ago, President Bush is obtaining congressional backing for a war with Iraq even before he has faced a direct military threat, assembled an international coalition or received support from the United Nations.

Moreover, unlike 1991, passage of the resolution does not mean that a war is imminent. Indeed, as the vote neared, Bush and members of his administration in recent days have deliberately toned down their tough rhetoric. The notion that Iraqi President Saddam Hussein must be toppled has been shoved in the background, while instead officials argue that the best way to prevent a war is strong support from Congress and the U.N. Security Council for a possible war, because it will demonstrate to Hussein that he has no choice but to give up his weapons of mass destruction.

It's an argument that swayed many skeptical members of Congress and which administration officials say in

*See ANALYSIS, A8, Col. 1*

President Bush: Iraq's "outlaw state" days are "coming to an end."

## Overwhelming Approval Gives Bush Authority to Attack Unilaterally

By JIM VANDEHEI and JULIET EILPERIN
Washington Post Writers

The House and Senate voted overwhelmingly to grant President Bush the power to attack Iraq unilaterally, remove Saddam Hussein from power and abolish that country's nuclear, chemical and biological weaponry.

Moving the nation closer to a possible second war with Iraq, 77 of 100 senators and 296 of 435 House members voted to authorize the president to "use the armed forces of the United States as he determines to be necessary and appropriate in order to defend the national security of the United States against the continuing threat posed by Iraq."

The president needs no further congressional approval to deploy troops, order airstrikes and wage a ground war with Iraq.

"The gathering threat of Iraq must be confronted fully and finally," Bush said after the House vote yesterday afternoon. "The days of Iraq acting as an outlaw state are coming to an end."

With Congress's debate behind him, the president will focus on the United Nations. He is pressing the world body to adopt a new resolution demanding that Hussein immediately dismantle his weapons of mass destruction or face possible military action.

Not since Congress passed the 1964 Gulf of Tonkin resolution—which helped bring expansion of the Vietnam War—has a president won such broad and flexible authority to carry out an undefined military operation, historians say.

The bipartisan endorsement of Bush's

*See RESOLUTION, A6, Col. 2*

■ U.S. weighs occupation plan to reshape post-Hussein Iraq. | *Page A11*

# Va. Shooting Confirmed as Act of Sniper

## From Sports Teams to Tourists, Great Outdoors Loses Its Appeal

By MONTE REEL and NURITH C. AIZENMAN
Washington Post Staff Writers

Many Washington area schools scrapped all outdoor activities through the weekend, several tour groups canceled plans to visit the capital, and home-delivery services thrived yesterday as people tried to protect themselves from a deadly sniper they feared could strike again.

The impact of a week of shootings on daily routines could be felt almost everywhere in the region, but particularly where children were involved. Northern Virginia school districts canceled all outdoor athletic events, including varsity football games, through Sunday, and

Prince George's and Anne Arundel counties moved their weekend football games to Monday. The association that governs sports in D.C. public schools was to make its decision today.

Montgomery County school officials said today's football games would be played tomorrow and all other weekend events would go on as scheduled.

Many youth recreational leagues also took unscheduled mid-season breaks, despite concerns from some league officials that it might be an overreaction.

"It's not an easy decision," said Howard Kohn, commissioner of the Takoma Park Neighborhood Youth Soccer League, which has 2,000 players and

*See DISRUPTIONS, A25, Col. 1*

## Fear Comes to Pr. William

*Slaying Drives Home Painful New Reality*

By ERIC M. WEISS and CHRISTINA A. SAMUELS
Washington Post Staff Writers

A single shot on a rainy night served a sharp notice to Prince William County and residents of Washington's other Virginia suburbs: The trouble has arrived.

Wednesday night's sniper killing of a gas station customer also reinforced painful new facts for the region, according to scores of interviews yesterday: Bright lights meant to make service stations safer also provide illumination for a gunman. A close interstate isn't just a convenience but the means for a quick getaway. And 30 miles of highway is hardly insulation from "city" crimes.

"Everyone's upset, everyone's wound up," said Roy Fuentes, 64, a car salesman who works a few driveways from the Sunoco station on Sudley Road where Dean Harold Meyers, 53, of Gaithersburg was killed. "The guy's on a

Prince William Police Chief Charlie T. Deane answers questions from media.

rampage. You don't know what the hell he's up to. But it knock away from where I work—my God."

Fuentes moved to Manassas three years ago from Fairfax County. "I thought I could get a better deal out

*See VIRGINIA, A26, Col. 1*

## Death Toll at 7 In Attacks Across Anxious Region

By JOSH WHITE and CAROL MORELLO
Washington Post Staff Writers

Bullet fragments taken from a customer fatally shot at a service station in Prince William County on Wednesday evening were conclusively linked yesterday to the sniper who now has claimed seven lives in nine days and has changed the way the Washington region goes about its everyday chores.

Although authorities had suspected all along that the sniper was responsible for the death of Dean Harold Meyers, 53, a Gaithersburg engineer, they confirmed it only after ballistics tests matched fragments from Wednesday's shooting to the .223-caliber bullet fragments removed from the bodies of several previous victims, officials said.

Like the two shootings before it, the Prince William attack occurred next to a major highway, allowing the killer to come and go quickly, a shift from the seven earlier shooting incidents.

However, investigators said they did not find a tarot card or any other communication from the killer as they did at Monday's shooting site, at a Bowie middle school. They also did not find a shell casing, as was the case in Bowie.

Confirmation that the sniper had struck for the second time in Virginia and the first time in Washington's more immediate Virginia suburbs widened the circle of fear that has caused many residents to go about their most mundane activities with caution. Gov. Mark R. Warner (D) urged people to be alert to their surroundings and be vigilant about the whereabouts of their children.

Prince William Police Chief Charlie T. Deane said: "Everyone has been keeping their fingers crossed that this would be resolved before the next one.

*See SNIPER, A24, Col. 1*

Investigators look for evidence near a Prince William Sunoco station where a customer was shot dead.

■ Attack locations allowed quick getaways. | *Page A25*    ■ Shootings fuel fear at area gas stations. | *Page B1*    ■ Shootings cause soccer tournament to cancel. | *Page D1*

## States' Budget Woes Fuel Medicaid Cuts

*Poor Lose Coverage and Services*

By AMY GOLDSTEIN
Washington Post Staff Writer

Oklahoma will mail letters soon to nearly 78,000 poor residents—some families that recently left welfare, others people who are disabled or old—telling them that, as of March, they no longer will be eligible for Medicaid.

In Illinois, Medicaid officials last month began to require patients who need a popular anti-depressant drug, Zoloft, to get tablets that are twice as strong as they need, then break the pills in half.

And Missouri's Medicaid program last July stopped paying for adults to get eyeglasses or for doctors to perform circumcisions on newborn boys.

**INSIDE**

**Bomber Is Foiled**
One woman was killed, but a suicide attacker's plans to bomb a bus near Tel Aviv went awry thanks to the bus driver and a doctor.
WORLD, *Page A29*

**Election Reform**
The House overwhelmingly passed legislation to provide almost $3.9 billion to overhaul the federal elections system.
FEDERAL PAGE, *A35*

**Giants Go Up 2-0**
The San Francisco Giants beat the St. Louis

*Weekend*
**25**

**Silver Weekend**
On Weekend's 25th Anniversary, reflections on how we have fun, from adventure sports to DVDs and ethnic dining to DJs.
WEEKEND

## Welcome for U.S. in Gulf No Longer Quite So Hearty

*Perceived Bias in Mideast Feeds Resentment*

By RAJIV CHANDRASEKARAN
Washington Post Foreign Service

KUWAIT CITY, Oct. 10—In the early 1990s, Kuwaiti shopkeepers would give American customers the "George Bush discount," a few percent off to express thanks to the United States for leading a military coalition to expel Iraqi invaders. Americans still are welcomed here, but feelings on the street are notably less enthusiastic and universal than they were a decade ago, according to Kuwaitis and longtime American residents. Many Ku-

vacate this Persian Gulf country, sentiments highlighted by the shooting of two U.S. Marines here on Tuesday by Kuwaiti gunmen identified as Islamic activists.

Similar anti-American attitudes have been building forth in other Persian Gulf countries allied with the United States, including those closest to Washington. The resentments pose complex new challenges for the region's leaders, who seek to maintain close ties with the United States, and for U.S. military planners who hope to use Persian Gulf nations as bases in the event of an attack against Iraq.

Fear characterized this front page of the *Washington Post*. (© 2002, *Washington Post*)

"Dire reports" had communicated the dreadful news, and the *Post* dramatically stated: "The attacks left scenes of horror to be discovered by stunned passersby and morning commuters on a gorgeous morning."

Amplifying the feeling of horror was the *Post*'s breathless account of the sequence of events that had left one person after another dead. Details about the killings emphasized the instantaneous demise of the victim at the hands of a sniper. Essentially, the newspaper reported that the victims lay murdered without anyone really to attend to their wounds or death throes; the gaping wound of James "Sonny" Buchanan was mentioned. Yet despite all this depressing news and reaction, the *Post* article closed with a note of hope by noting the capture of other serial killers.

Most other *Post* accounts concentrated on the nature of the murders and the fright in the community. To be sure, Montgomery County Executive Douglas Duncan urged people to be vigilant, observant, and to take precautions, but not to stop their daily lives. Schools in Montgomery County would, in fact, open, the paper reported. And one of the shooting sites was planning for "business as usual" despite the events that had happened there.

Yet overshadowing this attitude were many other stories that emphasized fear. The *Post*'s front section contained a story on the schools which began with an anecdote of a Rockville family that normally let their middle-school child walk home from the bus stop. On this day, however, Jane Batwinis was waiting for her daughter Kathryn at the corner when the bus arrived. The paper quoted the mother: " 'We gave each other a big hug. She knew she was safe.' " The relief narrated in this account suggests the extent of the fear, upon which the *Post* proceeded to focus. Some parents had gone to their children's schools right away to pick them up; others had arrived in time for the closing bell. The schools kept the students inside, or at least in places not visible from the street. High school students ate in the cafeteria instead of being allowed to leave campus for lunch. At Georgetown Preparatory School, students prayed. Even as schools projected an aura of calm against the storm, the *Post* emphasized the threat.

In a column appearing on the front page of the Metro section, Marc Fisher[5] fleshed out this theme of widespread fright. After beginning his

5. *Washington Post* columnist Marc Fisher has written for the paper since 1986. He currently contributes to the Metro section of the paper; writes a column about radio, music, and culture for the Sunday Arts section; runs a blog and

story about parents and children with the notion that all were accustomed to tension, presumably from the 9/11 experience, Fisher emphatically declared that the community was not used to such violent
eruptions, and gave two examples. He focused on tenth-grader Karen
Quiroga, who usually walked home from school. On the day in question,
however, Karen's mother paced rapidly in front of the school. Marta
Quiroga had hurriedly left her business to find her daughter and make
sure she got home just fine. Marta, "taut with stress," according to
Fisher, smiled after finding her daughter. "They hurried into the car,
and the fear immediately swept over the mother's face once more: They
were off to the next school, to pick up the family's younger child. All
would not be right until everyone was back together." Fisher then continued by chronicling the general desire of the public for information
and the worry about "not knowing," as had been the case during the
events of September 11: no matter how much was known, it was still not
enough. Fisher concluded by noting that above all was a desire for
understanding "not just who did this, but why, and what do they want
from us, and do they want to kill me, too?" Such anecdotes spoke as
strongly about fear as any story in the *Post,* but in case readers had not
grasped Fisher's opinion, he concluded, "No one was okay, and the
next stop was home, where the TV reporters dispensed the same shop-
worn shreds of information, over and over, and we all spooned ourselves
another helping of helplessness."

Thus opened the *Post*'s coverage, which emphasized fear more
than any other theme. If many readers to this day might deem Marjorie
Williams's column cavalier and insensitive, others—probably a small
group then, but perhaps a larger group now—might find that the anal-
ogy to 9/11 in the Fisher piece and the panic purveyed in the paper
overstated the case. Yet the *Post* relentlessly wrote on this theme, even
though at times some articles presented countervailing influences.

In fact, the very repetition of expressions of fear is so easy to ascertain that the remainder of this chapter is devoted to illuminating
the various discourses that ran in another direction. Appeals to courage, or at least resistance, appeared, although many of these were in
letters to the editor that expressed the need for a different kind of
coverage. Immediately before the capture of the snipers, this less fear-

chat program on washingtonpost.com; and appears on Washington Post Radio.
Prior to joining the *Post,* Fisher, a Princeton graduate, wrote for the *Miami Herald.*
(Source: Marc Fisher website, http://www.marcfisher.com/author.php.)

ful orientation seemed to gather steam among reporters, perhaps motivated by the recognition that life could not indefinitely remain in
suspended animation. As the crisis continued into the third and even
fourth weeks, isolated voices began to be heard questioning the focus
on fear. For example, an article on October 19, entitled "A Region
Running Scared," asked whether the collective response to the events
was appropriate. The article focused on an interview with Barry Glassner, a sociology professor at the University of Southern California, who
argued that the initial shock of the community would give way to the
question of the future of the community. According to Glassner, this
change in orientation toward less fear had not yet occurred, but with
time it might. The story also referred to a few individuals who had
already decided that the time to move beyond anxiety had arrived. Retired D.C. deputy police chief William Ritchie, for example, noted that
the community, along with the police, would have to take charge of
their lives. The article went on:

> Some impatience with all the caution could be witnessed heading
> into the third weekend of sniper anxiety. In today's *Washington
> Post,* a parent of a student at Sidwell Friends School took out an
> advertisement in the Sports section that states, "Sorry Sidwell
> Friends' homecoming is cancelled due to paranoia and bad judg-
> ment." The school, along with the visiting opponents, chose to
> cancel games scheduled for the weekend because of the sniper,
> though the homecoming dance will still be held.

This marginal counterweight to the emphasis on the climate of fear
would have been noticed by few. What might have been more evident
was an emphasis on community that emerged as a correlate, or anti-
dote, to fright.

Interestingly, connected to the coverage of the region's anxieties, an
approach that most likely increased residents' suspicions of one another, the *Post* alternatively propounded a strong emphasis on cooperation. While many articles suggested or implied societal ties, some articles in the *Post* directly articulated the value of community. After the
shooting at the Falls Church Home Depot, on October 14, a story in the
next day's *Post* described the aftermath. Even as people, fearful for their
lives, had tried to take cover and depart, they had found their exit
blocked by more than fifty police vehicles. Assembled in this way, the
crowd, made up of patrons from various stores–Home Depot, Star-
bucks, the bookstore–all began to talk together, "bonding . . . as strang-
ers brought together by sudden catastrophe are wont to." Moved by

disaster, the community could also pull together in supporting the financial needs of the victims. On October 18, the *Post* reported that Radio America, a Spanish-language station, had broadcast a story about two families that needed assistance to transport family and friends to funerals. Within twenty-five minutes, people from very different walks of life had donated $7,000. In other cases, businesses provided free goods. Montgomery County's victim services coordinator, Bianca Kling, stated that she had witnessed incredible solidarity from business. Both the U.S. Chamber of Commerce and the Council of American-Islamic Relations began to raise relief funds, and the latter group explained its role in communitarian terms: "Our families live here just like everyone else. We want to . . . support the victims of his attacks." Another interviewee stated that such generosity could be explained in terms of vulnerability: " 'We want to make sure there's some good that comes out of this. . . . People are scared, but this is one way they can help.' " The story also suggested that the federal government might join in to support the community.

On October 16, Metro columnist Courtland Milloy[6] drew the most explicit connection between the sniper crisis and a renewed commitment to community. The shooting of a boy, a man mowing a lawn, a shopper, and a man filling his gas tank all reminded of us of ourselves. "We are no longer black or white, city or suburb" wrote Milloy. "All that matters now is our red blood, and it is boiling. Geographic lines matter less than the lines of grief in the faces of our neighbors, and in their eyes we see reflected the loss, the anger and determination that is our own." Milloy also quoted Douglas Duncan's comment that bureaucratic turf had dissolved in the desire to solve this case. A former FBI official argued that helping was a basic human desire. And Milloy added:

> Indeed, everyday people are working hard to uplift the spirits of our community. There are prayer vigils and impromptu memorials along with group counseling sessions. Some schools report that parents are visiting classrooms like never before, looking out for all kids, not just their own. Neighbors are running errands for one another, offering to take out the trash for the elderly and even mow their lawns.

6. Metro columnist Courtland T. Milloy Jr. has been with the *Washington Post* since 1975, initially joining the paper as a reporter. His current column debuted in 1983 and explores issues in the African American community. (Source: *Washington Post* website, http://discuss.washingtonpost.com/wp-srv/zforum/02/metro_milloy040802.htm.)

For the most part, this community born of tragedy was a secular one, but some *Post* articles linked the new sense of community to religion. Of course, most funerals were held in churches and there religion served as a bulwark for the mourners, but other, more explicit comments also pointed to religion. In an October 15 article, a description of individuals who visited the Home Depot out of respect for the victim killed there was termed "a pilgrimage of grief." On October 24, reported in the *Post*, a minister resorted to religious nomenclature to describe Douglas Duncan, who had attended all the funerals of the victims, as "the chaplain of Montgomery County."

Probably more often than showing how religion boosted community life, the *Post* endeavored to show how religion helped individuals. One article, on October 24, documented how religious parents relied on their faith as an aid in giving their children strength. One mother's rationale was that she was accepting God's will. In an October 14 story, entitled, "Time of Fear, Words of Comfort," the reporters Hamil R. Harris[7] and Eric M. Weiss[8] visited three churches, in Bowie, Maryland, Fredericksburg, Virginia, and Kensington, Maryland. Here, the ministers dispensed religion as a source of comfort for the fearful. At Bowie, John W. Brooks had entitled his sermon "When God Disappears." Yet he reassured members of his congregation that they should turn to God: " 'All things work together for good for those who love God.' " And he reminded them that, despite the carnage that consumed the world, God's love never wavered. The Reverend Larry Lenneu in Virginia, some fifty miles southwest of Bowie, had discarded his sermon after the October 12 shooting in Manassas, because he believed that religion at such times must speak directly to his parishioners' concerns. He urged his congregants to recognize and accept that they were not in control. Meanwhile, some sixty miles north, in Kensington, preacher Ann Har-

7. Hamil R. Harris has been with the *Washington Post* for more than seventeen years, covering community issues in the Washington, D.C., metro region. In addition to local news, Harris is known for exploring religion and race relations. He chronicled his experiences at the *Post* in his book, *Career Diary of a Newspaper Reporter*. (Source: Career Diary of a Newspaper Reporter: Gardner's Guide Series website, http://www.ggcinc.com/publishing/careerdiary/cdfull009.html.)

8. Reporter Eric M. Weiss wrote for the *Washington Post* from 2002 to 2009, covering transportation issues in the Washington, D.C., metro region. A former press secretary on Capitol Hill, Weiss attended Columbia University Graduate School of Journalism in New York. He is currently public affairs officer at the U.S. Department of Transportation. (Sources: Linked-In website, http://www.linkedin.com/pub/7/76/74b; e-mail, Weiss to author, July 15, 2008.)

rison held a "healing" service that asked: " 'How do we deal with the fear? Do we lock ourselves away?' " She answered, " 'I learned in hard times I had to depend on God. I am challenging myself. Can I do the same with the sniper?' " Parishioners found these words, and their trust in God, a salve. However, it is worth noting the somewhat secular conclusion to this account. While appreciating the songs and services at the Bowie church, a worshipper had her own prayer for the Lord: "I am praying that they can catch this guy before next Sunday." Elsewhere, reinforcing the commitment to religion, was the repeated denial in various sections of the *Post* of the sniper's claim to be God.

The *Post* articles further strengthened community by creating boundaries. On the outside was the sniper. And on the inside were his targets and victims. Examining how the *Post* dealt with these two entities illustrates how the paper shored up community sentiment in the way it defined the shooter. Five main characterizations of the sniper competed in the paper. Two of these seemed linked – the "deductive" which, indeed, could lead to an assertion of bewilderment, or "puzzlement."

Several times the *Post* analyzed the hard evidence available and tried to estimate carefully the identity of the sniper. Although "deduction" – and the other profiles of the sniper – appeared in a myriad of articles, an October 12 story by *Post* staff writer Stephen Hunter epitomized this approach. The article began by emphasizing the limited knowledge available. Hunter claimed, "The only certain thing known at this writing is that 'he' shot 11 times, hit 10 people, and killed 8. We know the caliber of the weapon, the targets on the body, and the range from which the shooter fired." From this, the article argued that the shooter was neither a novice marksman nor a trained professional. Arguing against the notion that this was the work of an experienced rifleman the writer noted the wide availability of the ammunition that had been used and the limited recoil of the weapon, which made it relatively easy to use. Claiming that the sniper was "unlikely to be a trained operative or terrorist," the article noted that because the rifle recoiled little, the shooter could watch the bullet strike. In his closing phrase, the columnist then dropped his dispassionate analysis and claimed: "He's planned it so he can watch the dying." Similarly, on the next day, on the front page of the Sunday paper, staff writer Serge Kovaleski[9] used a

---

9. Serge F. Kovaleski, a graduate of the College of William and Mary, was a staff writer for the *Washington Post* in 2002. He covered D.C. politics for the paper before joining the staff of the *New York Times,* where he is currently an investi-

similar technique, one that began from ignorance. Kovaleski examined elements of the crimes to develop his analysis, but he was even more cautious than the previous day's writer in offering insights: he suggested that the sniper had planned his murders but that the victims were random.

By applying reason and assuming that the shooter had acted rationally, this kind of patient approach granted rationality to the criminal. But another viewpoint, what I term "puzzlement," related to these punctilious analyses, seemed to exclude the sniper from the community. Many articles were infused with the notion that nothing relevant could be known about the sniper. This lacuna suggested that the shooter was both unpredictable and outside civilized society. Some articles explicitly underlined this viewpoint. In an October 15 editorial, written by a forensic psychiatrist, the writer noted: "This fear, the one that permeates the lives of Washingtonians, is worse than most because of the unpredictability of the threat. When cognitive psychologists tell us that risk seems greater when it is catastrophic and unpredictable, they might well have had circumstances like this in mind." Another article, appearing on October 21, just before the capture of John Muhammad and Lee Malvo, also attested to the unpredictability of the sniper. Although this article implied rationality, it made the sniper seem ominous and threatening.

Yet other visions of the sniper painted a picture that far more clearly pushed the perpetrator totally outside the bounds of society. There was the notion of "anger," a characterization of the sniper upon which President George W. Bush, quoted on October 8, and Police Chief Charles Moore, on October 15, both relied when they claimed that the sniper was "evil." Despite the fact that several professional profilers (see the *Post* edition for October 13) discouraged such characterizations, because they might antagonize the shooter, who might then retaliate, this view too resonated in the *Post*. The most thoroughly developed version of this discourse emerged in Colbert King's column for Sunday, October 12, entitled "He Is Not God." The passion in this article makes it worth considering at length. First, King mocked the sniper's claim to be God, claiming that God would not make schools go

gative reporter. (Sources: *Washington Post* website, http://www.washingtonpost.com/wp-srv/liveonline/01/magazine/magazine_kovaleski071601.htm; and http://www.washingtonpost.com/wp-dyn/content/discussion/2006/01/13/DI2 006011300555.html; *New York Times* website, http://topics.nytimes.com/top/reference/timestopics/people/k/serge_f_kovaleski/index.html.)

into lockdown, make parents worry for their children, or cause drivers and walkers to take special care.

Instead King asserted that these events occurred because responsible people had to deal with a mentally ill person who deemed himself important. "In reality, he's nothing but a dweeb with some bullets and a rifle." The columnist labeled the shooter an "egomaniac" who was absolutely nothing without his weapon. King continued: "The predator pulling the trigger, mean and contemptible as he is, will be a forgotten figure within a few years of his capture. He was of little moment before taking up arms against people who have done him no wrong. He will, in due course, return to insignificance after his reckoning with justice. No amount of planned violence can win him the stardom or the distinction he so desperately craves." King declared: "These senseless slayings will end." His commentary prophesied, "He will be brought down." Eloquent in its passion, this piece clearly revealed a vision of the sniper as utterly beyond redemption. King described him: "He may operate in a different moral universe from the rest of us but he is still in our world." He was in the world, but not part of the community. So inconsequential was he that his motives need not be uncovered. To be forgotten would be his fate.

In evidence contained within the *Post* articles for October 8, though far less than in many television shows, were the insights gleaned from criminal profilers–a fourth way of cataloging the sniper. Readers of the paper learned about the categories of "serial killer," "mass murderer," and "spree killer." Analysts wrestled with the appropriateness of applying such categories given the changing circumstances that accompanied each slaying. The analysis that seemed most to resonate–and that kicked off Colbert King's analysis cited above–was that the criminal, by shooting from afar, did not have to reckon with the psychological ramifications of the carnage caused by the bullet. (This, of course, contradicts the thrust of the previously described analysis by Stephen Hunter.) Furthermore, the sniper's eluding the police made the events appear as a game. While other versions of these characterizations emerged, all suggested that the shooter was a totally aberrant being from outside society.

Finally, even though frequently debunked, the notion that the attacks were the work of terrorists never really disappeared from the *Post*. And in fact, two articles that appeared on October 16 and 18 took this possibility quite seriously. The first, headlined "Experts Look For a

Link to Al Qaeda Attacks," carefully examined the likelihood of such a
tie, concluding in the end that it was less, rather than more, likely. But
an op-ed piece by Caleb Carr,[10] who had written a book on terrorism,
argued in favor of this possibility. After dismissing the categories outlined by the profilers, Carr argued that terrorists had behaved similarly
to the sniper. Beginning just before the anniversary of the U.S. invasion
of Afghanistan, the Washington-area assaults coincided with intelligence predictions of resumed al-Qaeda activity. The sniper's tactics
resembled paramilitary tactics in which a cell might carry out the killings. By using only one weapon, the terrorists created the illusion of a
superhuman killer. Additionally, these attacks in the capital showed the
power of the terrorists. Even the failure to claim responsibility fitted the
pattern established by al-Qaeda. Indeed, Carr claimed that Americans
must confront "the . . . terrifying possibility that a new kind of enemy is
conducting an unprecedented campaign within our borders – and is, for
the moment, winning it."

   More thoroughly than any of the other visions, this last one placed
the sniper outside the community. In fact, overall, the imagined sniper
projected by the *Post* mainly depicted this individual, or occasionally
individuals, as looming beyond the walls of society and threatening it.
As this sniper was excluded, the community could then constitute itself
as pure in its defense. The established border created a stronger interior
for society. Even the notion that the perpetrator was white – a point that
I have not mentioned here because it was less a part of the *Post* reporting than elsewhere – served to keep the community whole. Had the *Post*
identified the attacker as non-white, or, more particularly, as African
American, the sniper might be said to have emerged from social fis-
sures existing in the region and the nation. With a sniper coming from
within, from prior struggles, the crisis would have seemed inherent
to society. As white, though – and depicted as unjustifiably angry – the
sniper seemed crazed.

   Ironically, while such negative treatments of the sniper added to

10. Author and military historian Caleb Carr has written several novels and
nonfiction books, including his 2002 work *The Lessons of Terror: A History of
Warfare against Civilians*. In addition, he is the author of numerous works for the
stage and screen. Currently a contributing editor of *MHQ: The Quarterly Journal of
Military History*, he has taught military history at Bard College. He has also appeared on the PBS series *American Experience* as a commentator. (Source: Wikipedia: The Free Encyclopedia, http://en.wikipedia.org/wiki/Caleb_Carr.)

the threat, the same position occupied by the sniper as outsider allowed the *Post* to strike a number of themes that attested to a unified and strong community. First and foremost was the posthumous treatment of the killed. The obvious model for the assessments of such individuals is the obituary. For public figures, these attempt a balanced view of a life. Private individuals receive a listing of their positions and achievements, but seldom do they receive either plaudits or criticism regarding their personal traits. Yet the coverage of the sniper's victims, full of encomiums and compliments regarding their character, approximated that of war casualties. As the ultimate antithesis of the sniper, his targets emerged as beacons to the community. Furthermore, they strengthened the sense of community, because everyone else–other than the sniper–could relate to them. Such an emotion was amplified because of the nature of this event. Clearly, the victims were involved in everyday activities that no one could really avoid–mowing the lawn, shopping, going to school, taking a walk, waiting on the bus, and pumping gas. So often, individuals feel immune from unfortunate disasters because they are not in similar circumstances. But in this case, these tasks constituted American everyday life, and created empathy with the victims. Second, the geographic and ethnic uncertainty of the shooter created an association that embraced everyone in the region. Thus, the method of reporting about the victims, coupled to the indiscriminate killing across activity, area, gender, and ethnicity, created a bond knitting together those in the Washington, D.C., and Richmond, Virginia, corridor.

Specific elements in the coverage of the dead–both the news of their demise and the funerals–enhanced the notion that these were members of the readers' community. Repeatedly, the *Post* stressed the helpfulness of the victims. Sarah Ramos, killed in the first day of the shootings, was a "doting mother to her seven-year-old son, Carlos, Jr., a dedicated member of local church groups, a beloved babysitter to several area children" (October 8). And "acquaintances described" Dean Meyers, who was killed in Manassas, as "a quiet friendly man who jogged through the development and was always ready to lend a hand" (October 11). Kenneth H. Bridges, murdered at a gas station in Spotsylvania County, was "an uncommonly decent man, the kind who welcomed newcomers to the neighborhood with a basket of homemade chocolate cupcakes" (October 12). As for the student wounded at Tasker Middle School, "Neighbors and classmates described the wounded child as a sweet-natured, well-behaved boy, always quick to help others" (October 7). By making service the most consistently noted characteristic of the victims, the *Post* emphasized community ties.

In addition to helpfulness, other qualities mentioned included a love of children, family, and spouse. Also, the characteristic of humility was common to the descriptions of the victims (October 20). Of course, as noted, they died doing normal, everyday activities, but the *Post* frequently mentioned that this humbleness was a commonplace in their regular lives. James D. Martin, the sniper's first victim, was known as "just plain old Jim." At the funeral, the pastor noted that Jim would have been embarrassed by the attention. The minister stated, "I know he'd be hanging around today, saying, 'You're overdoing this. This is not what I had in mind'" (October 10). Similarly, one young man at the funeral for James "Sonny" Buchanan remembered the help James had given him at the Boys and Girls Club ten years earlier. Although he officially served as a mentor, James just tried to be his friend (October 10).

By characterizing the victims as loving, helpful, and modest, the *Post* constructed something of a secular icon for the community. As noted, this praise was not accompanied by any criticism. This pattern held even in the treatment of Kenneth Bridges, who was deeply involved in African American economic empowerment. By labeling his efforts "internal reparations," Bridges was, to some extent, indicting white indifference (October 12). Some of the *Post* readers may have felt some hostility toward such efforts, but the *Post* did not acknowledge the potential unpopularity of Bridges's work. This silence left the place of the victims undisturbed, so that they could be both a reflection of and an inspiration to the community.

To sum up the tendency to lionize the victims, one need only return to the Colbert King column that placed the snipers in a "different moral universe." In contrast, King pointed to the victims as people "of real consequence . . . well-liked and deeply loved." They had been killed by sneak attacks. Even as profilers conceded that the snipers were competent, King argued that they were not merely evil-doers. And King continued, regarding those who had been killed: "They are the ones whose lives are valued. They are the ones who will be remembered. To them goes the glory." In his assertion that losing them had been a "defining event" for the area, King signaled that their deaths were crucial to the community.

Further strengthening the sense of community was the frequently expressed assumption that children had been the main victims of the sniper. The angry reaction of Montgomery County, Maryland, police chief Charles Moose[11] to the wounding of the Tasker Middle School student–that this was getting personal–repeatedly found resonance in the *Post*. Articles expanded variously on this subject, and an editorial cartoon of October 12 depicted a child who carried a giant backpack marked FEAR. Another story quoted a psychiatry professor who opined that students were at least as traumatized by the shootings as they had been by the events of September 11, 2001. Likewise, a poll reported in the October 24 edition of the *Post* revealed that parents were particularly concerned for their children. One in four parents had decided to keep their children home from school or had picked them up early. One in six no longer sent their kids on the school bus. This repeated theme of threatened and frightened school children further marked the boundary, by vilifying the object of fear, the shooter, and indirectly elevating the community for its defense of children.

The major ambivalence that articles in the *Post* showed about community came, it seems to me, in how the authorities seeking to manage the crisis were depicted. To be sure, the paper purveyed a great deal of reassurance, much more so than was the case with many television news shows. Some journalistic attention was focused on the operation of the task force, which appeared, over time, to be doing its job more efficiently and more rapidly.[12] Furthermore, the *Post* reported in its story on the poll mentioned above, the public endorsed law enforcement. Eight out of ten people found the efforts of the police to be either "good" or "outstanding." But it was the public face of the police, Chief Moose, who drew the most attention. And he was the recipient of some positive reporting. On October 6, for example, Maryland State Attorney Douglas Gansler, a sometime critic of Moose, noted that the chief had been very accessible to the media. The *Post* quoted Gansler as saying that Moose had "responded both to well-thought-out as well as

11. Charles Alexander Moose has been in law enforcement since 1975, when he joined the Portland Police Bureau in Oregon. He had earned a bachelor's degree in history from the University of North Carolina at Chapel Hill, a master's degree in public administration from Portland State University, and a doctorate in urban studies and criminology. Moose was named police chief of the Portland police force in 1993, and remained in that job until 1999, when he joined the Montgomery County, Md., police force as chief. After resigning his position in 2003, Moose authored a book about the D.C. sniper case titled *Three Weeks in October: The Manhunt for the Serial Sniper*. He later served with the D.C. Air National Guard and was a member of the Honolulu Police Department. (Source: Wikipedia: The Free Encyclopedia, http://en.wikipedia.org/wiki/Charles_Moose.)

12. Cf. the *Washington Post* for October 12 and October 17.

naïve questions in an even-tempered, positive manner, and that's important because this is a difficult case." Another article, a few days later, presented an exceptionally moving characterization of Moose, who, it was reported, broke down, a tear trickling down his cheek, after the incident at Tasker Middle School. The *Post*'s report emphasized the silence that followed Moose's show of emotion, and then his embrace of his deputy as they left the news conference. This portrayal communicated solemnity, which was underlined by the comment that Moose's sincere response had made Montgomery police officers proud because it showed his compassionate side. When Moose later apologized for this emotional break in his professional demeanor, the *Post* cited those who approved his reaction. The article concluded with a description of Moose pushing past his own anger to continue the business of capturing the sniper.

Contrasting with the glowing reports on the police were outbursts of critiques. Not surprisingly, as the crisis wore on, expressions of frustration with the police force emerged. After the slaying of a bus driver on October 22, the *Post* the next morning quoted one local resident as declaring, "Can't they just find this guy?" Two articles and many comments attacked various aspects of the investigation, particularly the coordination and efforts of the consolidated force that included many different elements of law enforcement. Complaints centered on the inefficiency of the system for receiving tips from the public, the lack of sharing among the various partners in the investigation, and the ineffectiveness of the dragnets that were thrown up after shooting episodes. The *Post* interviewed police officers who expressed real anger over how poorly the structure of the team worked. Some policemen were vocal in their criticism: " 'It's a total bureaucracy, with guys who have never worked a homicide wanting to know every little detail,' said one Prince George's county detective. 'We have all these hurdles to jump, just a lot of BS to wade through.' 'In some instances, there is duplication of work, and it's just a mess,' a Montgomery officer said. 'It's not a situation that's presented in the press conferences.' " The majority demanded anonymity to avoid retribution. Another article discussed possible violations of civil liberties that were occurring through overzealous police stops (October 21).

Despite occasional positive reports, articles in the *Post* were especially critical of Chief Moose. Appreciation for the capture of the snipers and then a controversy over Moose's decision to write his own book about the events may have somewhat obscured the earlier barbs. These included the view that even though Moose sought the limelight, he gave only cryptic, unhelpful answers. The biggest flack, however, came over Moose's anger with the media for printing information about a tarot card left at the scene of the Tasker Middle School shooting. For example, Marc Fisher devoted his entire October 10 column on the Metro front page to an attack on Moose. First, Fisher claimed that every time Moose lost his temper, the sniper reveled in this success. Then Fisher went on to castigate Moose in a sarcastic barrage of criticism about his "almost constant briefings." After referring to Moose's "petulant little tantrums," Fisher continued:

> Then yesterday, he got the morning off to another bizarre start with a rant against Channel 9 and *The Washington Post*, which had performed a public service by getting word out about the tarot card found near the site of the last shooting–information that could spark a memory in someone who knows the killer.
>
> But all the chief could think about was his pride. "I have not received any message that the citizens of Montgomery County want Channel 9 or *The Washington Post* or any other media outlet to solve this case," he railed. "If they do, then let me know. We will go and do other police work, and we will turn this case over to the media."
>
> If you can't take the heat, bud, turn the investigation over to the professionals.

Fisher contrasted Moose's effort with that of the Prince George's police chief, Gerald Wilson, who was not "wasting his time hanging out with and haranguing the assembled TV mob; we can assume that he is actually supervising police work." Reacting to Moose's warning about journalists giving information that would alert or upset the sniper, Fisher retorted: "The chief should have listened to his own advice: It was Moose himself who spent the hours before Monday's shooting of a 13-year-old boy talking about morning rush hour as a 'target-rich environment.' "

As a conclusion, Fisher dwelt on the chief's temperamental past, not only in Portland, Oregon, but even in 1999 in Montgomery County, where Moose once responded to a reporter: "I guess you all think I'm an (expletive)." Finally, Fisher restated his accusation that Moose's behavior had only energized the sniper. Yet another volley of criticism occurred after the chief did not inform the public of another threat against children, in the wake of the final shooting on October 22.

A lack of trust in the authorities at times destabilized the sense of community which much *Post* reporting had encouraged. And there were many articles that expressed significant fear, including some that focused on very high levels of anxiety. Based on a series of interviews, one October 6 story reported how area residents equated these events with 9/11 and experienced equivalent feelings of hopelessness and fear. Elsewhere, despite a few defiant and resistant customers, business was reported to be dreadfully off. On October 16, one businessman was reported to have said that he no longer even trusted his own customers. Yet another article, on October 21, while conceding some residents were immune, described the expanding zone of fear as the snipers extended their range of activities. These pieces continued a string of stories in the *Post* that detailed the spread of anxiety into specific areas as attacks occurred. For example, on October 11, an article following the shooting of Dean Meyers began with the headline "Death Toll at 7 in Attacks Across an Anxious Region" and chronicled the series of shootings. Countering some hopeful reporting about the police response was the ongoing commentary about problems with the witness report hotline.

Appearing in the *Post* were other stories which, while still emphasizing fear, focused far more on coping strategies being used. Perhaps the most interesting was the account that appeared on October 8 and featured zigzag walking as a way to reduce the sniper's opportunity. While a practical effort, this method forced the individual at every step to admit the presence of fear and the possibility of being shot. Likewise, an account on the reaction at Benjamin Tasker Middle School documented how the teachers, who themselves wavered between confidence and fright, were dealing with nervous, excited schoolchildren. An editorial on the same day, chronicling the "new level of fear," opined: "This is what terror is about, after all: The randomness of violence that makes everyone a potential victim and any activity, no matter how prosaic, potentially fatal."[13] Yet this same opinion piece argued that helping the kids demanded more than that. A final example of feeling fear but not completely giving into it was an article that discussed fear in terms of trying to overcome it. The title, though, was not encouraging: "Be Afraid of Being Afraid." It would seem one simply had a choice of which fear to embrace.

13. Ibid., October 20, 2002.

More than simply sharing a lack of confidence common among the press, the *Post* writers published extensively about a compelling fear or the fear that required some sort of active response. And, as it seemed to Marjorie Williams, the preponderance of the articles emphasized fear. Moreover, they made much clearer statements than did the encouraging stories that the *Post* published regarding a concerned but effectively coping public. As most of the later stories provided oblique support by their emphasis on community spirit, these stories were not as powerful as were those that documented and editorialized about fear.

In the end, one should not expect coherence from a paper whose coverage was somewhat decentralized and included editorials, letters to the editor, analysis, and many news reports. Moreover, these articles sprang from the context of the events occurring around them. Yet, a general pattern of articles emphasizing fear and a sense of community emerged, with the former more evident, indeed, evident enough to cast a consistent pall over whatever strengths were revealed.

As we shall see in succeeding chapters, other publications, both electronic and print, also emphasized fear in a manner similar to that of the *Post.* Interestingly, though, the rest of the media reported far less about community in relation to the sniper than did Washington's major paper. Before exploring the shared emphasis on fear in the rest of the press, it is worth explaining why the *Post* undertook far more community reporting. First, the *Washington Post* conceived of itself, contrary to its reputation for national impact and focus, as a distinctly local paper. As Jo-Ann Armao, Paul Duggan, and Craig Timberg pointed out in their interviews with me, the Metro section possessed the largest staff of any division at that time. Second, the reporters noted, unlike its natural competitor the *New York Times*, the *Post* remained so committed to its own region that it had not, and still has not, committed to national distribution. Unlike the *New York Times*, the *Wall Street Journal,* and *USA Today*, the *Post*'s publishers still have not attempted the common local delivery all across the United States. Indeed, even in regard to the website, the *Post* was much later than the *New York Times* to commit major resources to developing that medium, which would clearly appear to those outside its delivery area and thus create an incentive to reduce local reporting. All these factors put together showed the *Post*'s greater concentration on a broad concern with community affairs. Given the *Post*'s superior resources, compared with any other local outlet in the area affected by the sniper, no other publication could mount significant competition. Competing publications barely had sufficient resources and/or space to cover the incredibly complex and ever developing crime story. Thus, as we shall see, the focus of the rest proceeded without the same moderating influence of a sustained focus on community relations.[14]

14. Only the *Baltimore Sun* came close to the *Post* in terms of resources, but it still did not have the same large number of reporters to commit to the story. And indeed, although the sampling necessary to this project omitted a systematic analysis of the *Sun,* studying that paper would not have changed the overall impression of the difference between the *Post* and the mass of periodicals and television stations.

## Continuous Coverage

At the height of the events related to the snipers, there seemingly were more journalists reporting on the events than there were police personnel investigating them. And the reporters, their editors, and their photographers turned out an inexhaustible supply of words, images, and sounds to explain what was occurring. In doing so, these media representatives constructed a contemporaneous narrative of the events. This narrative both contained and embellished a growing sense of mystery and wariness. In many regards, this was axiomatic, given that the identity or identities of the shooter or shooters were not known and what could be reported was limited to the additional deaths and woundings that occurred and what the police were discovering as events occurred.

An important way to analyze this constructed narrative is through the continuous, or wall-to-wall, coverage that was at times available on television. By identifying broadcasts of two hours or more of breaking news, we gain the best vantage point from which to comprehend the narrative of the developing story. In most other sorts of coverage, minutes, hours, or even days elapse between events and publication, and this lends a degree of historical reflection to stories. Continuous coverage, on the other hand, creates a plotline that accompanies the viewer through some sort of chronological span of time. Literally, one feels time pass as reported events occur. In other media venues, however, time usually collapses into a series of complex stories, or something akin to a Bruegel painting. Chronology does not disappear, but its overall impact is reduced, since the reader is required to expend greater effort to link the episodes and create the narrative suggested by them.

In addition to creating the sensation of time ticking away, continuous coverage, when repeated over several periods, as it was in October

2002, also made the sniper event more whole. In other words, present-ing a plethora of information developing moment by moment pre-sented the killings much more clearly as an unfolding narrative. It also increased the personal agony and involvement, and permitted a more profound–indeed a more stark–type of memory. Continuous television coverage in particular doubtless created much more of the meta-narrative than did reporting by the other media. By studying these periods of continuous television coverage, we can see the story develop-ing and deepening its themes. Furthermore, the intensity of this re-porting allows us to understand better than any other way how this news appeared to and impacted upon its contemporary observers.

This continuous coverage also demands attention because it is a significant factor in analyzing what makes the coverage of the sniper different from the reporting of other, equally serious, prior events. While television previously had turned its cameras on other stories for long periods of time, only in the preceding couple of decades had this kind of saturation been so compelling and so frequent, enabled in large part by the emergence of 24-hour news channels. Further analysis probably could place coverage of this event among its peers, in terms of length of broadcasts and numbers of viewers, but at the very least, the coverage of the sniper events must be included in any consideration of a substantial vaulting up in this kind of media blitz.

One more advantage of considering continuous, or wall-to-wall, coverage is the analytical novelty. While students of television have for some time been able to study the medium, only quite recently has tech-nology made it possible to see television as it actually existed, commer-cials and all, at the time of broadcast. Earlier, much of the spontaneous coverage that had gone on was completely inaccessible to scholars. Although networks and even local stations have preserved increasing amounts of programming, accessing this material has been very diffi-cult and/or prohibitively expensive. The emergence of Shadow TV, which at this moment records and then makes available to subscribers much of the programming over a significant period in major markets, including several cable channels as they existed in New York City, has changed this situation.

To analyze coverage of the sniper events, I focused on the main sources of continuous coverage–Washington's major broadcast-ing channels (ABC, CBS, FOX, and NBC) and cable news channels (CNN, FOX National, and MSNBC). Unfortunately, Shadow TV was a less stable medium in October 2002, when it was in its infancy, than it later became, so the local channels were not always recorded. Further complicating research is the fact that this was a service not then distributed by universities, which made the cost of access substantial for an individual. Finally, watching this coverage can potentially consume huge amounts of time, as one has to consider the images, the words, and the overall impact. Of course, voluminous note-taking becomes necessary.

For this analysis, I isolated all the periods of continuous coverage, of which there were eight in all. For half of these, only cable news was available. After spot-checking for comparison's sake, I found that relatively little difference existed among the three main cable channels, and so selected CNN. For the other four episodes, I relied upon the local channels alone. Although how these channels analyzed events did differ from the analysis offered by the cable channels, the main thrust of reporting was similar enough that it was possible to focus on the local channels. The main deviation in my approach to local units—as opposed to utilizing a single cable channel—was the use of all four of the Washington stations, even though all were generally similar. Yet, by watching all four, I gained insight into how these local TV stations competed in their own market. Further comparative research could yield a similar payoff regarding the cable channels, but that work was not part of this project. Time constraints and financial considerations argued otherwise.

According to Steve Hammel, then vice-president for news at the local ABC affiliate, electing to go to continuous coverage cost the stations considerable revenue at the time, at least in the short term, yet they did it on several occasions during the weeks of the sniper incidents. While competition certainly played a leading role in the decision to go on the air in this way, and also in when to return to regular programming, it seems that, in part, the local channels also made their decisions as a matter of public service and perceived obligation. For all-news cable stations, the specter of financial loss was also present, as they had to focus resources, yet this remained a good story and higher ratings did follow its broadcast. All in all, continuous coverage was an approach that was significant on eight days in October. So prevalent was this form that Michael Buchanan,[1] an early-morning anchor for WUSA, the CBS

1. Broadcaster Mike Buchanan anchored the local news for the CBS affiliate in Washington, WUSA9, for thirty-three years. He then spent a year—2004 to 2005—as a general assignment reporter with WJLA, Washington's ABC affiliate. In 2005, Buchanan left his full-time job in television to join the world of radio, although he remains as a part-time contributor to WJLA. Looking to escape the daily grind of

affiliate, was relieved during the sniper killings when he awoke to the sound of advertisements being run on his television. This signaled that no additional shootings had occurred.

Yet for all the emphasis on these broadcasts, which in the most exuberant situations ran well over twelve hours straight, substantial similarities emerged–at least in terms of the basic structure. Stations came on the air with a loud fanfare heralding important and significant developments in the sniper case. The logic or teleology of the initial announcement was that something big had happened. Staying on the air suggested that something else was going to occur live–at the least, new information, but ideally, a resolution to the case. On the whole, however, these outcomes proved elusive. In any case, new information remained scarce because of the nature of the shootings. There was little the reporters could ascertain about the snipers or the shootings. Ballistics evidence took many hours to process. And the police became increasingly tight-lipped as events wore on and the search for the shooter or shooters grew more tense. Good images oftentimes were even difficult to obtain, because of a lack of action. Moreover, the distance of the shooter or shooters from the victims pushed out the parameters of the crime scenes so far that getting a good angle for the cameras was nearly impossible. At some scenes, reporters rented rooms in buildings with better views.

In this environment, news outlets sometimes had little new to report, and tended to recycle information from earlier news reports. Over a long period, information was repeated. As material trickled in, older information was replaced, so that after several cycles a largely new report was constructed. But this took a long time to accomplish, and, in the end, all the broadcasts, even the finale with the capture of John Muhammad and Lee Boyd Malvo, simply tended to fade out. As Steve Hammel later explained, the station stayed on until there were no prospects of any new developments that would have forced it back on the air

---

local news coverage, Buchanan now critiques the absurdity of everyday life in his daily "rant," *The Buch Stops Here,* on WTOP Radio. Describing his goal as telling good stories with humor, he targets overpriced ballpark fare and slow checkers at the supermarket–in the express lane. "We're going to pick on the weatherman," Buchanan said prior to debuting his show. "We're going to pick on people." According to the *Washington Post,* Buchanan can be described as "boisterous, unpredictable and slightly rumpled." (Sources: WTOP.com website, http://www.wtopnews .com/index.php?nid=62&sid=511634; *Washington Post* website, http://www.wash ingtonpost.com/wp-dyn/content/article/2005/04/28/AR2005042801947.html.)

in the immediate future. The end of a continuous-coverage episode or session, then, was mainly a matter of news personnel giving up hope for an immediate resolution. In short, these broadcasts generally were very demoralizing to a regional population hoping for relief.

Yet this general pattern of reporting cannot account for all the specific aspects of the wall-to-wall coverage. Beginning with the morning of October 3, this study considers the phenomenon in detail. By analyzing each of the efforts at continuous coverage, up to the night of the capture, the chapter reveals an ebb and flow of levels of fear, punctuated by some hope. But only with the capture of Malvo and Muhammad was anxiety seriously relieved, and replaced with relief. Thus, when balanced against the coverage of the *Post,* this kind of television moves the overall reporting much more in the direction of fear.

Yet beyond the fear, as noted at the very beginning of this chapter, this kind of coverage did create a story, in four parts. The first events encouraged only fear, but in the central period, lasting some ten days, the focus on the police created some sense of forward progress. With the spate of problems in the last few days leading up to the capture, despair reemerged. Finally, by seizing the snipers, the police provided redemption. In this genre of reporting, we can truly see a narrative. One cannot overstate the positive middle of the story, since every investigation, prior to the denouement, ended in failure. Indeed, when we contrast this description with that implied by the actions of the schools, we see a resiliency in the latter that is stronger and more consistent than in continuous coverage. Further, lacking the community aspect of *Post* reporting, continuous coverage was decidedly more fearful.

• • •

Already on the evening preceding October 3, Muhammad and Malvo had fired a shot into a Michael's store in Wheaton, Maryland, and had then killed James D. Martin in a nearby grocery store parking lot. The next morning, in an effort that attracted the notice of the media, the two men killed a string of individuals: at 7:41 a.m., James L. "Sonny" Buchanan; at 8:12 a.m., Premkumar Walekar; at 8:37 a.m., Sarah Ramos; and at 9:58 a.m., Lori Ann Lewis-Rivera. Although Muhammad and Malvo had already apparently killed five and wounded four others in preceding months in a national crime spree, it was these four shootings on that Thursday morning that crystallized and created the public phenomenon of the sniper as the Washington community and then the nation came to know it. Doubtless, the geographical and temporal concentration of the murders played strong roles in the impact of the events.

While local stations were the first to start covering the story, their broadcasts are not accessible, and I must turn to CNN. To supplement CNN, a network that clearly began covering the story later than did the local outlets, I secured and will use the coverage of the Washington all-news radio channel, WTOP. In later sniper shootings, with the story better understood as important, the gap between local and national outlets diminished, and this makes the use of CNN sensible as a general marker. Yet here, in this one, admittedly important case, CNN paid less attention than did the locals and stayed on for a shorter time. It can, however, serve as a reasonable approximation.

Early in the morning, WTOP was reporting the previous evening's shooting of James Martin, but it was not until 9:20 a.m., well after the deaths of three new victims, that WTOP mentioned the additional violence. At 9:20 a.m., the anchor reported two victims, but did not refer to the initial killing that morning at 7:41.

Breaking with this partial and illusory coverage came the first substantial report, at 9:52 a.m., just over half an hour after the initial report. With seemingly no reporter on the scene, the anchor announced that a manhunt was underway for the shooter, whose victims now numbered three. Rather gruesomely, the second victim had been killed by a shot to the head, the anchor reported.

This slowly emerging story then began to swim into focus at 10:21 a.m. when WTOP reporter Kristi King[2] arrived at the scene of one of the shootings and announced that four individuals were dead. She then connected the four more-recent victims to the victim of the previous evening, making a total of five dead. Over the next forty-five minutes, her repeated reports, which varied somewhat, began to construct themes that showed perseverance. Most notably, when listing each victim, she rather forcefully added "shot and killed." This repeatedly emphasized phrase drove home the finality of death with an omi-

2. Kristi King has been a member of the WTOP news team since November 1, 1990. Prior to her move to the Washington, D.C., metro region, King worked as a reporter for a Jacksonville, Fla., radio station. When she was transferred from news to traffic coverage, she realized that the fun of reporting from an airplane high above the city wasn't what she wanted and she was drawn back to news. Ironically, her first job in Washington was as a traffic reporter for WTOP Radio. Her time monitoring D.C. traffic lasted only five months, however, as the outbreak of the first Gulf War brought her back into the newsroom, where she remains. In July 2008, King took her reporting to another level, jumping out of an airplane with the Army's Golden Knights. (Sources: WTOP.com website, http://www.wtop.com/?nid=74&sid=598 739; wtop.com, http://www.wtop.com/?nid=25&sid=1446686.)

nous tone. Further emphasizing fear was a report about police officers working with tears in their eyes. The radio also initially reported that a truck–identified as an Isuzu–had been the escape vehicle. Despite the emergence of a seemingly horrific and potentially related set of crimes, King's report underlined that the police knew little about the events. Furthermore, these reports came in during a scheduled one-hour interview with D.C. police chief Charles H. Ramsey. Although interviewer Bruce Alan[3] asked the chief his opinion about the crimes, the interview concentrated on numerous other questions.

Only after 11:00 a.m. did WTOP really pull out the stops and begin heavy coverage of the newly emerging sniper story, taking breaks away from it for some other stories and for weather and traffic updates. Another reporter, Steve Eldridge,[4] arrived at the Shell station where Lori Ann Lewis-Rivera had been fatally shot. His report, which mentioned abandoned booster seats beside the victim's car, brought home the tragedy to listeners. Furthermore, the anchor interviewed Brian Porter,[5] of the Montgomery County Public Schools, who announced a lockdown of the system, adding further gravity to the situation depicted by the coverage. For forty minutes, WTOP focused almost entirely on this

3. Bruce Alan has been a news anchor for WTOP in Washington for seventeen years. He has covered breaking news, as well as performing myriad interviews with subjects ranging from politicians to Hollywood celebrities. Alan was also the host of WTOP's award-winning *Ask The* series–including "Ask the Governor" and "Ask the Mayor." He is the recipient of numerous awards, including an Edward R. Murrow Award and several Achievement in Radio awards. (Source: WTOP.com website, http://www.wtop.com/?nid=73&sid=598762.)

4. Reporter Steve Eldridge has spent many years focusing on transportation issues in the Washington, D.C., metro region. He has written for the *Washington Examiner* and currently writes an online column titled "Sprawl and Crawl," which is hosted by CommuterPageBlog. (Source: CommuterPageBlog.com website, http://www.commuterpageblog.com/sprawl_and_crawl_with_steve_eldridge/index.html.)

5. Brian Porter has a master's degree in Education Administration and a bachelor's degree in Journalism. He started his career as a reporter for a local newspaper in Washington, D.C. Porter was the Montgomery County Public Schools Director of Communication and chief spokesman for fourteen years, becoming chief of staff in July 2004. In August 2007, Porter announced his retirement to work full-time on a doctorate in education policy and leadership studies at the University of Maryland. (Sources: Porter interview; Montgomery County website, http://www.montgomerycountymd.gov/mcgtmpl.asp?url=/Content/RSC/BCC/Summaries/071904.asp; Gazette.net website, http://www.gazette.net/stories/082407/polinew14705_32360.shtml.)

story and scarcely mentioned any other news, which is very unusual for this station whose coverage at the time tended more toward sound bites – a series of headlines with very brief stories.

This high degree of concentration by the radio station specifically signaled the seriousness of the situation. Other than the nature of the crime, however, much was left uncertain. Listeners heard little about the perpetrators or the police response to the events. Following the initial burst of coverage, the radio station emphasized the story, but then, as the afternoon began, it covered other stories as well.

As WTOP gathered steam that morning, CNN started to pick up the story. All through the morning, CNN clearly was planning to spend the time focusing on Hurricane Lilli, which was headed into the Gulf Coast. But as Lilli fizzled and lost her punch, news of the shootings began to surface. At the top of the eleven o'clock news hour, CNN ran a brief note on the five murders. Within twenty minutes, the coverage shifted to a news conference with Montgomery County police chief Charles Moose, in whose jurisdiction the murders had occurred, and for the next hour and a half, CNN substantially featured the emerging sniper story. While the channel did not move into a pure wall-to-wall mode, as would become normal with later events, the cable network allowed this story to predominate in its news coverage until one o'clock in the afternoon. Limited attention was devoted to the impending Iraq war and to Hurricane Lilli. Even ads ran, though infrequently.

Several features of CNN's reporting are worthy of attention. First, in this initial coverage, CNN had no camera crew of its own and relied on feeds from stations in Baltimore and Washington. More importantly, CNN's live shots were particularly unenlightening. Mainly, they pictured the two gas stations where the victims had been hit. From across the street, only pumps, several cars, and significant yellow tape were apparent. Exceptionally, one victim, covered up, was shown. Still, the scene was more confusing than it was ominous.

On the other hand, CNN's reports directly and indirectly emphasized the fear gripping the area. For example, an interview with the owner of the Shell station was particularly gruesome in the description of the murder scene. Since the slain woman had slipped under her car, the corpse had to be dragged out from beneath the automobile. Further, at several intervals, commentators mentioned that the scene seemed unusually gory for a murder scene. The Shell station owner admitted that he felt "shaky" and pretty bad. When CNN reporter Bob

Franken[6] first arrived in Montgomery County, anchor Wolf Blitzer[7] questioned whether there was a great sense of fear. Franken replied that there was "huge" apprehension.

As we shall see, local and national coverage often produced mediocre images that then were paired with the reporters' more-powerful words. This was, in the jargon of Washington TV, a better "tell" than "show" story. Furthermore, even during this early coverage, some differences emerged that require discussion. At the beginning, CNN broadcasters had to explain the story to their national audience. Not only did they use a map to show Montgomery County's location, they also felt it necessary to explain that this area was prosperous. This, of course, would not have been necessary for local channels. However, as the crisis continued, CNN's reports presumed that viewers knew as much as did local-area station viewers, and so the earlier difference in the amount of basic information evaporated. One other element of this mention of the wealth of Montgomery County deserves comment. That is, an unspoken assumption seemed to be that such crises are linked to poverty or impoverished areas. By noting the high economic status of the area where these events were occurring, the correspondents seemingly changed the story from one which most watchers could imagine did not pertain to them to one with which most would identify. In a sense, as many commentators and journalists remarked, what differentiated the sniper story from most crime stories was that it undermined the tendency by most of the audience to use the characteristics of a crime as a way to figure out how to avoid it. As these murders occurred in such places, fewer would feel they could escape. More would feel fearful.

A persistent difference between CNN and the local Washington channels was the inclination to analyze the situation. CNN immediately

6. Bob Franken is a former CNN political correspondent and an Emmy Award–winning journalist. He has covered a range of political and breaking news stories over several decades, including both Iraq wars, Guantanamo Bay, and the activities of Congress and the Supreme Court. He is currently a correspondent for MSNBC. (Sources: Washington Speakers Bureau website, http://www.washingtonspeakers .com/speakers/speaker.cfm?SpeakerId=2397; Wikipedia: The Free Encylopedia, http://en.wikipedia.org/wiki/Bob_Franken.)

7. Reporter Wolf Blitzer has been with CNN since 1990, where he has performed a variety of roles. In addition to serving as the network's military affairs reporter, Blitzer has anchored the Sunday morning program *Late Edition with Wolf Blitzer,* as well as *The World Today* and *Wolf Blitzer Reports.* He currently hosts *The Situation Room,* a daily program focusing on current world events. (Source: Wikipedia: The Free Encyclopedia, http://en.wikipedia.org/wiki/Wolf_Blitzer.)

called in one of its own criminologists, Mike Brooks, to comment on and explain the events. This effort to interpret did, as we shall see, exceed that of local broadcast channels. Furthermore, the locals were more likely to rely on journalists than professionals trained in relevant fields. Nevertheless, Brooks could add little. In fact, like WTOP, the cable network felt its way forward, as it encountered a difficult, even frightening, situation. This uncertainty and fear deepened in successive wall-to-wall reports.

The next outbreak of continuous coverage occurred on Monday, October 7, after the early morning, nonfatal shooting of a thirteen-year-old junior high school student. This incident built upon the fears engendered by the first shootings that, in the interval, had been exacerbated by ballistics tests that linked all of the deaths to a single weapon. Certainly, the report of the ballistics tests contributed to decisions to go to wall-to-wall coverage of this event, signaling, as it did, the ongoing and expanding nature of the events. Yet another factor contributed to the coverage. Montgomery County Police Chief Moose had reassured the public the preceding Friday by asserting that the schools were safe. Now, a middle-school child had been shot on his way from his aunt's car to the doors of the school building. Later, commentators on the series of events would question whether Moose's comments were not a red flag to which the snipers responded. In any case, the still-echoing but failed reassurances probably played a role in decisions to open continuous coverage of the events, alongside the facts of these particular events themselves.

At 8:09 a.m., Iran Brown arrived early at Benjamin Tasker Junior High, in Bowie, Maryland (Prince George's County), and was gunned down by shooters crouched just to the north of the school. His aunt, who was a nurse, had dropped him off. She immediately returned when she saw him fall. She drove him directly to medical facilities. By the time the school's principal arrived from inside the building, both boy and aunt were gone. The principal, John Lloyd,[8] did not know what had

---

8. At the time of his interview, John Lloyd had been at Benjamin Tasker Middle School for nine and a half years, six and a half of those years as principal. Previously, he had taught and coached basketball at High Point High School in Maryland. Lloyd resigned from Benjamin Tasker in January 2004, citing the lack of support from Prince George's County in running an overcrowded school. A spokeswoman for the school system, Lynn McCaulley, said of Lloyd: "It's been rough. Ever since the [October sniper] shooting, it's been tough on that principal. I think it was all a lot of pressure for him." (Sources: Lloyd interview; Gazette.net website, http://www.gazette.net/gazette_archive/2004/200404/bowie/news/198281-1.html.)

happened at first, and neither did anyone else. In a little over half an hour, the press would begin to cover this case. All four local channels were on the air before 9 a.m. and basically continued coverage until the local evening newscasts picked up the story.

A careful analysis of the first half-hour is valuable. The themes that developed in those early minutes persisted throughout the day. Coverage began by 8:45 a.m. In the first forty-five minutes, the stations scrambled to get their reporters into position. Channel 7 was the first to go into substantial coverage, relying upon its correspondent already located in Rockville in Montgomery County, where the sniper task force was centered. Despite this initial lead, only at 9:26 a.m. did Brad Bell[9] actually arrive at Benjamin Tasker. Impressively, the NBC affiliate, long seen as the dominant player in local news, had a police spokesperson on the phone at 8:50 a.m., then showed live shots from a helicopter at 8:55 a.m., and finally relied upon Megan McGrath[10] at task force headquarters at 8:56 a.m. But like Channel 7, it took a while for Channel 4's Brian Mooar[11] to arrive on scene, at 9:29 a.m. Although

9. Maryland reporter Brad Bell has been with Washington's ABC affiliate, WJLA, since 1991. He also worked at several additional news organizations prior to joining WJLA, including as field producer for the Washington bureau of the Independent Network News. A general assignment reporter, a State House reporter, an environmental reporter, and a documentary reporter and producer, he is currently Prince George's County, Md., bureau chief for WJLA. Bell has won five local Emmy Awards, including one for his breaking news story about Pfisteria contamination in Maryland waters. (Sources: Wikipedia: The Free Encyclopedia, http://en.wikipedia .org/wiki/WJLA-TV; WJLA website, http://www.wjla.com/pageloader.html?js= wjla&page=talent&pagename=brad_bell.html.)

10. Megan McGrath has been a general assignment reporter for Washington's local NBC affiliate, NBC4, since 1999. A native of Maryland, McGrath began her journalism career at a weekly newspaper before moving to broadcasting. She worked at several television stations in Prince George's County and Baltimore, Md., and at WJLA in Washington before joining NBC4. She is known for her comprehensive coverage of the September 11 attack on the Pentagon, beginning with the event as one of the first reporters on the scene and extending weeks into the aftermath. McGrath is the daughter of Patrick McGrath, a national correspondent for FOX 5 in Washington. (Sources: NBC Washington website, http://www.nbc4.com/meet thenewsteam/1198848/detail.html; Wikipedia: The Free Encyclopedia, http:// en.wikipedia.org/wiki/WRC-TV.)

11. Brian Mooar has been a reporter for the *Washington Post,* an early morning reporter for NBC4 in Washington, and a reporter for MSNBC. Mooar currently works for the Washington Post Company as a reporter. (Sources: Zoominfo website, http://www.zoominfo.com/Search/PersonDetail.aspx?PersonID=56089462; NBC

FOX News had previously announced the shooting, it began to broadcast substantial details at 8:53 a.m. with its own helicopter in the air above the scene. Likewise, while the station had personnel in Montgomery County, nearly an hour elapsed before FOX could broadcast a live shot, from Benjamin Tasker. Although last to come on the air, at 8:55 a.m., with no helicopter shots, WUSA was first in putting a reporter at the scene, as at 9:15 a.m. Gary Reals[12] called in by phone. Shortly afterward, a second reporter showed up, but live shots were not broadcast until 9:49 a.m., with more cameras following shortly.

In a period of around forty-five minutes, a pattern of reporting developed that was often replayed during the next three weeks. Anchors provided the center of the broadcast. Because this was "breaking news," announced with significant fanfare, it had to assume a quick tempo and present new material. Consequently, the rhetorical style was for the broadcast to move from source to source–reporters, interviews, officials on and off camera, and more. All this produced a rapid, staccato pace that fed the viewer's expectation of news and excitement to come and, as a result, created anticipation and even anxiety. Ironically, because of the paucity of information for relatively long stretches of time, oftentimes the camera invariably found its way back to the anchors. Selected because of their ability to strike a personal connection with viewers, anchors are generally reassuring. Michael Schudson and other scholars have argued that the role of the anchor is to be a rock of

---

Washington website, http://www.nbc4.com/news/1165623/detail.html; *Washington Post* website, http://www.washingtonpost.com/wp-dyn/content/ article/ 2006/02/22/AR2006022202169.html.)

12. Reporter Gary Reals has spent four decades covering news in the Washington, D.C., metro region. After service in the U.S. Marine Corps following his high school graduation, Reals attended George Washington University for a degree in Urban Affairs. His career began in radio when he joined WMAL-AM in 1970. He worked behind the scenes before breaking into news reporting for the station in 1975. Reals's television run started in 1980 as a reporter for WUSA9, then known as WDVM-TV 9 in Washington. He then worked at WJLA, the region's ABC affiliate, from 1983 to 1990, before he again joined WUSA9 in 1991. In addition to his coverage of the September 11 terrorist attacks, Reals is known for his years of political coverage in the nation's capital. He was involved in reporting the 2000 election–both the Florida controversy and the Supreme Court decision–as well as the 2004 presidential election. Reals was the WUSA9 reporter assigned to cover the trial of John Muhammad for his role in the D.C. sniper case; he left the station in January of 2009. (Source: WUSA9 website, http://www.wusa9.com/company/ bios/story.aspx?storyid=37267&catid=133.)

stability in crisis.[13] This was born out during the continuous coverage here. As their particular contribution was to fill in the spaces between reports, they often had to ad lib what was known to their peers. This act of summary seemed to be calming in and of itself in that it flattened out some of the sharp edges of what was being reported. Moreover, they endeavored to speak in neutral, calming tones. However, the effect was counteracted by the frenetic air of the field reporters.

The first instinct of all the broadcasters was to purvey basic information about the events. All the newscasts announced that a child had been shot with his mother on the scene (it would be some time before they recognized the woman as his aunt) and that the child had been transported to medical facilities. Furthermore, the school system had requested that parents not rush to pick up their children. While anchors speculated that this shooting was connected to the sniper, they repeatedly said there was yet no evidence to that effect. For the most part, they did affect a calm demeanor, and the customary camera distance from the anchors tended to deemphasize eye contact and emotional impact.

One channel departed from this approach. While WUSA did all the things that the others did, its coverage also revealed more anxiety. The anchor, veteran newsman Mike Buchanan, evinced considerable anguish through his body language – adjusting his tie, holding his head. As he himself later imparted during an interview, Buchanan found Washington's experiences with terrorism in the previous year to be all too much. He was referring to the jet that was flown into the Pentagon on September 11 and the anthrax-attack letters that were sent out just a week later and resulted in the deaths of five persons, including two Washington postal workers. Anchoring his station's coverage of the Iran Brown shooting that day, Buchanan, whose experience as a police reporter was considerable, queried a police spokesperson who was giving the press release: "Basically, Corporal, you do not have any lookout [any one individual under suspicion]?" Then, remarking that the entire thing was unbelievable, Buchanan added that it was necessary to find the shooter and find him fast. The on-site reporter, Gary Reals, with his voice seeming to crack, described an almost surrealistic exodus from Benjamin Tasker school. Regardless of school policy, parents were arriving at the school to take their kids home. Responding to a question from Buchanan about the existence of roadblocks, Reals noted that

13. See Michael Schudson, *The Sociology of News* (New York: W. W. Norton, 2003), 125.

none had been put in place. In this exchange, which occurred between 9:15 a.m. and 9:20 a.m., WUSA had replaced a measured uncertainty with skepticism and a depiction of fear.

Shortly afterward, an event occurred that emphasized the themes of fear and also of doubts about the police and their work on the sniper shootings. In addition, the incident highlighted differences in the coverage by the competing television channels. At 9:25 a.m., FOX announced that six or seven police cars had left Benjamin Tasker at high speed. Unconfirmed reports indicated they were responding to a second shooting, said FOX's broadcast. From the helicopter's perspective, viewers were shown a speeding police convoy that proceeded directly to a Walmart only a couple of minutes away. At 9:30 a.m., FOX reported that customers were still entering and leaving the store. Although ambulances were on the scene, they arrived without sirens blaring. So, because people were on edge, this incident was overstated. The coverage of the NBC affiliate paralleled that of FOX, except that it began at 9:29 a.m. and ended at 9:35 a.m., with the conclusion that nothing new was occurring. Still later, but without the benefit of the helicopter, was WUSA's coverage, beginning at 9:29 a.m. and not pulling the plug on this episode until 9:38 a.m.

Channel 7, the ABC affiliate, created additional anxiety for its watchers. At 9:51 a.m., reporter Brad Bell, at Benjamin Tasker school, noted the report of an additional shooting, just as had the rest of the television news teams. Four minutes later, the anchor confirmed that indeed two shootings had occurred. At 9:42 a.m., after all the other stations had abandoned this story, Channel 7 broadcast a new map labeled "New Shootings," which included a second shooting that day. Quickly recapping, the anchor spoke in a grimly ominous tone. Finally, five minutes later, the second shooting was discredited–but not before the coverage had raised new worries.

Even the rather short digressions–not to mention that of Channel 7 –communicated a degree of frustration and failure on the part of the police. As the designation of breaking news implies, something exciting –even something that might lead to solving the crime–might occur. The racing off of police to another "shooting" presented two starkly opposing possibilities, that of a possible capture and that of more death. That neither occurred seemed merely to signal, notwithstanding the reasonable police reaction, a degree of ineptitude that reinforced remarks like those of Buchanan. Moreover, the speeding cars conveyed dread to the viewer over what they might uncover. Even though the final outcome at the Walmart was relief, the incident raised or rekindled fears about another round of serial shootings.

Following the Walmart incident, the reporting seemed to contain fewer caveats and hesitations, and it focused more often on scenes that produced concern. One of the main themes of the reporting through the next half-hour, until a few minutes after 10 a.m., concerned the children at Benjamin Tasker. Various camera angles showed parents and their offspring streaming out of the building. To all appearances, this seemed like fright producing flight. Reporters conducted some interviews with terrified parents and children that depicted the latter shaken and grateful to be going home. In one WRC interview, the child said he was happy that his Dad came to get him. The father added that God and the country would prevail; the police were doing all they could.

Such confidence was little in evidence in other reports, all of which mentioned how little the police had learned and how this event had created great fear and concern. Mike Buchanan took the pessimistic view that, if this case were connected to the sniper, the police would be worried. According to Buchanan, even the search for the white box truck (the focus of police attention at that time and almost to the end) seemed futile. At WJLA, Brad Bell noted that false alarms (like that of the events at Walmart) indicated the high level of tension. When questioned by the anchor about whether the police had any evidence, Bell replied that no one was saying anything–a situation that was eerily similar to prior shootings.

Broadcasts throughout the day struck an ominous note regarding the status of the investigation and the anxieties of the area. Simply remaining on the air with little new information indicated how important the channels thought this shooting to be. But in the end, they had little more encouraging or informative to say than had been available at ten o'clock that morning.

Shaken by this shooting and its coverage, the region had little opportunity to recover. On Wednesday night, October 9, the snipers killed Dean Meyers at a gas station just off I-66. Once again, the police found little evidence, despite an extensive search of the scene and the first well-coordinated dragnet in which officials shut down major routes heading out of the area. Although the press covered this story as breaking news, they did not settle into a prolonged period of continuous coverage.

The next event with major implications for the press coverage of this whole chain of events stemmed from the aftermath of Iran Brown's shooting. In the woods from which they had fired, the snipers had left a tarot card symbolizing death. Acting on a confirmed tip, and after checking with the Prince George's County police department about whether the station could proceed, Mike Buchanan announced the existence of this card and its menacing statement: "I am God." The *Washington Post* confirmed the existence of this message and also published its contents. Although the actual phrase on the card was, "Call me God," and not quite what the reports said, the police actively involved in the investigation became very upset, because the card had also included the snipers' demand that the police not release its contents to the press. Already facing allegations from some quarters that he had attracted the snipers to the schools with his remark that the children were safe there, Chief Moose excoriated the news media for publishing the tarot card leak.

It was in this context of vociferous criticism from the chief–along with two shootings in the previous four days–that the press had to cover another murder, on October 11, just south of Fredericksburg, Virginia, along I-95. Shot and killed in Massaponax at 9:28 a.m., Kenneth Harold Bridges had been pumping gas at an Exxon station. A police officer was standing just across the street working on an entirely different case. The police immediately put into action a plan that placed a stranglehold on escape routes from the scene. Still, no arrests were made.

Within a half-hour, the four local channels went on the air. The most obvious focus of their stories was the shooting site, fifty miles south of Washington. Given that it was a dreary rainy day that made aerial coverage impossible, for the four hours between 10 a.m. and 2 p.m. that most of the channels pursued this story, the available images and information came primarily from reporting about the large-area dragnet the police had put into place. The most indelible scenes came from the "mixing bowl," where I-95 merges with the Washington Beltway in Springfield, Virginia, about fifteen miles south of the capital itself. Other sites appeared as well, some identified or identifiable (e.g., the American Legion Bridge crossing the Potomac northwest of Washington), while others were unidentifiable to the average viewer. All of these images depended on the TV stations' use of traffic cameras set up by state agencies. While the anchors and reporters discussed the police search and many related subjects, these pictures of traffic either flowing or backed up by police stops provided the dominant visual aspect to the coverage.

As an example, WJLA (the ABC affiliate) rotated its coverage through a number of cameras poised high above the event, communicating a range of emotions. First, they showed an organized police effort to catch the perpetrators. This represented an important shift from uncertainty and disorganization. However, through indirection, these same images also undermined and replaced this positive view with fear and concern because, while the elevated positions of the camera communicated an omniscience, the rain and mist made everything look quite fuzzy. Even color cameras seemed to transmit only black-and-white images, as the weather conditions made colors more difficult to perceive. More importantly, viewers saw vast stretches of concrete populated by large numbers of cars being stopped by small stick figures—the police. The organization of the work sometimes was clear, but more often was not. At times, the officers seemed to pull over only the white vans generally under suspicion, letting others pass through without inspection. At other times, the review of vehicles seemed far less systematic. Reporters and anchors increased this uncertainty as they too struggled to interpret what they were observing on camera.

Moreover, images from traffic cameras increased trepidations. Despite the distance, viewers could see the police working. What if there were another shooting? What if they made a mistake? The enormity of sorting through the vast number of cars caused the entire scene to seem quite problematic. Finally, as earlier discussed, the entire logic underlying continuous coverage is that a conclusion will be reached. The fact that for over four hours cars were progressing through the roadblock but no one was arrested could only deepen concern. As a supplement to all the available images, the local channels maintained contact with various police departments that narrated about their intense efforts and even about suspicious vehicles stopped. Hope was raised but not fulfilled in these phone interviews. From the beginning of its coverage, WUSA stated that the whole point was to catch the madman who had caused this scene. Signing off without success signaled a disappointment if not an outright failure.

The other linchpin of continuous coverage was the crime scene, which camera crews and announcers were able to picture around midway through the coverage. As the roadblocks and miles of traffic made getting there difficult, the channels endeavored to deal with this problem by seeking comments and descriptions from either businesses located near the crime scene or from police sources. One enterprising FOX reporter turned Josh Mitchell, manager of a Hooters restaurant, into a fellow reporter. To her questions he responded that he had heard all this police activity between 9:45 a.m. and 10:00 a.m. He then explained the geography of the Exxon station. At 10:30 a.m., WRC (NBC) talked with the local sheriff by phone; he said that law enforcement officers were investigating a shooting that closely resembled those elsewhere. Furthermore, he indicated that a white van had escaped from the area by bullying other cars out of its way. These accounts were anything but systematic, leaving the sources largely unmediated. In the case of the local sheriff, part of his news, about the white van and its bullying its way out, appears in retrospect to have been in error.

Finally, the reporters arrived in Massaponax. This was no easy task. One Channel 7 cameraman, for example, was forced to use his extensive local knowledge of side roads and, in the end, even his willingness to cut through private property in order to make it around the stalled traffic to the scene itself. Channel 7 reporter Gail Pennybacker[14] found her journey on I-95 to be tedious, but she used her time to good purpose by discussing the roadblocks facing northbound traffic as she wended her way southward.

Upon arrival, these reporters did deliver news reports. Although the perimeter set up around the crime scene was very large, reporters at least could describe the scene–including the rather chilling vision of the victim's car with the driver's door still open. The expansive deployment of yellow tape often pushed cameras beyond the limits of their picture-taking abilities and deprived the audience of up-close images. According to Pennybacker, and confirmed by Marty Doane, also of WJLA, eventually, at least one news team rented a room in an adjacent motel to get better images. Most importantly, for the impression it made of the police, the local constabulary held a news conference that was widely covered. Virginia State Police spokesperson Lucy Caldwell

14. Reporter Gail Pennybacker has been with WJLA since January 1986. After earning a degree in journalism from Kansas State University, she began her career as an anchor and reporter for several television stations, including KOTV in Tulsa, Okla., KTSB in Topeka, Kans., and KTUL in Tulsa. She has covered local and national news during her tenure at WJLA, including the September 11 terrorist attacks and the Iraq war. Pennybacker is the recipient of numerous journalism awards, including an Emmy Award for her coverage of the inauguration of the first African-American governor in the United States, Doug Wilder. She has also received Dateline Awards for Excellence in Journalism, Associated Press Awards, and a Quill and Badge Award from the International Union of Police Associations. Pennybacker is involved in several community organizations, such as the Alzheimer's Association and the American Diabetes Association. (Source: WJLA website, http://www.wjla.com/pageloader.html?js=wjla&page=talent&pagename=gail_pennybacker.html.)

**Marty Doane and Gail Pennybacker, a long-term team for WJLA in
Washington.**

announced that thousands of officers were working the case, including
one who would shortly be on the scene. She claimed that the police had
closed many ramps and had located an eyewitness. To a question about
traffic stops on Route 1 (parallel to I-95), Caldwell admitted that monitoring that major arterial road was more difficult. Other interviews
similarly expressed confidence in the police effort.

   In fact, then, despite doubts raised by the oral and visual reports
about the dragnet's efficacy, the crime scene permitted a more positive
view of the effort to track down the shooter, leading one to wonder
whether this somehow related to the previous police criticism of the
press. Perhaps such was the case, for the anchors noted without comment that the police had asked, and they had agreed, not to reveal the
location of specific roadblocks. This seemed to signal a tacit agreement
that the media concurred in allegations that they had overstepped their
bounds in reporting on these crimes. Perhaps chastened, the press had
turned down the heat on the police. If this were the case, it may have
been unintentional; no reporter later interviewed for this study acknowledged trimming a report because of the attack by police chief
Moose. Moreover, Brian Mooar of WRC still insisted that terror was
permeating the area of the shooting, despite the positive reporting that
was coming from it.

       • • •

Relatively speaking, the snipers took a long break after the Massaponax
killing. In fact, the succeeding Thursday and Friday slipped by without

incident, and the weekend as well. Because many speculated that the lack of a Saturday or Sunday shooting to date indicated that the sniper had personal or work obligations on those days, a tendency existed for the community to brace itself for Monday. When nothing happened that day and the police seemed somewhat upbeat about their investigation, a certain optimism crept into area residents. But hope was shattered that day–October 14–at 9:15 p.m., when the sniper gunned down Linda Franklin, a forty-seven-year-old woman shopping at a Home Depot store in Falls Church, Virginia. When CNN's Aaron Brown,[15] based in New York, came on the air at 10:00 p.m., the shooting topped the news before he turned to other stories. Until 10:17 p.m., Brown tried to combine this story with other important matters but he finally succumbed to the flow of news from the shooting. He then continued broadcasting, with no commercials, until 2:03 in the morning.

CNN's broadcast followed the usual pattern of an anchor wending a path through a series of reports, followed by a recap. It served the double purpose of knitting everything together for viewers who entered the show at different times and of acting as filler when no new information was available. Furthermore, CNN and other national news shows tended to turn to experts who would bring academic or professional knowledge to the task of analyzing the situation.

One major difference between CNN's coverage of the Franklin shooting and its coverage on October 3 was the limited attention given this time to geographical background information. While the network used maps to show Falls Church, it did not try to situate viewers in the general arrangement of the region. This seems to indicate that the network personnel had become educated to the snipers' movements and the area in which those movements were occurring and they believed that audiences had, too.

But the largest and most significant change from previous coverage was the central positive position the police pursuit occupied within

15. Beginning his career reporting local news for a Seattle television station, Aaron Brown spent many years as a reporter for ABC and was the founding host of the station's *World News Now*. He joined CNN on September 11, 2001, and subsequently received an Edward R. Murrow Award for his coverage of the terrorist attacks. He is currently an anchor for the PBS documentary series *Wide Angle,* hosts *The Aaron Brown Show* on public radio, and is a professor at the Walter Cronkite School of Journalism and Mass Communication at Arizona State University. (Source: Wikipedia: The Free Encyclopedia, http://en.wikipedia.org/wiki/Aaron_Brown.)

the coverage itself. Visually, as helicopters delivered images from high above the scene, viewers could survey the activity of the police, which was resulting in roadblocks spreading out over a great area. At night, in these circumstances, what stood out were great stripes of cars where the killer might be hiding. Watching the search could spread a sense of encouragement among viewers, even anticipation that this ordeal might end here and now. Of course, the job was daunting. And the inability to see specific details, as with the preceding dragnet, could change viewers' impressions. Still, encouraging a positive interpretation were the reports from the scene noting the careful checking by the police as well as the rapidity of their response. One CNN expert, Mike Brooks,[16] remarked that the roadblock was the largest he had seen in his twenty-six years of experience. He further noted that everyone knew what to do and the pieces fell together quickly because everyone was aware of his or her role. Furthermore, the reports indicated that the police had appealed to eyewitnesses and put out a description of a white Astro van with specific characteristics. They seemed even to have a general description of the shooter. The massive effort appeared to be generating results.

One of the interesting sidelights of this recognition of the enhanced role of the police was a series of remarks regarding the relationship between the police and the press. In an exchange between reporter Kathleen Koch[17] and anchor Aaron Brown, Koch noted that fewer and

16. Mike Brooks worked for the Washington, D.C., Metropolitan Police Department for twenty-six years, was a member of the FBI Joint Terrorism Task Force, and has instructed numerous safety courses for the general public. He became a part-time analyst for CNN in 2001 and a full-time correspondent in 2003, focusing on current news and law enforcement issues. Named Journalist of the Year by the National Association of Emergency Medical Technicians in 2004, he remained at CNN until 2005, when he moved to freelance journalism. He has since appeared on FOX News Channel, MSNBC, and *ABC News Now*. Brooks is also currently a security consultant. (Sources: http://masc.state.sc.us/Resources/PIOmtg_0107 .htm; Wikipedia: The Free Encyclopedia, http://en.wikipedia.org/wiki/Mike _Brooks_%28journalist%29.)

17. CNN general assignment reporter Kathleen Koch began her career at a local news station in Biloxi, Miss. Before joining CNN, she worked as a general assignment reporter for several news organizations in the Washington, D.C., region. She has covered a range of breaking news stories during her tenure at the station, including the September 11 terrorist attacks, the crash of American Airlines flight 587 in New York, and the 2004 spate of deadly hurricanes in Florida. She also followed the campaign of George W. Bush prior to the 2004 presidential election and the lead-up to the outbreak of the Iraq war. She currently focuses on aviation reporting for CNN and serves as a back-up political corre-

fewer police briefings were occurring, either because the police did not wish to share information or because they wished to deprive the sniper of the pleasure of seeing the effect of his bullets. To this, Brown responded that reporters do not blame the police for this seeming lack: they do their job and we ours, he implied. Later in the broadcast (at 1:27 a.m.), he added that the community was terrorized and needed to know the current state of knowledge. He opined that the media tried to do their job carefully, but that he understood the irritation of the police. To some extent, the main press briefing by Tom Manger, then police chief of Fairfax County, appeared to add weight to Brown's depiction of two sides each doing its job. In that press event, the chief said that although they had no specific new information, officers were making great efforts to apprehend the culprit. Offering little, he then was besieged by media questions fired in staccato fashion, to which he responded that he didn't know, he wouldn't say, or it was too early to tell. This seemed vividly to define the relationship. And the police version of its role dominated.

If such coverage generally seemed to accept the police's determined role, a few off-message moments still took place. First, questions surfaced about the changing description of the white van under suspicion. And Brown termed the evening encounter between taciturn officials and inquisitive journalists as "strained." Moreover, two stories at least took the spotlight off the police. CNN interviewed a couple who had seen the victim fall. They claimed that the police had detained an eyewitness to the actual shooting. Also, two young men told CNN that they had seen the police handcuff and interrogate a suspect. The interviewees pronounced themselves very nervous and labeled the detainee "shady." Such descriptions showed those from the press trying to penetrate the police screen erected between them and the story, rather than their simply accepting what the police wanted them to have.

While the police became the protagonists on that night's telecast, the basic framework for everything that happened and was broadcast remained fear. That Linda Franklin had been shot in the head vividly reminded all viewers and participants that the situation was dreadful, and deadly. Many reporters commented on the fear exhibited inside the Home Depot store as people in the parking lot headed for the store at the time of the shooting screamed in fright. The couple whose inter-

spondent. (Source: CNN website, http://www.cnn.com/CNN/anchors_reporters/koch.kath leen.html.)

view was noted above also mentioned that the large amount of blood on the scene was shocking. They wondered whose mother, sister, or wife the victim might be. Brown likewise offered that even if this event was not "terrorism," it had terrorized the community. For him, this shooting brought back Americans' worst fears–which were especially painful after the lull in the shootings. And, of course, the station's signing off of its continuous coverage with no resolution to the situation could not produce anything like confidence.

Five calm days passed after the Franklin shooting. A reference during the continuous coverage became, at first, more definite: the police had a witness who had seen an olive-skinned man standing outside a white van shooting a weapon like an AK-47. But the witness, Matthew Dowdy, could not be more precise. Eventually, the authorities found that Home Depot cameras had filmed Dowdy inside the store when the shooting actually occurred. The manhunt continued, but with indefinite clues. Inside the investigation, even greater disappointment existed as the police saw promising leads evaporate. Still, this would be the longest interval without a shooting.

On October 19, at 7:59 p.m., the snipers wounded Jeffrey Hopper outside a Ponderosa Steak House near I-95 some fifteen miles north of Richmond. The restaurant sat in a strip of commercial buildings with woods in the rear that furnished cover for the shooters. At the time, speculation held that this episode was meant to encourage further the notion that the shootings had no pattern and thus that no one was safe. No earlier victim had been shot on a weekend, yet this was a Saturday. Furthermore, the police had announced that the government was using a spy plane to track suspicious actions in the Washington metro area. Perhaps, it seemed, this locale was an effort to attack beyond the range of aerial surveillance.

Coverage of the event as a strenuous police effort further accelerated, although more direct criticism began to appear than had previously been the case. This ebb and flow becomes apparent from tracing CNN's coverage, which began at 9:32 p.m. and lasted virtually commercial free until 2:04 the following morning.

Right after the basic details of the shooting were announced, the theme of the police response surfaced and remained prominent throughout that night's coverage. Daryn Kagan,[18] reporting from the

18. Daryn Kagan became a news anchor for CNN in 1994 and soon after made a name for herself with a wide range of political and international reports. In

Police Task Force headquarters in Rockville, Maryland, announced that police had altered their tactics. Now every shooting was assumed to be related to the snipers, and the police officers would act accordingly, she said. If it turned out they were wrong, the police later would reconsider. Furthermore, before the Franklin shooting, Fairfax County had thought itself immune from the sniper's activity. Afterward, the police had conceived a plan for every area, in order to speed their response to sniper events anywhere, anytime throughout the larger Washington region. At 9:50 p.m., CNN contacted Raymond Loring, a worker in a store near the shooting, and even he noted the rapidity of the police response–three seconds after a witness had dialed 911 from his store, Loring said. Of course, someone else may well have already called, but Loring's comments served to illustrate the larger approval of the handling of the situation by the police. At the top of the hour, Jeanne Meserve[19] noted that the police already had a plan when they arrived on the scene and had changed tactics to include enlarging the dimensions of the crime scene as well as other measures which were not revealed. Further, the authorities were attempting to educate the public about how to be competent eyewitnesses. As CNN's broadcast went on, news about the police effort continued to predominate. As reporter Gary

---

addition to covering presidential and mid-term elections, Kagan covered the second Gulf War from the Middle East and traveled to Africa to report on AIDS and famine. She was also the anchor of CNN's news show *CNN Live Today* for eight years. A graduate of Stanford University, Kagan worked for a local television station in Santa Barbara, Calif., prior to breaking into national network news. She left CNN in 2006 and started her own website, DarynKagan.com, to cover what she describes as inspiring news stories. In 2007, she debuted her first documentary, "Breaking the Curse, with Daryn Kagan," on PBS, which subsequently won the 2008 Gracie Award for Best Documentary. Her first book, *What's Possible!* was released in 2008. (Sources: Wikipedia: The Free Encyclopedia, http://en.wikipedia.org/wiki/Daryn_Kagan; Daryn Kagan website, http://www.darynkagan.com/index.html.)

19. CNN correspondent Jeanne Meserve has reported breaking news stories for the network and currently covers homeland security for CNN's America Bureau in Washington, D.C. Prior to joining CNN, Meserve worked at various local news stations throughout the eastern United States, including three years at ABC News as a correspondent for the State Department. She was an anchor at CNN, and began reporting on the security of America's ports, chemical plants, airports, and borders following the September 11 terrorist attacks. She contributed to the network's coverage of Hurricane Katrina, which subsequently earned CNN a Peabody Award. In addition, Meserve was a reporter for CNN's specials "Is America Prepared? Lessons of Hurricane Katrina" and "Is America Prepared? The Next Disaster." (Source: CNN website, http://www.cnn.com/CNN/anchors_reporters/meserve.jeanne.html.)

Tuchman[20] made his way toward the crime scene, he phoned in the report that a number of unmarked police cars had passed him at more than 100 miles per hour. Regular traffic was also moving south toward Ashland, perhaps to allow the Task Force to reach the scene, he said.

Images broadcast during the coverage reinforced this concentration on the police effort. Numerous shots of the crime scene appeared, but received little in the way of explanation. True to their word, the police had extended the perimeter of the scene to the point that little could be viewed. And, as the images photographed by the helicopter were shown, little could be seen except traffic stops at a distance. With the crime scene basically invisible, the police were even more so the sole center of attention.

Little new emerged until nearly 11 p.m., when Dan Clark, a former FBI investigator, commented on his understanding of the operations at the crime scene. He was especially impressed by the size and coordination of the Task Force. As reporter Gary Tuchman showed up in Ashland, he came on to provide more specific details. While reiterating what many said about the shooting's lack of a definite link to the sniper, Tuchman gave a more detailed portrayal of the seriousness of the police response. In particular, he noted that traffic on Virginia State Route 54 had been at a standstill since the police arrived. On this road, which leads to I-95 and crosses in front of the Ponderosa, occupants of the vehicles still remained in their cars. The disquieting news came from CNN's Jeanne Meserve, who noted that no one had actually seen the shooter. She also noted that despite the efforts, it was difficult to make roadblocks work, adding her hope that they would be successful. Over the next half hour, commentators and reporters all expressed greater optimism that the multiple roadblocks could compensate for the complexity of the effort. Moreover, the broadcasters noted, the motivation

20. With CNN since 1990, national correspondent Gary Tuchman served as an embedded journalist with the Air Force in Iraq, traveled to Afghanistan, and reported from Ground Zero in New York following the September 11 terrorist attacks. Tuchman has contributed to several CNN stories which won awards, including a Peabody for the network's coverage of Hurricane Katrina, a CableACE award for his work on the Oklahoma City bombings, and an Emmy. Prior to joining CNN, Tuchman worked as an anchor and political reporter for a local Florida television station, receiving Associated Press awards for his work in documentary, enterprise, and spot news reporting. (Source: CNN website, http://www.cnn.com/CNN/anchors_ reporters/tuchman.gary.html.)

of the police remained so high because they felt responsible for the safety of both families and neighbors.

The main core of the next hour of the broadcast (11:30 p.m. to 12:30 a.m.) played, considered, and reconsidered a press conference given at the crime scene. Here the police stated, and the press reported, that no suspect had been apprehended and the police were going to let traffic start moving again.

This official concession turned the tide and altered the tone of the broadcast, as it presaged the rather disappointing reports that came to characterize the remainder of CNN's coverage of the night and early morning of October 20 and 21. Anderson Cooper,[21] anchor throughout the evening, discussed with other analysts how the police arrival at the Ponderosa seemed to have taken only two minutes and thirty seconds. Though fast, probably as fast as it could be done, Cooper pronounced it not rapid enough. With a sniper as capable as this one, he said, too many avenues of escape remained. A map was shown to reveal the many access roads available. A further discussion supported the coordination of the task force but also still raised doubts.

Somewhat later, Cooper wondered aloud if the perpetrator could be captured. Because he fired at such a distance, he left almost no evidence. Also, the police investigation of the nearby woods, so necessary because the attackers might have fired from there, possibly had destroyed evidence. Cooper directly asked panelist Kelly McCann,[22] if the shooter would ever be caught. McCann replied that he was unsure, but that he believed the police effort possibly elated the sniper.

Not only did this coverage contain a certain despair, it also projected an image of the sniper as mocking authorities, the press, and

21. Anderson Cooper has been with CNN since December 2001, initially as a weekend anchor and later as a prime-time reporter. In 2007 he co-hosted CNN's documentary "Planet in Peril," a four-hour program exploring environmental issues threatening the Earth. He currently anchors *AC360°* on CNN. (Source: Wikipedia: The Free Encyclopedia, http://en.wikipedia.org/wiki/Anderson_Cooper.)

22. J. Kelly McCann has a long history in security preparation and training. He served in the United States Marine Corps, specializing in hostage situations and responsible for training counter-terrorist forces. He has also worked for the U.S. Department of Defense. From 1985 to 1986, he helped to develop techniques for dealing with domestic hate groups. McCann has released several instructional videos on safety and has also appeared on CNN as a security analyst. He is currently senior vice president of Kroll's Security Services Group. (Source: Wikipedia: The Free Encyclopedia, http://en.wikipedia.org/wiki/Jim_Grover_(martial_arts).)

even the public. At 1:04 a.m., another police news conference began with the assertion of a clear plan, but then coupled with it the same lack of information regarding the sniper. In fact, the entire news conference commenced with the spokesperson admitting at its beginning a lack of knowledge, but asserting a willingness to answer questions. While this press conference lacked the testiness that characterized those in Rockville, the result remained the same—a lack of information.

The concluding wrap-up (from 1:59 a.m. to 2:04 a.m.) summed up the awful situation. Ashland had been terrorized, and despite the enormous effort, including a thorough search still underway, little was known. Casey Jordan,[23] a CNN expert, openly admired the response, but then ironically credited the shooter's skill. Perhaps, she noted, he'll be equally impressed with the efforts of the police, and slip up. Although her remark smacked of desperation, her wish soon would be realized. Little could she have imagined the topsy-turvy reporting that would proceed during the next few days.

At the close of coverage in the early morning hours, most viewers would carry away a message that did not imply good tidings. Even though only a few remarks considered or characterized the temper of Ashland and the region, the conclusion of the reporting came back to the threatening aspects of the events. So few results despite such extraordinary efforts implied an area still under the gun. That this gunman menaced anyone and everyone was underlined by coverage that had proceeded virtually nonstop for four and one-half hours.

But in the shadows, mostly hidden from public and press view, opportunities were gradually emerging for the police. Already on October 16, and as many as a half-dozen times on October 18, the men who would be caught and identified as the snipers, Malvo and Muhammad, had tried to get in touch with the authorities or someone who would lead them to government officials. The Ashland shooting, in the evening of October 19, finally led to contact. In fact, the search of the

23. Criminologist and attorney Dr. Casey Jordan has been in the industry for more than twenty years. She has taught at the university level, published numerous pieces on forensics and crime, and performed legal and forensic consulting. Her specialties include behavioral analysis, offender typologies and case evaluation, jury selection and trial strategy through reverse engineering, criminal law, and high conflict mediation. She has appeared on CNN as an in-house criminologist and has consulted with hundreds of news outlets over the years, including for the ABC News programs *20/20, Good Morning America,* and for MSNBC, FOX News, Court TV, *America's Most Wanted,* and the *New York Times.* (Source: LinkedIn website, http://www.linkedin.com/pub/4/014/346.)

woods behind the Ponderosa uncovered a Ziploc bag left by the shooters. By 2 a.m. on October 20, the plastic bag was in police possession,
but officials decided, in order to preserve evidence, to open it carefully.
The four-page note contained the code words "Call me God" and notified the police of an upcoming call at the Ponderosa, at 6:00 a.m. on
the 20th. Unfortunately, the number was incorrect and the hour of
6:00 a.m. had already passed. Finally, at 9:40 a.m., on October 20, one
of the shooters called the FBI hotline demanding that someone be at the
Ponderosa in ten minutes. Because the hotline operator had no idea
what was transpiring, and no information about the possible sensitivity
of the phone call, no one was sent to receive the call at the Ponderosa.

However, the snipers and police finally managed to connect. At
7:00 p.m. that evening, Chief Charles Moose, head of the investigation
unit, held a news conference in which he gave out a cryptic message
asking the sniper to try again. By this time, the police had comman-
deered both the correct and incorrect numbers back at the Ponderosa
that the snipers had indicated. The next morning (October 21), at
7:57 a.m., Malvo called and talked to FBI agent Jackie K. Dalrymple.
After reading a thirty-eight-second statement, he hung up. Despite de-
lays, by 8:07 a.m., the Task Force knew the address of the pay phone
used by Malvo, which was located on the corner of an Exxon station
in West Richmond. Law enforcement officials ordered the Henrico
County Police to move in on the location, which they did in force. By
8:30 a.m., the bust was made, but Malvo was long gone. Unfortunately
for two unsuspecting men, Jose Morales and Edgar Rivera Garcia, they
were there and in a van. Thus, they became, if only for a brief time, the
chief suspects.

At 9:38 a.m., more than an hour after the takedown which the
police had hoped would be the end of the sniper menace, CNN had a
camera view of the scene but no reporter there. Immediately, the anchor, Paula Zahn,[24] expressed hope that this action would resolve the
case. In a discussion that ensued between analysts and broadcasters,
speculation emerged that this occurrence at the gas station seemed to

24. Paula Zahn has anchored or reported for ABC's *World News This Morning*
and *Good Morning America,* CBS's *CBS This Morning* and *48 Hours,* and *The Edge
with Paula Zahn* for FOX News. She joined CNN in 2001, and in 2002 began
hosting a morning news program titled *American Morning with Paula Zahn.* She
premiered *Paula Zahn NOW* in 2003. She resigned from CNN in August 2007.
(Source: Wikipedia: The Free Encyclopedia, http://en.wikipedia.org/wiki/Paula
_Zahn.)

be connected to Chief Moose's desire, expressed the previous evening, to receive a call from the sniper. Further, the panelists knew that the police had detained an individual (CNN did not yet know that two men were in custody) about whom there was interest. The drift of this discussion reached a focal point at 9:56 a.m. when the group concluded that this kind of response indicated "tremendous interest." Further, though the van differed in some respects from previous descriptions, its appearance was similar enough to encourage the belief that the sniper had been apprehended. Despite caveats about the certainty of the identity of those arrested, the experts and journalists expressed confidence that this was it. One expert speculated that this arrest indicated the perpetrator wanted to give up because his capture was inevitable.

Interestingly, in the absence of a reporter on the scene, CNN relied on a local resident, who merely happened to be in the vicinity and had dialed the network on his own accord. Using a cell phone, R. E. Dotson, of Richmond, gave a detailed and interesting report. In his description the entire scene appeared ominous. It was a dreary, rain-swept area with a heavily armed police presence. Dotson did what any reporter would do, pressing as close to the crime scene as possible. He even noted that the suspected white van lacked both a state inspection sticker and a locality sticker. While CNN and other channels had interviewed many eyewitnesses, Dotson acted more like a station employee.

At 10:09 a.m., Moose's news conference temporarily burst the hope that the ordeal had ended. Moose simply read a brief, mysterious statement that he claimed was a response to a message received. Moose's action, in which he evidently acted as though the sniper was negotiating with police, undercut any notion that the culprit was in custody.

Zahn then wondered aloud if this lead about the van was false. CNN's Kelly McCann was reassured that a raid of this magnitude would not have been launched without certainty. Otherwise, the target would be scared off. In fact, by this time, at the headquarters of the investigation in Rockville, many, including Chief Moose, suspected that no bust had been made. Some were already worrying about the damage that this operation could do to the overall effort to apprehend the sniper.

For the next hour, indeed until nearly 11:30 a.m., CNN continued to debate the significance of the arrests. More information was assembled through interviews with eyewitnesses, including another report from R. E. Dotson. The image shown did little to change the perception of uncertainty. The rain was preventing any aerial shots that might have created a greater sense of omniscience. Further, the overcast gray skies, along with mist and rain–as well as a substantial perimeter for the crime scene–eliminated even the possibility of very interesting camera shots. Beginning just after 11:30 a.m., there was a series of upbeat assessments. Eric Haney,[25] a criminologist based in Atlanta, noted that the police soon would be questioning two men. Proud of what they had done, these two killers, in his opinion, would soon be telling everything. CNN's Kelli Arena[26] added that although reporters did not know whether these men were the killers, sources inside law enforcement had told CNN that "We sure hope so." Another CNN reporter, Jeanne Meserve (who had spent considerable time covering this case), said that an official told her: "It looks very, very promising." She further indicated that a real sense of movement had come to exist. And from the Joint Task Force in Rockville, Daryn Kagan reported a real feeling of energy there that had come from the previous night's events. Moose's announcement, the call for communication by phone, had invigorated the case. She called the events the biggest bombshell that we have had. At 11:43 a.m., Eric Haney again insisted that those in custody would not stop talking for days. Phase one was the crime and investigation, he stated, declaring that now events had entered into phase two, which would lead to the trial. In a paraphrase of his previous argument, Haney described these men as intelligent and aware that this crisis had to end. They were simply exhausted.

25. Eric L. Haney spent twenty years in the United States military in front-line combat units and has since worked in security, traveling throughout the Middle East and Latin America to protect high-level government and corporate employees. Haney also has experience in hostage negotiation and has worked for international oil companies providing security. He lists his skills as the mastery of numerous activities including close-quarter combat, counterterrorism, explosives, and surgical explosive breaching. He has appeared as a guest analyst on various networks and programs such as CNN, CBS News, FOX News, and *Larry King Live*. (Source: Eric ND108,0L. Haney website, http://www.erichaney.com/bio.html.)

26. With CNN from 1984 to 2009, Kelli Arena joined the network as an intern and in 1985 became a production assistant. During her time at CNN, Arena covered numerous high-profile events such as the domestic wiretapping program, the U.S. war on terrorism, drug trafficking, and the resignation of Attorney General Alberto Gonzales. She was a member of the reporting team that received an Emmy Award for the network's coverage of the September 11 terrorist attacks. Arena has received several awards for her work, including a Peabody Award, a CableACE award, and a "Best Correspondent" award at the New York Festivals. In addition, she appeared four times on *The Journal of Financial Reporting*'s Top Journalists Under 30 list. (Source: CNN website, http://www.cnn.com/CNN/anchors_reporters/arena .kelli.html.)

Although anchor Leon Harris[27] reminded viewers that all this was speculation, he too would fall into it before signing off. Possibly the strongest endorsement of positive movement toward an arrest and thus a resolution to the whole episode came from another report by Jeanne Meserve. She asserted that though the case was not necessarily closed, one could observe, since the previous night, a strong optimism among police that was notably different from the anger over the tarot card. In addition, the setback over the false witness at the Franklin shooting at Home Depot had been put to rest.

At noon, Wolf Blitzer took over as anchor. Although the correspondent remained the same, the tone changed. In her report, Kelli Arena gave much more information than she had previously reported about the note found at the Ponderosa. The reporting moved away from the Exxon in Richmond. When Arena mentioned this, she noted the importance of being cautious, as the individuals apprehended might have had nothing to do with the case. At 12:48 p.m., Blitzer likewise recommended taking a deep breath, as the suspects might be irrelevant to the case. For the first time since 9:48 p.m., CNN started to run advertisements. Finally, the coverage simply petered out. Howard Kurtz,[28] the *Washington Post* commentator on television and the media, later noted that CNN's case on this particular occasion seemed to be one of maximum coverage with minimum information. Just after 1:00 p.m., Kelli Arena noted that no police confirmation had been received and that the individuals picked up in West Richmond were not involved with the

27. Broadcaster Leon Harris spent twenty years at CNN, where he anchored *CNN Live Today, Prime News, CNN Presents,* and *American Stories.* He has reported on many breaking news stories during his career, including the crash of TWA Flight 800, the Los Angeles riots, the 2004 Asian tsunami, and the September 11 terrorist attacks. The recipient of numerous awards including several CableACE awards and Emmy awards, a National Headliner Award, and a National Capital Area Emmy Award for Best Anchor, he currently anchors for WJLA and is a co-host of the news program *Capital Sunday.* (Source: WJLA website, http://www.wjla.com/pageloader.html?js=wjla&page=talent&pagename=leon_harris.html.)

28. Howard Kurtz, a graduate of the Columbia University Graduate School of Journalism, has written for numerous publications, including *Vanity Fair,* the *New Republic,* the *Washington Monthly, New York Magazine,* and the *Columbia Journalism Review.* He joined the *Washington Post* in 1981 and has served as New York bureau chief. Since 1990, Kurtz has focused his work on the objectivity of the media. He currently writes a column for the *Post* called "Media Notes" and hosts CNN's *Reliable Sources.* (Source: CNN website, http://www.cnn.com/CNN/anchors_reporters/kurtz.howard.html.)

sniper case. In fact, the authorities must have known the error for some time, but no one wanted to admit it openly. At 1:10 p.m., CNN quietly returned to regular broadcasts.

Because earlier coverage became so optimistic and had been so positive, leaving this story without a whimper must have left viewers both unsure and disappointed. In fact, this ending must have left some misgivings in the press and public about the police effort and the likelihood of its succeeding. Lack of confidence in the police, coupled with the continued existence of the sniper murder spree, could only have produced anxieties. This conclusion continued a narrative in which, after a long succession of events, the apparent failure of efforts must have tended to fray nerves.

Apart from its effect on viewers, the broadcast of the gas station arrests had to be one of the low points in the reporting on the entire sniper situation. To be sure, the press always was working in the dark, even far more than were the police being covered. And the pressure of wall-to-wall coverage more than other situations encouraged a situation in which information was broadcast, regardless of its accuracy. Nonetheless, the press usually remained reasonably accurate, by limiting what was said and just repeating it as much as necessary to fill up the time while waiting for a new development. In the case of the Richmond gas station arrests, these journalists were grasping at straws, providing assurances without any observable verification from the police. And when the story unwound, little acceptance of responsibility followed. Happily, this was an extreme, not the norm of continuous coverage.

Returning to an analysis of television's continuous coverage shows that matters became far worse the very next day–October 21. Several factors combined to create problems. First, Malvo and Muhammad began to get quite anxious about making additional phone calls. Apparently, they had immediately decamped from Richmond after the call on the 20th. By 10:00 a.m., they were in Montgomery County. When Chief Moose held a news conference at 4:17 p.m. asking them to call back, the two were likely already planning their next response–a shooting.[29] Furthermore, this shooting took place in a rather unfortunate context for the police. The attempts to communicate with the sniper had raised

29. For the narrative here and in subsequent pages, see Sari Horwitz and Michael E. Ruane, *Sniper: Inside the Hunt for the Killers Who Terrorized the Nation* (New York: Random House, 2003).

hopes, but one detail of the Ponderosa incident caused a lot of trouble. The sniper's letter had closed with the line, "Your children are not safe anywhere or anytime." At a discussion on Sunday (October 20), the Task Force members appeared ready to release this information. Even though the police chief of Richmond thought this inadvisable, he went ahead and warned area schools, which then decided to close. But the Task Force members changed direction and did not make public the contents of the note, and other school systems remained unaware of the threat posed by the sniper's note. The alerted systems did not leak the reason for their shutdown, but the Tuesday morning edition (October 22) of the *Richmond Times-Dispatch* announced it. Consequently, the decision of the snipers to claim a victim coincided with the news that the Task Force had not warned people outside of the Richmond area of the harsh and threatening words contained in the letter found at the Ponderosa.

At 5:55 a.m. on Tuesday, October 22, the snipers struck again, this time back in Aspen Hill, where the entire affair had begun. This shooting occurred less than one mile from one of the earlier killings and less than two miles from two others. Firing from nearby woods, the snipers shot Jamaican immigrant Conrad Johnson in the upper abdomen. A bus driver, Johnson had been preparing for his usual route. After the shooting, he seemed in good shape upon arrival at the hospital, but the internal damage, in fact, proved fatal. Most of the local channels narrowly focused their reporting only on Johnson's shooting and the resulting police effort. Just before 6:30 a.m., one local station announced a shooting and within a minute or so quoted an Associated Press report that the victim had been shot in the chest. Ten minutes later, the announcer noted that a bus driver was being transported to a trauma unit. Accompanying this news was information about the clogged traffic arteries.

Of all the coverage of all sorts that appeared that day, the images from the air in the dark during the first hour of coverage were exceptionally striking. As usual, Channel 4 rapidly put a helicopter in place. A number of overlapping images communicated fear. First, viewers instantly saw strings of cars moving toward the horizon. In the dark, the stationary headlines told the tale. While earlier the same image had communicated the police stopping the sniper, now, with more dragnet failures, the picture resonated differently, illustrating the sniper's ability to bring the entire region to a stop. Two closer shots reinforced and developed this general image. From the air, one could see a roadblock spanning the entire width of Connecticut Avenue. From the helicopter looking toward the street closure, viewers saw first a string of tail lights, and then moving on, a string of headlights. These appeared to be streaks of red turning to white and vice versa, depending on the position of the helicopter. Many watchers would not have been blamed had they seen it as a silver river turning bloody–symbolic of the region's emotions.

Another vivid image concerned a roadblock strung completely across the Beltway. From the helicopter's angle, the image appeared similar to that of Connecticut Avenue. Yet because of the far greater breadth of the roadway and the substantial division between lanes in opposite directions, the lines of cars did not blend. Instead, what was most evident was the stoppage of cars, their headlights illuminating the highway before them but quickly fading into black. It really seemed as though thousands of cars were poised to go sailing into a blackness that appeared as an abyss. Such a shot only reinforced the other gloomy possibilities.

As daylight arrived, around 7 a.m., different images emerged, including a better shot of the bus, but very little information was available. Announcers speculated rather pessimistically that this shooting reinforced the disturbing notion that one could not ascertain when the sniper would strike. More time was spent on a dismal appraisal of the efficacy of the roadblocks. They all seemed to rest on the hope that the sniper might be stuck in traffic. Other images and examples emerged to show a rather porous police effort. In another sign of desperation, WRC's Brian Mooar noted that the last shooting, with its proximity to the site of others, revealed a lot of local knowledge by the sniper.

WRC reported the end of the roadblocks after 9:15 a.m., but had after that very little new to offer and tended to repeat earlier observations. Using an earlier interview with neighbors, stations provided a few eyewitness reports. One bus driver referred to the "paranoia" in the air. A television anchor also found a high level of anxiety. He opined that while some people had become short-tempered, most just wanted an end to these events. Also put forward was the notion that the anxiety would simply have to be endured until the culprit was captured.

Primarily concentrating on the progress of the investigation, WRC had little to say, and even less to add that was positive. Just before 11 a.m., the station returned to local programming. While all of the stations covered other elements of the story later in the day, these morning reports were the primary effort at continuous coverage of this particular episode.

FOX News followed in much the same vein and emphasized the victim, the crime scene, and especially the traffic tie-up. If anything, this channel more emphatically described the mess that travelers faced. Although FOX did not emphasize the shortcomings of the roadblocks or the randomness of the shooting, it developed a series of other themes that made its coverage anxiety-producing. While FOX had aerial shots and showed the same images as its NBC competition, it also focused the camera on its reporter inside the helicopter. This was eerie, to say the least. Out of pitch blackness emerged only the face of the reporter into a very tight shot. This close-up generated a connection with the viewer and amplified the emotional aspect of covering this event. More important, as the reporter came into view, she seemed to materialize out of nothing—rather like the Cheshire Cat in Lewis Carroll's *Alice in Wonderland.* The effect was frightening. Also contributing to the climate of fear was FOX's statement that the station was cooperating with the police in not revealing the specifics of the dragnet. This might bring home to viewers the impression or sense that this was a situation they could neither know about fully nor fully understand and yet one that threatened their lives.

Beyond the general pattern used by both WRC and FOX News, the latter station also emphasized some other areas. FOX gave considerable coverage to the schools, varying it between presenting unconcerned students and showing frightened parents and children. For example, as a reporter was covering a traffic tie-up, a passing school bus inched by. As it did so, the kids pressed toward the windows, mugging for the camera. The reporter, taking an aside from reports on the gravity of the situation, remarked on the innocence of children. An hour later, FOX reported on a teacher who called the students terrified. She said they wanted to close the blinds. This was all they could think about. Following this report, the anchor questioned Montgomery County Schools official Brian Porter about the situation, asking whether closing the schools would be best. Porter demurred, noting that the schools would remain open, with parents electing not to send their offspring if they wished. A later report found a middle ground that accepted the situation and the staff's problems in getting to work, but also noted that student absenteeism was only 7 percent and that parents were pitching in to assist. In another clip, reporter Karen Gray Houston,[30] likewise,

30. General assignment reporter Karen Gray Houston has been with FOX5 since 1994. Throughout her career she has been a reporter, writer, and editor,

indicated strengths and weaknesses, with some schools ready while others were not.

The theme of coping in difficult circumstances received increased attention in an interview with a psychologist. In the interchange with the anchor, the health professional noted that people should accept vulnerability at this time. One should not obliterate this anxiety, but rather try to deal with it by engaging in other meaningful activities. Finally, turn off the television and move on to other matters, the psychologist lectured.

FOX News also spent some time profiling the sniper, described by criminologist Brent Turves as clever and flexible enough to keep law enforcement on its toes. Furthermore, Turves believed the motive of the sniper to be his desire to show he was in control. With the breakdown in communication with police, the shooter took the initiative to set the tone. Turves suggested being civil with him in order not to encourage further outrage.

For FOX News, Chief Moose's press conference formed a part of the channel's continuous coverage, and it mainly contributed to the impression of uncertainty. Lasting only about thirty minutes, the Rockville interchange with the media started by summarizing the information already largely known about the shooting, including the name of the victim (whose death had already been widely announced), and the effort to capture the shooter by using traffic stops. However, much of the reportage was fairly unrelieved gloom. Moose allowed that police had no "lookout" for any individual. This shooting, continued the chief, was similar to past ones and the police would determine whether it was linked. He cautioned that the killers would kill again, but also assured his audience that Americans were resilient.

The remainder of the press conference degenerated into chaos. Although FOX News had not mentioned the shooters' threat, published in the Richmond paper, the journalists were obviously obsessed with it and made it their main area of questioning. Was the report true? Moose, and later Duncan, tried to deflect this question by stating that everyone was in danger. Finally, one journalist cornered Moose by stating that parents would want to know if a specific threat existed. After

---

and she currently specializes in D.C. politics. The winner of several awards, she has been a member of the reporters' Committee for Freedom of the Press and is a member of the National Association of Black Journalists. (Source: MyFoxDC website, http://www.myfoxdc.com/myfox/pages/InsideFox/Detail?contentId=5772&version=15&locale=EN-US&layoutCode=TSTY&pageId=5.3.1.)

Moose said he would release what people needed to know, the reporter countered with: "You'll pass along a specific threat, in other words." Moose stonewalled. To another set of questions about the actions of the Richmond schools, the chief offered little, saying different communities made different choices. In this interchange, to worrisome questions, Moose, and Duncan as well, could only adhere to the decision that the Task Force had made not to release the snipers' threat. In the midst of this confusion, a reporter asked if this should be a federal case, suggesting a loss of confidence in the likely success of a locally led investigation.

That all these questions were followed by a short summary gave a final punctuation to coverage by FOX News, which ended at 1:06 p.m. In the main, the station had pursued the outlines of the case by following police activities and had arrived at coverage that generated considerable anxiety. Except for the press conference, coverage had been a little less fear-inducing than was that carried by Channel 4, the NBC affiliate, since the commentators had not directly deprecated the dragnet and had included reports that featured people coping with the crisis. Yet the two stations, and that of the Washington ABC affiliate, Channel 7-WJLA, all followed a similar pattern.

From 6:25 a.m. to 1:03 p.m., WJLA pursued the story in much the same vein as did FOX News, with coverage focused on police activity primarily but followed by growing dismay as events played out again without a capture or major lead developing. Even many of the subtopics remained the same for WJLA as for the others. Not only did the station speculatively profile the sniper, but it also took the exact same perspective. Yet WJLA did express skepticism about the efficacy of the roadblock. The single biggest difference was that Channel 7 had no helicopter and thus could not produce the same vibrant images. Like all of the rest of the ground shots of crime scenes, those of Channel 7 were remote. However, Channel 7's use of a ground camera to cover the congestion of the roads partially made up for its lack of aerial shots. A viewer at least could observe the real blockage of life in the area. On the other hand, this station had announced the reports of the sniper threat previously published, so that the tenor of its reports did not need to be more aggressive to be consistent with the other channels' gloom.

Channel 7 did make some poignant additions to overall coverage, however. When reporter Gail Pennybacker, then heading for work, heard about the shooting, she turned her car in the direction of the events. By 7:10 a.m., she went on-air in a somewhat personal conversation with the anchor. While this might have gone beyond the professional demeanor to which journalists subscribe, it proved to be revealing of the situation. The anchor asked Pennybacker what, as a parent, she could she tell her children. This must be difficult to explain at each shooting, the anchor said. Pennybacker said she had no response to this kind of event but that she tried to be at peace with everyone. Further, because the police lived as well as worked here, their motivation was the highest to catch the perpetrator, she said. The anchor then interposed that capture seemed nearer. Pennybacker pessimistically responded that there was then no lookout—no announcement that authorities were seeking any particular individual or individuals. The streets were dark at the time of the shooting, so eyewitness accounts would be few, she said. Furthermore, the complex mix of streets provided options for quick escape. It's just "heartbreaking" that this fell apart, she said. In this exchange, the reality and the pathos of the situation emerged as Pennybacker understood them. She had brought together her understanding of the situation with her place as a parent and a resident. In a much briefer way, reporter Brad Bell amplified the personal touch. Broadcasting from the scene of the shooting, he summarized what was known then and referred to a conversation he had had with someone he described as one of the top detectives in the county. "Sadly," he said, the response was not reassuring. When asked what he knew, the official said, "Nothing," and then added a few choice words, Bell said. This pithy response well indicated the circumstances that the rest of the coverage sought to communicate.

Coverage by WUSA-Channel 9, the CBS affiliate, ran from 6:15 a.m. to 1:04 p.m., and seemed quite similar to that of Channel 4 in that it too featured the crime scene, the victim, the overwhelming public response, and interviews with fearful citizens. Notably, because it only gained access to helicopter shots in daylight, Channel 9 lacked some of the most frightening images. And it took a greater interest in the schools and noted that it was deliberately withholding information about the traffic stops in order to not reveal their location to the sniper. Overall, however, its coverage resembled that of Channel 4 and, indeed, all of its competitors.

However, more than did Channel 7 and in different ways, WUSA deepened the creative side of its reports. To be sure, Channel 9 used the traffic jams to describe what was occurring. Further, like all of the channels, it sought to pull the story together by rehashing what had already been reported. But in this segment of continuous coverage,

WUSA really extended its reach. In the process, it showed a level of independent thinking that was deeper and more candid than usual. Discussing this involves selecting some of the best examples.

At 8:14 a.m., WUSA broadcast a report from a witness who rather excitedly related that children were walking to school in a neighborhood near the shooting of the bus driver. Mike Buchanan, one of the anchors, quickly questioned Montgomery County's Brian Porter, who was on the phone, about kids walking to school. "What if the killer is still out there?" Buchanan exclaimed. Porter answered that Montgomery County Public Schools operate as a system, not area by area. The other anchor, Andrea Roane,[31] queried whether the schools had asked for more police help. Porter noted that police had flooded the area. At that point, the less-than-reticent Buchanan lectured Porter that the school system should change its policy. Yet, upon reflection, he noted, some parents might not necessarily be at home to stay with their children. Thus, he said, you are "damned if you do and damned if you don't." His vignette's point was that, like the other reports on the schools, the situation was mixed. However, no one was more emphatic and open about debating what authorities were doing, or even debating with authorities, than were those at Channel 9.

Later in the morning (from 9:51 a.m. to 9:56 a.m.), veteran newsman Dave Statter[32] indicated the threats reported in the Richmond

31. Andrea Roane has been with WUSA for twenty-six years. Prior to becoming a broadcaster she taught English in middle school and high school. In addition, she was the coordinator of cultural services for the New Orleans Parish Public Schools and was administrator/principal of the New Orleans Center for Creative Arts. Roane has covered a wide range of news stories throughout her career, from breaking news to politics and from sports to education. She has also made a name for herself as an advocate of breast cancer awareness, and was named a "Washingtonian of the Year" for her work on the cause. She has received numerous local and national awards for her service to the community. Roane currently co-anchors WUSA's 9 News Now. (Source: WUSA9 website, http://www.wusa9.com/news/news_article.aspx?storyid=37259.)

32. General assignment reporter Dave Statter has been with WUSA since 1985. Prior to joining WUSA, Statter worked for several radio stations in Maryland and Virginia. He reported live for the first time for WTOP Radio after the 1982 Air Florida crash. Statter has covered breaking news and politics for 9 News Now, but is best known for his work on fire prevention and safety issues. His blog, "STATter 911," follows firefighters and EMTs in their daily activities and has received worldwide recognition. Statter has won numerous awards for his work, including a local Emmy award, a "Best of Gannett" award, and an Emmy for Feature Reporting. He

paper. Clearly, here the station also went beyond the reporting of Channel 4. Buchanan, who had first reported the tarot card left at the scene of the Benjamin Tasker shooting, regretted his prior leak. Although Statter concurred that leaks were regrettable and argued the police should all speak on one key, he also indicated that the station would report the threat on children because others had. The station had suppressed the Richmond news, but now it would go forward. Wryly, Buchanan noted that journalists stick by the rules for about a week. The journalists then turned to the dragnet, as Statter noted that police officers previously had said that a dragnet could not work. Agreeing, Buchanan argued that too many jurisdictions were competing with each other within the investigation, resulting in a logistical nightmare. Moreover, concluded Statter, the police were so worried about leaks that they withheld information, undermining the investigation. Compounding all this was the Richmond arrest that alerted the sniper to the police tactics. This five-minute discussion was an interlude in coverage that otherwise looked much like that of the other stations. Not only was this interjection candid, it also was highly critical. One might say that it represented a departure. While television widely reported that the dragnet was not working, this report laid out the reasons much more plainly and seemed to assess blame.

To illustrate WUSA's effort, yet another exchange among Buchanan, Roane, Statter, and another seasoned reporter, Gary Reals, may be helpful. In a rather long sequence that began at 10:22 a.m. and lasted on and off for over thirty minutes, Reals began by stating that this shooting was the sniper's response to Moose's request for another phone call. The discussion veered off to consider whether the Ashland shooting might be credited to the sniper. Statter noted that at the request of the authorities, reporters had suppressed a lot about the Ashland investigation that authorities had now come to release. Summing up, he stated that fourteen bullets and a lot of gas had caused all the crisis. This remark sparked Buchanan to note that the region was basically being held hostage. And Roane added that this investigation might be too much for the police. Should federal authorities take over? After

---

also won *Washingtonian* magazine's "Best Crime Reporter" award in 1993. Statter served as a volunteer firefighter in Prince George's County, Md., for six years. (Source: WUSA9 website, http://www.wusa9.com/company/bios/story.aspx?sto ryid=37486&catid=133.)

further remarks regarding the sniper's demands, Statter concluded more or less where they had started, that the sniper was deliberately sticking it to Chief Moose with a shooting in his own backyard.

Again, while this sort of candor and direct analysis, as well as criticism, was largely confined to WUSA, it was surely not confidence-building either for the police or for a viewer's hope for a quick and calm resolution. Other channels did allude to some of these problems, but WUSA provided more information and many more judgments. The final round of continuous coverage would bring similar analysis–but little satisfaction.

This difference among the channels' coverage raises the question of how what they broadcast was different from or similar to what the cable channels carried. In fact, WUSA was pursuing an approach that somewhat resembled the independence exhibited in CNN's reporting. And, in fact, CNN's reporting for October 22 paralleled that of the CBS affiliate, WUSA-Channel 9. We might reasonably speculate, then, that if all of the local channels' broadcasts were available for analysis, with no missing dates, the analysis likely would show less assertive reporting. Further, on those dates for which this overall wall-to-wall coverage analysis relies on local coverage, one ideally would supplement the generally more independent cable channels. But these differences should not be overstated, because even though WUSA's analytical barbs stung, this channel mainly followed the emerging story as sources created it. Most criticism came in simple added remarks that the local channels made, about how things were working. With an entire set of channels to draw from, one might find more basic reporting and more deliberate analysis, yet the overall impression might well end up the same–that weariness and wariness were becoming frequent themes of the discussion.

From the depths of frustration and anxiety there did emerge an end to this crisis, which was approaching its fourth week. By 5:00 p.m. on Tuesday, October 22, after the Johnson shooting and the contentious noon press conference, Chief Moose admitted to the press that the sniper's note had included a threat against children. In another press conference two hours later, after reports circulated that the Ponderosa note included financial demands, he spoke through the press to the snipers. He indicated that logistical problems made the demand for money impossible.

No response followed from the sniper, but finally the breaks that closed the case began to occur. Late on the evening of the 22nd, the police spoke with Robert Holmes, a friend of Muhammad's from Tacoma, Washington. Holmes mentioned a rifle that might have been used in the shootings, and also brought up Muhammad's anger at his ex-wife over custody of their children. Simultaneously, a breakthrough occurred in Alabama. In the communication directed at the authorities, the sniper had mentioned involvement with a shooting in Alabama. Now a fingerprint connected to the case pointed to Lee Malvo, and a search of computer data linked Muhammad to Malvo in a custody dispute. A chain of evidence leading from Alabama to Tacoma to Muhammad's wife was created. To strengthen this, police procured a photo of Muhammad. They also decided to examine a tree stump in Tacoma used for target practice by Muhammad and Malvo that might have bullets that would link to those taken from the sniper victims or found on the scenes of the shootings. And for safety they took Mildred Muhammad and her children into custody.

All of this sudden progress took place out of sight of the press, but by 7:30 p.m. on October 22, pictures of the FBI digging up the stump in Tacoma appeared on television. Such a large-scale maneuver and its cause could not be covered up. By this time, the FBI had also learned the license number and description of Muhammad's car. At 8:47 p.m., and again at 10:30 p.m., journalists could hear on scanners that a manhunt had begun. At 11:00 p.m., some stations had released this information. Chief Moose confirmed the targets of the search, and released the photo of Muhammad at 11:50 p.m. In addition, he spoke directly to the snipers, noting that they wanted him to say certain things, which Moose did: "We have caught the sniper like a duck in a noose," and, "Our word is our bond." He also reiterated a desire to keep communication open. Finally, and most importantly, Moose identified the hunted men as "persons of interest" rather than as suspects.

For once, the police and the press had specific information, but no one knew how soon it would be used. By 1:00 a.m., the suspicious car was spotted at an Interstate rest area. Within thirty minutes, the suspects would be sealed in. At 3:30 a.m., the police broke into the car to arrest the sleeping men. At 5:55 a.m., the car was towed in for an inspection that began just before 9:00 a.m. and shortly thereafter produced a weapon consistent with the one the police sought. Hours later, ballistics tests would indicate this rifle had been used in all the cases from which sufficient bullet fragments could be recovered. At 8:17 p.m., before a national television audience, Chief Moose announced the successful conclusion of the search.

All four channels covered all of these events for many hours. And all became decidedly more analytical, though FOX News remained far less so than did the other three. But more important than the differences between their broadcasts was the fact that the tone of both sets was anticipatory, optimistic, and, eventually, celebratory.

While WUSA raced back on the air to announce developments at 3:47 a.m., WRC came on with it at 4:38 a.m., and WJLA picked it up ten minutes later, it was 5:26 before FOX News started its coverage. At that point, through the broadcast of a police press conference and re-marks by the anchor, FOX summed up the developments, from Moose's late-evening statements through the information that the wanted men had been captured.

Then, in a theme that dominated the reporting of FOX as well as the other stations, the anchor opened with the stated hope that the individuals apprehended were indeed the snipers, linked to the shoot-ings perhaps through ballistic analysis. In coverage that became more aggressive as it sought background, the station linked the arrested men to a sniper training camp in Alabama and to the Tacoma tree stump. But clearly this was tentative information, and overlaid by a concern for official police confirmation.

At 5:56 a.m., FOX reporter Holly Morris[33] broadcasting from state police barracks in Frederick, Maryland, said the police were "ada-mant" that they could not yet link these men to the shooting. Although this might be the major break in the case, the situation was still evolv-ing and police would not comment about whether they had recovered weapons. Morris pointed out that many questions still remained about how everything had come together and culminated in these arrests, and she speculated that the police had more pieces than observers could see. Reinforcing this caution was Al Feinberg,[34] reporting from the

33. Reporter and anchor Holly Morris specializes in "live" reporting for FOX5, with topics ranging from local community issues to breaking national news. She worked as an anchor and reporter for a television station in Lexington, Ky., be-fore joining FOX5 in 1998. She has received several regional Emmy awards and a regional Edward R. Murrow Award. She currently contributes to *FOX5 Morn-ing News* and anchors *FOX5 News at Noon*. (Source: MyFoxDC website, http://www.myfoxdc.com/myfox/pages/InsideFox/Detail?contentId=5768&version=12&locale=EN-US&layoutCode=TSTY&pageId=5.3.1.)

34. Al Feinberg has worked as a news reporter and features reporter for FOX5 News. In 2001 he was nominated for Capital Region Emmy awards for his show "Al's World: The Collectors' Edition"on FOX5, for his report entitled "Try It; Buy It," and for his writing for the segment "Escort Service." (Source: NATAS website, http://www.capitalemmys.tv/nominations/nominations_2001.html.)

Rockville base of the Task Force, who said he was hearing very little. Perhaps symbolically underlining the approach of the station was the helicopter shot it broadcast. Restricted to a perimeter of five miles from the scene of the arrest, and at an altitude of 6,000 feet, the nighttime shot showed absolutely nothing of interest.

At 6:06 a.m., FOX brought in former investigator Lou Hennessey, who explained how the investigation likely was proceeding. Through careful, systematic procedures, the police tried to draw proper conclusions. Although the police were cautiously optimistic, he argued that authorities did not wish to identify anyone falsely.

Interestingly, during the next hour and a half, the station continued to vacillate between efforts to link the arrested men to the shootings and a variety of cautions, especially from Hennessey and Feinberg. But at 7:45 a.m., Amy Robach[35] noted that while the police still refused to call these men suspects, it did "look very, very good." Holly Morris reported that officers had found a gun in the car that had been tied to the shootings in Washington, D.C., on October 3. Amy Robach also pointed out links between Malvo's handwriting and that in the notes left at the scenes, as well as more connections to the shooter emerging from Tacoma, Washington. Although Feinberg, following the upbeat reports of Morris and Robach, still seemed hesitant to proclaim the case over, by 8:35 a.m., he too was joining in the excitement. Still awaiting "official confirmation," he announced that many were feeling cautiously optimistic that this was the major break in the case. Those troopers who remained silent were not afraid to smile. Reporter Paul Wagner's[36]

35. Amy Robach anchored the early morning and noon news for FOX5 in Washington prior to joining MSNBC as an anchor. At FOX5, Robach covered various news stories including the Iraq war, the September 11 terrorist attacks, and the war in Afghanistan. In 2000, *Regardie's Power Magazine* named Robach one of the "Most Powerful People in Washington D.C." At MSNBC, Robach has followed the Iraq war, Hurricane Katrina, and the 2004 presidential election. In addition to her work on MSNBC, Robach currently serves as a national correspondent for NBC's *Today* and co-anchor of *Weekend Today,* and is a frequent guest on *Imus in the Morning,* a radio show on ABC Radio Networks. (Source: MSNBC website, http://www.msnbc.msn.com/id/3080448/.)

36. Reporter Paul Wagner has been with FOX5 since 1999, specializing in investigative journalism. Prior to joining FOX5, Wagner worked as a radio DJ, a traffic reporter, a Capitol Hill stringer, and a reporter for the Associated Press Radio Network. He also worked for WTOP Radio for eleven years. Throughout his career, Wagner has covered breaking local and national news and high-profile criminal cases. He has explored dozens of "Cold Cases" for FOX5 since 2000, and his work in discovering the loss of evidence by D.C. police in numerous unsolved

sources concurred with those of Feinberg. By 9:00 a.m., the anchors were referring to the arrested as "suspects" in the case.

Despite a continued flow of information, FOX remained slightly reticent. At 10:12 a.m., the station quoted a Department of Justice source as saying that officials were "cautiously optimistic but no victory dance yet." Gradually, as the day wore on, assurance grew. Still the station waited for absolute certainty until Moose came on later that evening after 8:00 p.m.

Clearly in this coverage, FOX News exercised more independence than it had earlier in providing background and in pursuing sources, but it also still waited for the police to make the official final call. Even on the subject of the optimism and relief those at the station felt, they tended to report it through the reactions of the police. The "smiles" and "victory dance" were those of law enforcement. But it was joy nonetheless, in contrast to the gloom of every other incident of wall-to-wall coverage.

A somewhat different tone can be found in the reports of WRC, the NBC affiliate. Although the station had a head start, with continuous coverage from 4:37 a.m., the content of most of its first hour resembled that of FOX-Channel5. For example, at 5:33 a.m. reporter Brian Mooar confirmed that Muhammad and Malvo were those arrested. Cautioning viewers, he noted that there had been other people of interest who had proved to be dead ends. This was but an incremental move forward. Although there was a lot of excitement, Mooar admitted, he also re-minded viewers that the investigation remained in its early stages, and those detained were not fully declared suspects by the police.

However, after 6 a.m. the station began to show connections that could be established between Malvo, Muhammad, and the shootings. And although Mooar noted that the police still had much to learn, he too seemed caught up in the enthusiasm. Stating that some connection existed between the weapons charges on which the men were arrested and the sniper, he also pointed out that this was the first time in the case in which authorities had provided names of individuals who were of interest to the investigation.

At 6:43 a.m., reporter James Adams[37] seemed to pull together vari-

---

murder cases resulted in a D.C. law requiring such evidence to be held for sixty years. Wagner is the recipient of several awards, including three "Outstanding Enterprise Reporting" awards and an Edward R. Murrow Award. (Source: My-FoxDC website, http://www.myfoxdc.com/myfox/pages/InsideFox/Detail?con tentId=5757&version=10&locale=EN-US&layoutCode=TSTY&pageId=5.3.1.)

37. James Adams is a general assignment reporter and weekend anchor for

ous reports, noting that the pieces of the case had begun to fall together because of a shooting in Montgomery, Alabama. When a sniping incident in the state of Washington turned out to be connected to Malvo, who was suspected of committing the shooting in Montgomery, these two individuals were linked and then also were tied to the Washington, D.C., case, he said. Adams provided additional details, including the residence of Muhammad's ex-wife in Maryland and the presence of a car like Muhammad's at the shooting in D.C. While the elements were not quite assembled just as the police would do, Adams was very close to a correct version of the links and facts as the police knew them. Evidently, he was using sources within the investigation to create an understanding of the events prior to the arrests. He showed an independence that WRC had normally eschewed.

But Brian Mooar continued to instill a sense of caution into the broadcast. In a 7:06 a.m. report, he noted that law enforcement officials were more upbeat than they had been at any time in the past with this case. Yet, he still reminded his viewers that the progress might be tentative.

At 7:22 a.m., long before the police later claimed to have found the weapon and surely many hours before ballistics reports were received, a reporter at NBC Network News announced that police sources believed those arrested were the culprits. Six charges would be filed as early as that day. Not terrorists but spree killers, the serial murderers had been pushed by publicity and would not stop until they were captured. Another national correspondent, Pete Williams,[38] in the studio with

NBC4. He has been a Washington reporter since 1977 and has also worked as an investigative reporter for FOX5. He has covered Capitol Hill and the White House and has been a freelance journalist for CNBC, BET News, and BIZ network. Known for his focus on education reporting, he has received several awards, including Emmy awards, a Washington Area Mass Media Award, and a United Press International Award. (Source: NBC Washington website, http://www.nbc4.com/meetthe newsteam/1198788/detail.html.)

38. NBC Washington correspondent Pete Williams has been covering the Justice Department and U.S. Supreme Court since 1993. After graduating from Stanford University in 1974, Williams began his career in broadcasting as a reporter and news director for a local radio and television station in his hometown in Wyoming. He later became a press secretary and legislative assistant to Congressman Dick Cheney and Assistant Secretary of Defense for Public Affairs. Williams is the recipient of a First Amendment Award from the Society of Professional Journalists for his efforts to allow reporters into pre-trials in Wyoming and to allow the broadcast of Wyoming Supreme Court proceedings. (Sources: Wikipedia: The Free Encyclopedia, http://en.wikipedia.org/wiki/Pete_Williams_(television_correspondent);

the anchors, affirmed that the Alabama and Tacoma connections had provided the key. Added Williams, critics had said the Task Force was disorganized, but this was clearly not so. Ironically, it was a leak–getting the license from scanners–that led to this quick arrest. To this, the anchors replied that they had all been waiting for this information.

Skeptic Brian Mooar quickly fell in line. At 7:52 a.m., he noted that even with a hesitancy to say it out loud, authorities believed they had their men. So many intersecting lines of inquiry encouraged them. Already, the night before, they had enough to levy murder charges, but used lesser weapons counts to expedite the arrests.

The high note of these reports continued throughout the day on WRC as well as the other channels. And it should be noted that throughout these reports was a distinct lack of criticism of the police. Despite earlier doubts, especially at the Conrad Johnson shooting, all stations early on October 24 expressed confidence in the actions of the authorities. Probably the most exuberant was WUSA, which linked the captured men to the shootings very early–at 6:47 a.m. WJLA quoted the Associated Press in the same vein at 6:46 a.m. In fact, WRC's reporting looks similar to that of WUSA and WJLA in that regard. WRC, more than FOX-5, pushed harder into police sources and more aggressively appeared to sort through various pieces of information to present the case as it was emerging. In this moment, the local channels "connected the dots" like their national peers were wont to do.

Greater amounts of analysis and a positive outcome–such was the continuous reporting of October 24. This effort contrasted with all those that preceded it. While continuous coverage encouraged the notion of a happy ending, only this episode conformed to that rule. When Mike Buchanan woke up in the morning, he had come to wish to see advertisements, because then he knew that nothing tragic was occurring. Unfortunately, anyone who shared this view would have been often disconcerted from October 3 to October 24, 2002.

Despite their anxiety-producing aspects, these reports did have a rhythm and an evolution. The coverage of the initial shootings on October 3 and the wounding of Iran Brown on October 7 revealed considerable confusion and disorganization. Television broadcasts reported on the victims, the neighborhoods, and the police with little discernable order to the events. As the major dragnets that accompanied the Massaponax, Home Depot, and Ashland shootings provided some fodder for

MSNBC website, http://www.msnbc.msn.com/id/3689493/.)

television crews to cover, the story became largely a police story. Although some criticism of authorities was aired during this time, it was negligible. This coverage would have a similar focus toward the end of the events, but negative views of the police also would become more apparent in the middle of the narrative. The style of coverage afforded the siege at Richmond proved a poignant if still somewhat silent critique that became rather explicit at the Johnson shooting. All the local channels doubted the efficacy of the dragnet. Finally, in contrast, the capture and the end of the snipers' spree produced a police story with a happy ending. According to veteran CNN reporter and former Washington Bureau Chief Frank Sesno,[39] this pattern may be found in many big news stories: information, explanations, investigation, and recrimination. While the sniper story did not clearly follow in that order, it certainly contained all those elements and added its own exclamation!

How the stations devoted so much time, resources, and lost ad revenue to this story will be considered in chapter 4 of this book. For now, it is worth considering why the local stations and CNN (along with other national news channels) handled the story somewhat differently. The basic difference was a greater independence that often correlated with a more critical approach to law enforcement. Certainly, the greater resources of CNN played an immense role in this equation. With twenty-four reporters assigned to this story alone in the Washington area, CNN had a greater ability to dig into many facets of the story. In addition, the network had criminologists of all stripes at its disposal. Finally, CNN played to a national audience whose members may have wanted to know the background to the event more than did the locals, who were more concerned with avoiding both danger and traffic jams. Finally, insofar as independence translated into defying or irritating the police involved in the investigation, the news reporters of CNN were more likely to be indifferent. These reporters did not live in the town. No future relationship had to be maintained with authorities. Second, the power of the cable channel induced sources to be forthcoming, overcoming anger about past indiscretions or slights. In sum, CNN had greater resources and was more impervious to criticism. To be sure, the local reporters might compete against the resources by relying on experience, which gave them access to information on different terms. But for the local

39. In 2002, when interviewed for this book, Frank Sesno was a professor of Public Policy and Communication at George Mason University. Currently, he is at George Washington University in the School of Media and Public Affairs. (Source: Sesno interview.)

reporters to be indifferent to local hostility might prove difficult because in order to go on doing stories in the years to come, they could not afford to offend police sources. Furthermore, since the public was likely more sympathetic to the police, this also meant running afoul of their local constituency. That concern with public criticism was important, for local channels may be shown in the coverage of the capture. When the broadcast channels had pleasing news to report and did not fear police or citizen antipathy, they could, in fact, be more independent. Perhaps it was the link to the community that kept local stations less independent and less likely to aim attacks at authority.

One other characteristic worth pointing out is the relative visual poverty of the images shown in continuous coverage. The size of the crime scenes, the invisibility of the criminals, and even at times the foulness of the weather made this story visually unappealing. In part, it proves to be something of a testimony to the determination of television producers that they covered this story to such a great extent, even when it was not that well suited to the medium of television.

While this study is more interested in the message than its accuracy or timeliness, it is reasonable to say that, even with a fair amount of speculation that included errors, a very high proportion of what was said was accurate. Much was not particularly important, but was nonetheless frequently repeated. In addition, the speed of reporting was blinding. The police found this in their inability to keep secrets.

The ultimate message of continuous coverage was that of a morality play: evildoers brought to justice. In a nation accustomed to a war on terrorism described in such terms, this event could be understood and applauded. But in the short-term, and on a daily basis, the failure to capture the snipers and the uncertainties described in this coverage purveyed fear that edged toward or suggested pandemonium. Even the coverage of the incidents that featured police action and inspired some confidence, or at least coping ability, ended in defeat or deep mystery and concern. And this too could well be understood by much of the public in the wake of the attacks just a year earlier on iconic buildings in New York and Washington.

# THREE

## *The Nation and the World*

Despite the prominence of the *Washington Post* and television wall-to-wall broadcasts, numerous other purveyors of information interested themselves in Washington's sniper events. In fact, although numbers remain uncertain, there likely were more journalists than police officers directly reporting on and investigating the event. Any attempt to read all of these periodicals and electronic media, much less systematically discuss them, must inevitably founder. Consequently, this study takes a sounding, somewhat selected, of the vast sea of material containing many currents and uncounted depths of backwaters.

This chapter explores the journalistic efforts, with a section focused on outlets mainly interested in the news and a second section dealing with media primarily interested in opinion. Although important exceptions exist and variations in emphases abound, overall this coverage promotes a strong element of pervasive fear, although examples appear of coping in such a difficult situation. But what is mainly missing is any interest in constructing community. In this way, the main stream of the coverage does not provide even the main element of support available in the *Post*.

At the beginning of this chapter is a survey of local-area reports. "Local areas" are defined as those places, from the Washington suburbs through Richmond, that were directly affected by the shootings. Three daily newspapers, one all-news radio channel, and four local television channels in Washington with regularly scheduled newscasts were selected for analysis of this coverage. Subsequent sections consider national and international coverage.

Like the *Post,* local outlets, even television stations, tended to convey themes more than chronology. Yet a very important difference existed in this coverage. While the *Post* emphasized fear, it also countered with news of community spirit. Local competitors tilted far more to the former.

The great exception to this emphasis on fear was the fascinating reporting in the *Washington Times,* a paper which, though published in Washington, mainly focuses on national and international news and considers itself a conservative commentator on national and international affairs. Perhaps because of this orientation, the *Times* devoted relatively little to the sniper case. More unusual, however, was its perspective.

Although the paper would eventually map its own path, it began like most local outlets. It published one of its early stories on October 8, after the shooting at Benjamin Tasker School focused attention on the vulnerability of children to attack by the sniper. The article depicted one student's leaving the school crying and expressing his relief that his father was picking him up. The reporter matched this anxiety with Police Chief Moose's fighting back tears in his despair over that shooting. Another report featured a daughter who reminded her father that there was nothing one could do to be careful enough in such circumstances. Although the article expanded from news story into the realm of an editorial, which concluded by encouraging readers to push on with life, its tenor suggested panic rather than fearful accommodation. Diana West,[1] in an article published on October 11 about business in the suburbs, wondered aloud whether the sniper was a terrorist. The piece noted that while these questions remained unanswered, most doubted the violence came from terrorists. And it also described the height of the first wave of shootings, on Thursday, October 3, as filled with "barely contained fear and chaos." Particularly upsetting was the report that a truck fitting the description of the sniper vehicle had been allowed to make a delivery at an elementary school. This article also

---

1. Diana West, a *Washington Times* op-ed columnist from 1999 to 2002, is currently a weekly columnist for the Newspaper Enterprise Association. A graduate of Yale University, her work has appeared in numerous publications, including the *Wall Street Journal,* the *Weekly Standard,* the *Washington Post,* the *Women's Quarterly,* and the *Atlantic Monthly.* Although she has worked in feature writing, she is known for her criticisms of the hot-button issues of the day. Her work at the *Times* focused on American culture and society, government affairs, and political scandals. She continues to contribute to the paper, although she resigned her position in 2002. (Source: United Features Syndicate Newspaper Enterprise Association website, http://www.featurebank.com/?title=Bio:Diana%20West.)

concluded with the urging that people needed to continue on in the face of these fears.

This style of reporting could be found even as the event came toward its end. An October 23 article assessing the impact of the shooting of Conrad Johnson suggested complete panic. The manager of a shop across from an earlier shooting declared herself "shocked and frightened" by the assassination of Conrad Johnson. She concluded rather helplessly that all the public could really do was to hope that the sniper gave up his deadly chase.

Yet the *Times* more vigorously countered this theme of high levels of anxiety, which had similarly predominated in the *Post*'s description of community attitudes. To be sure, an element of schizophrenia existed in the *Times*. The October 15 edition of the Metropolitan section announced that fear had reduced attendance at the outdoor food festival, the Taste of D.C., by 25 percent. Only two days before, the same section had emphasized the large crowds at the event. While the earlier article documented the many visitors, it also concentrated on their indifference to the attacks. A couple said that they had every intention of attending. Moreover, one of the cooks observed, "There's a good crowd out here. . . . People are smiling, and they are coming out. The good thing is that people are here to eat, relax, and have some fun." Instead of a focus on fear, the reporter found indifference, or even willful ignorance, of the circumstances.

Of course, the *Post* had published articles about people who wanted to push ahead without being intimidated, but the *Times* took another important step. While stating that many were deeply concerned and frightened, the October 23 *Times* focused on analysts who argued that these fears remained unfounded. The last half of the article repeated the familiar argument that people were scared because of the random nature of the attacks, but that this very nature of the attacks made self-defense nearly impossible. This followed the opening paragraphs that painstakingly showed that fear was irrational. Quoting George Gray, acting director of the Center for Risk Analysis at Harvard, the *Times* announced the risks to be very small. In the metropolitan area, the risk of being shot by the sniper was 1 in 357,692, while that of being killed was 1 in 465,000. According to the paper, these possibilities should be compared to the risk of suffering a heart attack in any particular year, at 1 in 400, or of dying from a fall, at 1 in 5,304, and so on. Clearly this article intended to minimize the risk. It must be noted, though, that the rates for the other risks were based on annualized factors, while the probability figures for vulnerability to the sniper related to the three weeks the episode had been going on at that point. Even so, the casual reader likely would have been stunned by these numbers and surely would have been encouraged toward calmness. Reinforcing this view was another quotation that reminded readers of all those who had not been shot, and which then was followed by the reporter's own remark: "Yet people in the Washington and Richmond metropolitan areas are terrified." Here readers might be startled by the seeming ignorance of the fearful.

Furthermore, the *Times* identified the miscreant that had caused anxiety: television news. In two pieces of media criticism, published on October 22 and 24, Jennifer Harper[2] excoriated both cable and local broadcast news. She argued that although the police had adopted the proper tone, the electronic media had "become shriller than ever." FOX News even had interviewed serial killer David Berkowitz, "Son of Sam." Furthermore, to avoid the charge that they had gone beyond reporting to interfering in law enforcement, she noted, the press had relied on traffic cameras, instead of their own photographers, to observe police roadblocks. Harper deemed this a flimsy attempt to obscure their inexcusable involvement, done in order to fuel the fear-filled reportage.

Not only had the electronic media sounded a siren that instilled fear throughout the region, Harper charged, they did so for venal reasons. Ratings had soared, up more than 100 percent, and this regrettable approach had spread to the Internet. A New York company selling domain names advised that the following addresses remained available: "Beltway Shooters," "Beltway Crash Shot," and "My Beltway Sniper."

Seconding Harper's analysis was another piece of personal reaction in the Life section of the October 24 edition of the *Times,* written by journalist Tom Knott.[3] He asserted that cable news encouraged fear

2. Jennifer Harper is a national features reporter for the *Washington Times.* Her topics of interest include the Internet, popular culture, the media, politics, and health. (Source: Bulldog Reporter website, http://www.firmvoice.com/ME2/dir mod.asp?sid=8BDE5AAB10AE456A89CD20CCFB0C45AE&nm=Search+Media+ Organizations+By+Media+Type&type=Market&mod=MarketPlaceEmployees&mid= D9B179CABA074BD98CDAF992AF0CA838&tier=19&id=D46BA480EC6B46CD A26E94684DC4926 E.)

3. Tom Knott has written for the *Washington Times* since 1984, contributing columns to the Sports and Metro sections of the paper. Knott earned a bachelor's degree in psychology from George Mason University. (Source: http://www.tom-knott.com/about/.)

because of its need to fill too much airtime. Relying on mental health experts who had little to say that was not speculation, he said, the stations put out news which overstated the risks. Compared to the panic on the airwaves, the reality was, according to this article, that one had a better chance of dying in a wreck than from a sniper bullet. In this way, Knott backed up Harper's critique of the electronic media and also supported the position of the *Times* that fears were disproportionate. To this end, he concluded, "Living is risky business. More so with a sniper in our midst, but the alternatives to the risks are unacceptable. Stay home? Don't eat out? Don't hit the pub? Nah. I don't think so."

Even though this spate of stories in the *Times* counseled against fear, some other reporting mentioned panic, or even perseverance, but not anxiety. In essence, the bulk of the *Times* articles minimized the danger. Interestingly, its reporting did little to emphasize the contours of community which had been the *Post*'s unintended answer to the fear it depicted. No local news outlets followed exactly in the *Post*'s or the *Times*' footsteps.

In fact, the other local outlets selected for this study emphasized anxiety more than did either paper. None shared the optimism or the stoicism of the *Times,* and none provided the sense of community of the *Post.* This survey considers the message of the four Washington broadcast channels that devoted substantial effort to news, and that of the all-news radio channel in Washington (WTOP-1500 AM); as well as the *Montgomery Journal* (part of a major chain of Washington suburban papers); and the *Richmond Times-Dispatch.*

The four TV channels and their network affiliations are: Channel 4, WRC (NBC); Channel 5, WTTG (FOX); Channel 7, WJLA (ABC); and Channel 9, WUSA (CBS). Why these outlets did not generate a stronger, more coherent chronology requires some explanation beyond the general factors that influenced the *Post.* Of course, short references to other shootings provided a minimum framework, but little more. This did not provide background for those not already acquainted with events, while, in fact, suggesting more the need for it. Particularly episodic, the Montgomery periodical provided an extreme example of the story being created afresh daily. But the electronic media might have been expected to behave quite differently. For evening and nightly broadcasts, the main method of reporting was the presentation of brief accounts—one or two or even several—on a variety of topics. As such, the news on the sniper case emerged in kaleidoscopic fashion. Generally, it was up to the viewer to "connect the dots." Thus, news in this situation arrived as a jumble of discrete parts. Themes rather than an interpretation received reinforcement.

Somewhat different was WTOP Radio, which, it should be noted, played an important role. On the air for twenty-four hours a day, it was positioned to give the news at all times, including as it developed or broke. In later interviews, many journalists, including Steve Hammel[4] and Gail Pennybacker,[5] mentioned the station as guiding them, in terms of the emerging facts. Essentially, the station utilized a very constant rhythm, with the regular appearance of news "holes" throughout each hour. These were filled by short, self-contained reports, which in themselves would not encourage a sense of chronology because of their very nature. However, during the next hour, the station would replace a certain percentage of the earlier hour's stories with newer, updated versions, or altogether new pieces. Even so, this meant that most stories were repeated before they were phased out. Only when something dramatic occurred was a story quickly dropped or substantially updated. Essentially, the description of the sniper story evolved and, through this evolution, gave a devoted listener a chance to comprehend a daily story. Still, one should not overstate the significance of this story. In the introduction to this work, I discussed the necessity of not trying to pin down what readers might read other than what the placements (e.g., the front page) indicated. But in the case of WTOP, it is difficult to imagine anyone listening for hours (or even for two hours) without interruption. The structure of the news, with its repetition, indicates that the producers, as well, expected people to move on. Thus, hearing snippets, it is most likely that any listener produced little coherent narration. Furthermore, because of the commitment of the

4. Steve Hammel was vice-president of News (news director) for WJLA during the sniper investigation. He arrived in WJLA in May 2000. A native of Pennsylvania, Hammel started his career at a hometown radio station. He received a bachelor of science degree from Syracuse University, and at the time of my interview with him had been in radio and television for over thirty-one years. As a reporter, he has covered the Three Mile Island incident, has been on Air Force One, and has covered city council meetings. He became a news director at the age of twenty-four, in Harrisburg, Pa., at the local ABC affiliate. He was subsequently promoted to news director in a Syracuse affiliate, and then to the Dallas station. He then moved to Rochester, N.Y., for seven years as a news director before being promoted to a St. Louis station. In late November 2002, he left WJLA to become station manager at KPHO television station in Phoenix. About six months later he was promoted to vice-president and general manager of the station. (Source: Hammel interview.)

5. For Gail Pennybacker's bio, see note 14 to chapter 2.

station to breaking news and keeping close to the "facts" as the reporters understood them, the next day's reports had balkanized information very, very differently than had the preceding day's. Most often, only a fan who listened all night would be able to perceive an overriding structure within this presentation.

For the most part, the Richmond paper, by its broad and diverse coverage, emphasized themes over chronology, but a certain rhythm did emerge. Richmond, over a hundred miles south of Washington, and even further from the initial shootings in Montgomery Country, did not at first treat the story as a local one. In the initial few days, the paper relied on the Associated Press and a single correspondent in Fredericksburg (fifty miles from D.C.) whose beat extended into Northern Virginia. As the shootings migrated down the I-95 corridor, first to the Fredericksburg area and beyond, then to Ashland on October 19, the amount of news featured in the paper sharply increased. The arrest of two men at an Exxon station in West Richmond on October 21 furthered the crescendo of reporting, which then continued until the arrests of Muhammad and Malvo on October 24 and their subsequent arraignments. So, for the *Times-Dispatch,* the structure of the news communicated a message of creeping crisis that eventually threatened to envelope the city. Occasionally, during the month of October, the paper recognized this vision of a lesser danger expanding into a greater one. Early after the wounding of a woman on October 9 near Fredericksburg, the paper's headline worried that normalcy had evaporated in the affected county. Another article, published on October 14, quoted a central Virginia police lieutenant as saying, "The fear is flowing south very quickly today, and I'm not saying if it's a wrong thing." In a later article, published on October 22, following the Ashland shooting, Richmond columnist Ray McAllister[6] indicated that up until the attack, he had viewed events as an outsider. But he noted that his new vantage point had not happened all at once following the sniper actions around Fredericksburg. "Most people worried a little more, in other words, but not a lot," he wrote. People had been more cautious, but his article

6. Ray McAllister had been a newspaper reporter for fourteen years when he became a columnist for the *Richmond Times-Dispatch* in 1988. He is the author of three books, including his 2006 work, *Topsail Island: Mayberry by the Sea,* that grew out of one of his columns. McAllister left the paper in 2007 to write books full time. In addition, he became the editor of *Boomer Life* magazine in June 2008. (Sources: http://www.mayberrybythesea.com/; http://www.boomerlifemagaz ine.com/Pages/EditorsColumn.php.)

# Richmond Times-Dispatch

50¢

FINAL

RICHMOND, VIRGINIA

*VIRGINIA'S NEWS LEADER*
A MEDIA GENERAL NEWSPAPER

WEDNESDAY, OCTOBER 23, 2002

...

# SNIPER KILLS MD. MAN

## METRO SCHOOLS TO REOPEN TODAY DESPITE THREAT

### ASHLAND NOTE: 'YOUR CHILDREN ARE NOT SAFE ANYWHERE, AT ANY TIME'

*Leaders say the decision is up to parents*

**BY PAIGE AKIN AND MEREDITH FISCHER**
TIMES-DISPATCH STAFF WRITERS

Students have been asked to return to school today despite the sniper's written warning: "Your children are not safe anywhere, at any time."

Police Chief Charles Moose of Montgomery County, Md., yesterday revealed that message from the note left in the woods near Saturday's sniper shooting in Ashland.

But the administrators' decision stands.

"We cannot be a fortress. Our lives need to go on. Our kids need to be educated," Powhatan School Board Chairman H.A. Gideons said.

**TIP LINE**

**TO REPORT** information about the shootings, call the FBI's toll-free hot line at **(888) 324-9800.**

The details of the note caught local school and government officials by surprise.

They had decided an hour earlier to reopen schools, after conferring all afternoon with law enforcement.

"We realize now we probably had good reason not to have children going to and from school, but we recognize that we cannot do that forever," said Chesterfield County Supervisor Edward B. Barber.

Area superintendents said it's up to parents to decide whether their children should return to school today.

Some parents were stunned by the note's details.

"A very cold chill went down my spine," said Chesterfield County parent Wendy Lindberg. "I really feel that whoever this is knows exactly how to put terror in people's hearts. When you start going after children, that's the lowest of the low."

The Times-Dispatch reported yesterday that the note contained a threat to school children. Administrators decided to shut schools based on information they were given about the note.

Their fears were confirmed yesterday when Moose read the note's chilling words.

Schools were closed for the past two days in Chesterfield, Dinwiddie, Goochland, Hanover, Henrico, Powhatan and Prince George counties, as well as the cities of Colonial Heights, Hopewell, Petersburg and Richmond.

Barber, who has five daughters, said he's not sure how school officials would be able to quell parents' fears. "That's a huge question, and I don't have an answer."

Police have given no indication that the threat to children on Monday and yesterday is any different today. But local officials were more willing to open

SEE **SCHOOLS,** PAGE A11 ▶

Apartment residents near the bus stop look out their window at the crime scene while a federal agent goes door to door.

CLIFF OWEN/THE WASHINGTON TIMES VIA THE ASSOCIATED PRESS

## Moose's words aimed at caller

### 'We are waiting to hear from you'

**BY PAUL BRADLEY AND ANDREW PETKOFSKY**
TIMES-DISPATCH STAFF WRITERS

ROCKVILLE, Md. — As police tried to confirm whether a bus driver shot dead early yesterday is another victim of the sniper terrorizing the region, authorities again used the media to reach out to the person believed to be the gunman.

Montgomery County Police Chief Charles Moose appeared before television cameras last night to send a message to the person who contacted police by leaving a note in the woods near the site of Saturday night's sniper attack in Ashland, Va. Moose said he wanted to continue communications, but without more bloodshed.

"You have attempted to communicate with us," Moose said. "We have researched the option you stated and found that it is not possible electronically to comply in the manner that you requested. However, we remain open and ready to talk to you about the options you have mentioned."

Moose continued, "It is important that we do this without anyone else getting hurt. Call us at the same number you used before to obtain the 800 number that you have requested. If you would feel more comfortable, a private post office box or another secure method can be provided.

"You indicated that this is about more than violence; we are waiting to hear from you," the police chief said.

Moose declined to elaborate and took no questions from reporters.

The Washington Post reported yesterday that the note left in Ashland demanded a $10 million payment.

Earlier yesterday, Moose released a chilling post script to the note: "Your children are not safe anywhere, at any time."

Authorities said police are treating the shooting death of Conrad Johnson, a 35-year-old father of two, as another sniper shooting. If ballistics tests confirm the link, Johnson would be the 10th person to die at the hands of the serial sniper.

Johnson was gunned down just before 6 a.m. as he stood on the top step of his Ride On bus, preparing for his morning run. The bus was parked, on layover for cleaning and paperwork. Montgomery County's Ride On bus

SEE **SHOOTING,** PAGE A10 ▶

Johnson

Unidentified family members of Conrad Johnson comfort each other upon leaving a Bethesda, Md., hospital. Johnson, 35, is believed to be the 10th person killed by the sniper.

MATTHEW CAVANAUGH/THE ASSOCIATED PRESS

TWO AREA HISPANIC MEN CAUGHT UP IN INVESTIGATION NOW FACE DEPORTATION
Page A13

OFFICIALS CONFISCATE EXXON STATION'S SURVEILLANCE TAPES, RECEIPTS
Page A13

PREP SPORTS CALLED OFF FOR REST OF WEEK
Page F1

LOCAL REC, YOUTH SPORTS LEAGUES PLAYING WAITING GAME
Page B1

LATEST VICTIM LOVED SPENDING TIME WITH HIS TWO SONS
Page A10

RANDOLPH-MACON STUDENTS, STAFF STRUGGLE TO REGAIN SENSE OF SAFETY
Page A11

MOOSE, MEDIA BREAKING NEW GROUND IN NEGOTIATIONS
Page A12

BUSINESS IS SLOW FOR MANY AREA RETAILERS
Page C1

---

**WEDNESDAY**
ONLINE ▸ http://www.timesdispatch.com

Today's weather
Partly cloudy. High: 66.

Angels take 2-1 Series lead
Barry Bonds goes deep but the Giants come up short.
Sports /F1

Recruiting 101
Virginia's freshman

IN FLAIR TODAY

Changing gears
Shift into the light lane at the fast-food drive-through
It's in the bag

Russia, France balk at U.S. draft
Key Security Council members say latest resolution needs work.
World /A9

Premier Pet wins Impact Award

**COMING**
TOMORROW

First Fridays
Gallery tour brings the crowds out at night.
Weekend

The bear truth

---

The *Richmond Times-Dispatch* covers the reaction to the shooting of Conrad Johnson.

implied that such a view was quite likely to change. The bulk of the paper's readers could scarcely conclude from these remarks, as well as the intensity of the coverage, that they were in greater jeopardy than before. This shift in approach was subtle, and the clearest message from this and other like-media did not emphasize chronology.

Rather, the main theme sounded among the local outlets was that of fear. Many, many articles and broadcasts made this their principal emphasis. At one extreme lay the descriptions of chaos and helplessness. Leonard Pitts,[7] a *Miami Herald* reporter assigned to Washington, on October 18 reported in the Richmond paper a story that focused on the lost innocence of his own grandson. While Pitts promised young Eric that nothing would happen to him, and promised himself that this child would rebound from this experience, the story largely argued the reverse. In fact, Pitts labeled the reassurance that nothing would personally happen as a "crazy promise." Most of the remainder of the article described the pain of watching the new wariness of his community. Generally, his neighborhood had lost its walkers and joggers, while people in gas stations positioned themselves so that they could not be seen from nearby wooded areas. People in stores who gave change said "Be safe," instead of their earlier, more innocuous remarks. Still, to Pitts, the new limitations placed on children remained the most difficult to accept. For example, Eric "used to run out every morning to get the newspaper. Now he pauses at the front door, peers in every direction, darts to the tree in the middle of the yard, looks carefully around its trunk, then makes a dash for the end of the driveway. He snatches up the papers and sprints like hell to the back of the house." In Pitts's estimation, the sniper episode showed children that a real monster could look just like ordinary men and women. Although the writer's grandson still retrieved the paper, it is evident that this account focused on the pure terror he made manifest.

Fear could be generated easily in the manner in which murders or woundings were reported. Even though WTOP rarely injected much emotion into its coverage, reporter Kristi King announced the shoot-

---

7. Leonard Pitts Jr. has written for the *Miami Herald* since 1991. He began as a music critic and in 1994 debuted his syndicated column focusing on pop culture, social issues, and family life. Pitts was a finalist for the Pulitzer Prize in 1992 and was awarded a Pulitzer in 2004 for commentary. He is the author of the book *Becoming Dad: Black Men and the Journey to Fatherhood,* published in 1999. (Source: Leonard Pitts Jr. website, http://www.leonardpittsjr.com/biog raphy.html.)

ings on the morning of October 3 by naming each victim and then emphatically stating "shot and killed." The repetition through the four victims at least mitigated the episodic nature of WTOP coverage, by providing a rhetorical frame if not background. Yet this dance mainly created shock among listeners, a shock which may have deepened with the report that police had little to go on except the possible presence of an Isuzu truck. King punctuated this report by noting that police officers dealing with these victims were holding back tears.

No people appeared more terrified than did the residents of Aspen Hill in the aftermath of the October 22 shooting of Conrad Johnson. Since Aspen Hill had been the center of the first five murders, on October 2–3, the residents had over the following three weeks breathed a collective sigh of relief that the sniper had apparently gone elsewhere. His return deeply shocked the community. Feeding off this sentiment and reinforcing it were a number of reports, including WJLA's account. Reporter Nancy Weiner[8] noted that although the crime scene tape had been removed, normalcy had not returned. Playgrounds and fields were abandoned, and no kids were in sight. Here, as elsewhere in the region, parents were keeping their kids at home, "just in case." One parent interviewed admitted: "It actually terrorizes me." Another pronounced parents "horrified." A third interviewee took his three-year-old son out only in his arms and shielded by a pegboard. In Aspen Hill, a family "spent the afternoon indoors watching news updates with the blinds down and the doors locked."

The print press reported about fear, but in a more muted form. Articles described residents carrying on with daily life but modifying their routines to fit a high level of anxiety. Other reports found continuity in behavior that was accompanied by a strong sense of foreboding and expectation that something would occur. Such coverage most often was juxtaposed with other reports of abject fear in the community; it sometimes constituted an entire segment. In a story on October 22, which featured a variety of responses to the sniper, the *Montgomery Journal*

---

8. ABC News New York correspondent Nancy Weiner frequently appears on *Good Morning America, World News,* and *Nightline.* She joined ABC in 2003 as a Washington correspondent for NewsOne. Before joining the network, Weiner reported for WJLA, Washington's ABC affiliate. She has covered a variety of hard-news stories throughout her career, including the Middle East peace process, peacekeeping efforts in Bosnia, and the September 11 terrorist attacks. (Source: ABC Media Net website, http://www.abcmedianet.com/shows05/news/correspondents/weiner.shtml.)

profiled two workers who in different ways reacted worriedly to the fear. Tim Johnson worked on Rockville Pike wearing big yellow disks that were advertisements for a music store. After the shootings began, he took a week off from work. Back at the job, he varied between a world-weary fatalism that permitted his sad return and the calculation that he did not form a worthwhile target. Johnson functioned, bearing far more than the weight of his signs. Car salesman Matt Sullivan, though comfortable during the day, became frightened at night. The *Journal* quoted Sullivan: "Right now, I feel I have a view where I can kind of pan around . . . And if I see a white truck suddenly stop on [Route] 355 and some guy get out, I feel I have a chance to duck. It's at nighttime, after 6 o'clock, when it's dark and you can't see, that I feel most vulnerable." Despite his worries, Sullivan continued to work as a salesman.

In the wake of the shock over the shooting of middle-school student Iran Brown at Benjamin Tasker, anxiety was readily apparent throughout the region. But even in these difficult circumstances, the press provided accounts that mixed stories of fear with those about resolve. In fact, in the aftermath, most media reported Montgomery County Executive Douglas Duncan's admonition that fear should be leavened with steadiness. Although the press had little option but to report the words of a community leader of Duncan's importance, reporters also included other stories of a similar ilk that they elected to consider newsworthy. For example, in an October 7 broadcast, WJLA presented the advice of a security expert about what to do if one became the target of a sniper. This consultant urged citizens to put a bulletproof shield– whether a car, a telephone pole, or a mailbox–between themselves and the shooter. If necessary, he urged them to use their arms. Find another way to observe the shooter other than simply looking over the barricade, he said. If possible, use a mirror. In short, do everything possible to limit the shooter's ability to wound. No matter how ridiculous such strategies seem in retrospect, given what is now known about the snipers' modus operandi, these reports indicate a structuring of news that included an effort to confront personal fear. Likewise, as the *Times-Dispatch* reported on October 8, police in Spotsylvania County (near Fredericksburg) urged people to go about their lives, but to limit trips as much as possible by combining errands.

Many articles and newscasts included a variety of responses. As Aspen Hill recovered a day after the Johnson shooting on October 22, the *Journal* published a story about the neighborhood. This account described drivers and bus riders who were too frightened to leave home.

One bus driver noted that a lot of his peers had simply called in sick. One driver had to be removed from his bus because he was too upset to drive. Resident Cynthia Clarke decided, after some grocery shopping, that she had had enough and was going home to read a book. The whole event had simply been too close. Businesses had to respond, and a local book store closed its more vulnerable front doors, but this was scarcely enough–as the proprietor noted: "Right now it's . . . a ghost town." As Clarke had indicated, she had gone out before returning to her book, and others similarly had had to run errands, but they were afraid. Even as they had to attend to business, they still warily surveyed the situation and took precautions. One resident said, "I was very concerned when I left the house. . . . I was keeping my eyes open." Yet, another did say he was simply unafraid, arguing that the randomness meant nothing could be done. He also noted he did not focus on these matters.

In contrast to the various levels of fear that dominated much local reporting, there were those like the Aspen Hill resident who shrugged off these concerns. Most in this category were aware of the risk but, because they were fatalists, remained unconcerned. For example, traveler Shawn Reese stopped with his two young children at a Shell gas station on I-95 near the scene of a shooting to fill up his car for the trip from North Carolina to Pennsylvania. He said in an article in the *Times-Dispatch* on October 11 that he was not fearful pumping gas there because, "If something is going to happen, something is going to happen. You can't let that scare you." Several days later, in Ashland, seventy-one-year-old Ruth O'Brien expressed quite similar views, carried by the *Times-Dispatch* on October 23. In an October 17 story, FOX News talked with motorists from Williamsburg who reflected the attitude that you have to do what you have to do. If you were destined to be hit, so be it. What can you do? "Doesn't bother me and my friends a bit," said one.

The press also reported on those who, though fearful, completely pushed it out of their minds. In its coverage of a high school football game, the *Times-Dispatch* reported on October 13 that the homecoming queen successfully focused on not tripping and falling and also successfully did not think about the "uncertainty and fear" elsewhere. Similarly, *Times-Dispatch* reporter Gregory J. Gilligan[9] interviewed other teen-

9. Gregory J. Gilligan joined the *Richmond Times-Dispatch* in 1987. From 1993 to 2008, Gilligan covered the retail industry in Virginia and wrote a weekly column called "Biz Buzz." He is currently deputy business editor for the *Dispatch* and also teaches journalism classes at Virginia Commonwealth University. (Sources: University of Virginia McIntire School of Commerce website, http://www.com

agers, this time at a mall. Ryan Clarke was there enjoying himself, not letting "some crazy guy take my fun away." Related to these were reports that featured a desire to return to normal. Like those people who simply avoided thinking of threats, these people stressed similar activities but justified them by a need to find the customary and comfortable. Maryland's Governor Parris Glendening, widely covered in the press, counseled his constituents that they must not let one person disrupt life. As reported by TV-7, WJLA, on October 17, he also argued that young people, while acting carefully, needed to return to "normal schedules." The *Times-Dispatch* quoted a Richmond-area school superintendent's message, on October 23, that, "Our lives need to go on. Our kids need to be educated." The *Montgomery Journal* included similar comments from athletic directors in its issue of October 11.

Finally, some interviewees exhibited resistance, or simply a lack of anxiety. For example, the Richmond paper interviewed John Jackson on October 23, who said, "I guess I'm here out of defiance. . . . I can't talk to the sniper except through my actions." FOX News ran a story on October 17 about pumping gas, which concluded that "a lot of people are refusing to let the nameless, faceless murderer alter their plans. They are moving on." On October 18, the *Journal* published another article that indirectly suggested a safer environment. Staff writer Sara Michael[10] documented that criminal activity other than the sniper's had decreased, perhaps because of a generally enhanced police presence throughout the county. She further suggested that so many people staying at home lessened criminals' opportunities. One criminologist speculated that this change did not stem from criminals staying at home because: "They tend to be risk takers anyway." Interestingly, and ironically, the public might have concluded from Michael's contribution that life had become marginally safer with the snipers on the prowl than it was otherwise.

Still, in these newspapers, reporting on the stalwart paled beside

---

merce.virginia.edu/faculty_research/centers/PWC/Mock_Press/mockpress_speakers.html; Richmond.com website, http://www.inrich.com/cva/ric/search.apx.-content-articles-RTD-2008-06-30-0025.html.)

10. Sara Michael, a graduate of Boston University, got her first job in journalism in September 2001 at the *Montgomery Journal,* covering cops and fires. She moved to *Federal Computer Week* magazine in 2003, focusing on technology in the federal government, before going back to school to earn a Master's degree in journalism from Northwestern University. She wrote for the now-defunct *Baltimore Examiner,* covering health and the environment. (Source: Michael interview.)

the reports of terror and those where encouragement was mainly laced with fear and foreboding, like the story on the boy dashing to pick up the paper. Furthermore, unlike the *Post,* these news outlets spent relatively little time describing a community that came together. To be certain, the stories based on fear fashioned a simplified society, but one whose links came from fright. The *Times-Dispatch* openly recognized this circumstance in a piece authored by Peter Hardin[11] on October 23. Noting that the sniper was a "malevolent equalizer," Hardin wrote that, like a natural disaster "that hits a geographic region, the sniper has made no distinction between his victims, dispensing fear across a broad swath." Referring to Moose's warning of the previous day that children were not safe anywhere, Hardin found these remarks frightening to all parents and, in particular, to this region that was dealing with an indecipherable serial killer.

Although positive expressions of community life were few, the local media did pay attention to the factors that the *Post* had reported as part of the community. Expressions of great admiration for the victims created icons for the community under siege. Still, relatively little advice emerged about strengthening the community or about getting along. In fact, articles published in the Richmond paper on October 16 and 21, written by Mark Holmberg,[12] examined the effort by police in an ironic

11. Peter Hardin worked as a Washington correspondent for the *Richmond Times-Dispatch* from 1992 to 2007. A graduate of Hampshire College, Hardin is known for exploring social and cultural issues in America. His projects have included an examination of the impact of eugenics in the twentieth century, and black farmers' fight to end racism at the U.S. Department of Agriculture. (Sources: LinkedIn website, http://www.linkedin.com/pub/7/8/5b4; InRich.com website, http://washdateline.mgnetwork.com/index.cfm?SiteID=WSH&PackageID=46 &fuseaction=article.main&ArticleID=4927&GroupID=222.)

12. Mark Holmberg became a reporter for the *Times-Dispatch* in 1986. Born in California and a bricklayer by trade, he received his bachelor's degree in biology from the University of Mary Washington. His first job out of college was as assistant manager of a sewage treatment plant, a less-than-ideal career for his interests. At the time, he enjoyed writing and music, so he submitted a concert review to the *Times-Dispatch* when he was twenty-four. A few weeks later, he was invited to be a freelance music critic for the paper. In addition to music, Holmberg did some street-level features, and in two years was offered a position at the paper. He began with lifestyles writing, continuing until 1990 when he moved to police reporting and general assignments. In 1999, he began writing his Sunday metro column. In 2003, Holmberg was a finalist for the Pulitzer Prize for distinguished commentary. He left the paper and joined CBS 6 in Richmond as an investigative reporter in 2007. He describes his position at the television station as a video version of his

way, which tended to blur the whole rupture between the sniper and the public. In one article examining the police and public from an unusual angle, the journalist took up the plight of those who owned or drove white vans. Facing stares and doubts, they were regarded as freaks. In a sense, this commentary unsettled the demarcation that police were trying to draw between society and the objects of the investigation. Holmberg then discussed a female psychic who believed she could go to places where the sniper had been and make some sort of identification. Reported straightforwardly, the article on a psychic suggested a community resorting to desperate and unusual measures. Underscoring this last point was the man who, according to Holmberg, was trying to find the sniper simply by scanning the traffic.

References to religion as a source of solidarity were sparse. The one major exception to this was the coverage of a prayer service held following the October 22 Johnson shooting, when community morale had dipped dangerously low. Television channels gave this event significant play. Attending were religious leaders from a variety of faiths and denominations–Catholics, Sikhs, Jews, and Protestants–as well as a variety of political leaders. The local NBC channel covered the event and sent a strong didactic message in its conclusion:

> Obviously, we have to be very careful about our children and take
> care of them. At the same time, we have to say this will pass. It's
> not–this is not the end of the world. And, sure, you might even
> want to help your child some in a special way for a day or so, but
> let us all cooperate with the police. . . . Don't let us lose our
> hope . . . our confidence. . . . [Doug Duncan] offered tips for peo-
> ple trying to cope with these recent shootings . . . be with your
> families at the time . . . connect with your communities and your
> faith. Talk to others, especially those people in leadership roles.
> And lastly, to act, engage in some kind of role. And, if you have
> any kind of information, make sure you give police a call.

Thus would community be reinforced. The *Journal,* on October 24, interviewed one of the attendees, who offered that the service had been a great way to get everyone together in a time of need.

---

column. When asked why he focuses his reporting on society's downtrodden, he responded, "Society can only elevate itself as high as the bottom rung. Richmond is this absolutely fabulous place that has really been held hostage by the trauma and dysfunction in the underclass. The only way you can truly improve their lot is to fully understand it, and empathize–and that's the tough thing." (Sources: Holmberg interview; Richmond.com website, http://www.richmond.com/local-life/1108.)

Yet the message delivered by the service proved a thin reed to counteract the anxiety-oriented reporting that otherwise dominated. As the NBC-affiliated WRC-Channel 4 report suggested, another way to create community solidarity in the face of crime may have been active support of the police. But the local outlets seldom advocated this, and instead gave more space to critics. In fact, according to Mike Mc-Mearty,[13] WTOP broadcast a strong defense of the media that cast serious aspersions at least at Montgomery Police Chief Moose's conducting of the Task Force investigation.

This WTOP report is worth examining because it went beyond most local reporting. It is doubly useful because it illustrates a connection between media and law enforcement, considered at length later in this book. The context for the report–which actually was an interview–was Chief Moose's angry attack on the media at a press conference. As earlier noted, the police discovered a tarot card left by the shooters on October 7 at Benjamin Tasker Middle School. On the card was a written message, which included the admonition not to tell the press about this communication. But Mike Buchanan of WUSA learned of it through sources and reported that such a card had been found, with the wording, "I am God." Even though the card actually said "Call me God," Chief Moose expressed anger, most likely because he feared the media had undermined a potential connection with the shooters. He took to the podium to charge the media with disrupting the investigation and scornfully spoke of WUSA's action. Sarcastically, he said that the public did not want the media to solve the case. And, he said, if they did, let the police know and they would go on to other matters. This latter remark was certainly designed to put the press on the defensive and force them to back away from investigating the case.

Radio station WTOP asked Dave Roberts,[14] the news manager of

13. Mike McMearty has been at WTOP Radio in Washington since 1992. His radio career began at a small radio station in Prince Frederick, Md. He then moved to a station in Annapolis, all the while waiting tables, bartending, and cooking to earn additional income. His initial assignment at WTOP was as assistant editor. During his tenure, he has been an editor, producer, reporter, anchor, sports reporter, and assistant news director. He is currently news director for the station. (Source: WTOP website, http://wtop.com/?nid=82&sid=598731.)

14. Dave Roberts began his career in television as a production assistant at an NBC affiliate in Detroit in 1978. In 1986 he moved to an ABC affiliate in Dayton, Ohio. Shortly thereafter Roberts was promoted, becoming the first African American in Ohio to be a news director. He then joined an NBC affiliate in Baltimore in

WUSA, to respond to Moose's attack on October 9. The radio reporter aggressively challenged Roberts to defend airing Buchanan's report, and he responded in kind. Labeling Moose's remarks a "tirade," Roberts sympathetically noted that the chief was under a lot of strain. In fact, Roberts reached back to earlier relations and noted, "Moose has been on our station and is familiar with our staff; we have a good relationship with him." Nonetheless, during the press conferences in Rockville, which, according to Roberts, were held every three hours, the police and other authorities had given out meager handouts. The news director made it clear that the station's job was to go beyond them. "We have a very experienced staff and investigation is our job," he said. "In fact, Mike Buchanan, who broke the story, has great sources and is one of the best reporters around. Mike was simply doing his job." Although Roberts indicated that, as a member of the community, the station would not air material that posed a danger, he did not believe the information about the tarot card fell in that category. Furthermore, Roberts declined to explain how sources were cultivated or how stories might be checked out with authorities. Finally, he declined to change any of the station's approach to the story and offered that more good investigations would help solve the case. This last comment was a complete rejection of Moose's position that the police alone should handle the sniper case. Indeed, Roberts concluded by saying that good sources led to good journalism.

Of course, a strong case could be made that independent journalism is a necessary part of community. But in this circumstance, at least in the short term, the refusal here to be an unquestioning prop or conduit for the police weakened the impression of community solidarity. Its absence made the anxieties surrounding the police investigation more evident. This proved to be the most evident theme also in national reporting on these events.

• • •

---

1992, before becoming news director of a Gannett-owned NBC affiliate in Atlanta. In his positions as news director, Roberts achieved high ratings for his newscasts. In 2000, Roberts became vice-president and news director of WUSA, a Gannett sister station. During his time at WUSA, Roberts reworked the station's news lineup, had a number of reporters leave, and despite an initial climb in ratings, saw overall viewership for WUSA remain low. He resigned from WUSA in 2004, although it has been implied that he was forced out. (Sources: *Washington Post* website, http://www.washingtonpost.com/wp-dyn/articles/A35646-2004Aug2.html; BNet website, http://findarticles.com/p/articles/mi_hb5244/is_200408/ai_n19574239.)

Broadcast and cable channels, radio, and thousands of periodicals carried the sniper story all over the country. To understand how the rest of the nation witnessed the "facts" of this story, this study considers first a sample of national news programming–Greta Van Susteren's broadcast on FOX, CBS's *60 Minutes,* ABC's *20/20,* NBC's *Today,* CNN's evening show hosted by Aaron Brown, ABC's *Nightline,* and the evening news on both CBS and ABC. This analysis will then be supplemented with insights drawn from four important newspapers.

These various outlets produced news that, much like the local outlets, emphasized fear, though with even less attention either to a sustained narrative or to an emphasis on community bonding. One significantly different path was taken by *CBS Evening News,* anchored by Dan Rather.[15] Midway along in the crisis, on October 15, Rather noted, "We're dedicated to making our coverage . . . steady, reliable, and accurate, fact-driven, not rumor-filled." The maker of the show interpreted this approach to mean a careful focus on the police case, with virtually no attention to the human-interest stories, in particular, the attitudes of the public.

This lack of coverage of society's reaction did not prevent CBS from taking an interest in the shooter. Picking up the story on October 8, the network characterized the sniper as a Special Forces "wannabe" who sought to escape a lower status. His main goal was exhibiting his control, which this news story granted he had achieved: the sniper "is having it his way so far."

Coupled with this appreciation of the sniper's skill, even as he clearly was despised, was a certain level of dismay with the police. From the beginning, Rather and those at CBS pointed out Chief Moose's tenseness. They also reported on the meager evidence available at his news conferences and on the vast use of roadblocks, which they characterized as leaving no alternative routes available for motorists.

On October 11, the *CBS Evening News* examined the fear gripping the community for its one and only serious consideration of that subject. A report by Wyatt Andrews[16] directly bore in on community con-

15. Dan Rather has been reporting the news for over fifty years. He has covered the assassination of President John F. Kennedy, the Civil Rights movement, the Vietnam War, and the current wars in Iraq and Afghanistan. He is known as the "hardest working man in broadcast journalism." Rather is now the anchor and managing editor of *Dan Rather Reports,* which started broadcasting on HDNet in November 2006. (Source: HDNet website, http://www.hd.net/bio_rather.html.)

16. Wyatt Andrews joined CBS News as a correspondent in 1981. A former

cerns by focusing on the way children went to school. With her child instructed to walk in front of her, Jeannette May explained: "I make them walk in front of me in a straight line, so at least if he's behind us, he's going to hit me before he hits my children." A second-grader told her mother that the sniper was lurking, and "He will kill me." Andrews continued by pointing out methods used to avoid being shot at the gas tank, and a clip within his report showed a football coach declaring that kids were frightened, and "It's just a scary mood." Andrews reached a dramatic height in his conclusion about the escalation of fear:

> What's most striking about this level of fear is that before the sniper attacks, most Washingtonians would have told you they were used to living in the bull's eye. You live here, it's a certain risk; it comes with the territory.
>
> But nothing, not the Pentagon attack, not the anthrax scare, ever changed Washington like this. No other threat had parents marching kids single file into school.

Echoes of this report appeared in the next evening news, along with a retrospective about the fear engendered by the Son of Sam shootings in New York during the late 1970s. In an October 23 report, the last one before the capture of the snipers, Wyatt Andrews reported on the note threatening children that Chief Moose released—and indicated the fears it raised. But he concluded on a rather different note: "The attitude of parents has changed. They still want their children to run in to school, but say they've stopped running away."

Such reports about community anxiety were exceptional for CBS, which kept its attention on the police case. By emphasizing, as they sometimes did, the incompetence of the police and the sniper's expertise, these reports could create fear. Reports on October 18, 20, and 23 reflected a certain despondency about police efforts to identify and capture the sniper. Generally, the CBS crew simply reported, without comment, on police initiatives, a coverage that seemingly reassured viewers that action was underway. Overall, the reporting from CBS differed from that of other news outlets by its relatively high level of

---

CBS White House correspondent during the first Bush administration, Andrews has covered the State Department, nuclear arms control, Middle East negotiations, and U.S. relations with Mikhail Gorbachev and NATO for the network. He is currently a reporter for the *CBS Evening News* and has reported on the Supreme Court, politics, biotechnology, and the environment. He won a 2003 Emmy Award for his coverage of the Washington sniper case. (Source: CBS News website, http://www.cbsnews.com/stories/2002/10/08/broadcasts/main524773.shtml.)

focused crime reporting and relatively low level of coverage that carried indirect and direct messages about a terrified community.

To a varying extent, the reverse was true for the rest of TV news. Closest to the CBS coverage from my sample of TV shows was that of Greta Van Susteren[17] on FOX News. Perhaps because of her legal background, she tended to follow the investigation with laser-like attention and showed little concern about community reactions. At the other end of the spectrum was ABC's *20/20* and, interestingly, ABC's *World News Tonight with Peter Jennings.* While the relatively sensationalist coverage of *20/20* might have been predicted, there is no particular reason—other than some possible affinities and discussion among those in the same network—to imagine why ABC would have differed from CBS. NBC's *Today Show* took the same approach as did ABC. These shows spent relatively little time on the investigation and focused most of their coverage on community reactions and anxiety. While *60 Minutes,* with its long lead time, scarcely considered the sniper events, ABC's *Nightline* and CNN's Aaron Brown presented the most complex coverage in this group of TV broadcasts. Both divided their coverage between following the investigation and showing the community reaction. *Nightline* remained relatively modest in its coverage, while Aaron Brown's focus was intense.

Because a close scrutiny of all these shows would be repetitive, I present them as something of a group, showing characteristic examples. This approach also approximates the channel-flipping habits of most viewers. This analysis considers how national television considered the police and then the reporting on the community.

Television news, first and foremost, followed the police investigation, and most of its coverage was negative about police competency. At times, Aaron Brown indicated sympathy for Chief Moose; other times, he showed real doubt about the conduct of the investigation. On the October 23 show, after a summary of the state of the case, the anchor opined rather cynically that it seemed to be at a place where it had been before. If Brown tended toward the dispassionate, he also invited and

17. Greta Van Susteren has worked for the FOX News Channel since 2002, hosting *On the Record with Greta Van Susteren. Forbes Magazine* called her one of the world's 100 Most Powerful Women. She has won numerous awards for her work in broadcasting, including the Sandra Day O'Connor Medal of Honor from Seton Hall University and the American Bar Association Presidential Award for "Excellence in Journalism." (Source: FoxNews website, http://www.foxnews.com/story/0,2933,42016,00.html.)

aired the most critical barbs directed toward the police by any medium. To be fair, it does not seem from the October 22 interview with Jimmy Breslin, a former *New York Newsday* reporter who had been deeply involved in coverage of the Son of Sam slayings, that Aaron Brown anticipated how vitriolic his guest would be. Nonetheless, Breslin repeatedly accused the police of rank incompetence, while Brown quietly demurred. Breslin declared the investigators knew nothing, were uncooperative, and had missed the best opportunity by their failure to canvas neighborhoods. Known for his irascibility, Breslin forcefully asserted his opinions, including:

> They've [the police] had four dragnets, they tell me, right? They know less now than when they started, I think. Why don't they show, I mean, why don't they show anything? Put it out there. I don't believe in anything. If it isn't shoe leather, it doesn't exist.

Directing a tirade at Chief Moose, Breslin charged:

> You're not doing your job. You haven't caught him. You don't even know what he looked like. We don't know if it's a man or a boy or anything. I think you're doing a dismal job. You should be replaced but you haven't been.

Guests such as this, of course, tended to sap viewers' confidence in the police.

Elsewhere, other stations aired criticisms of the police. A story broadcast on October 23 on PBS's *NewsHour* justified press coverage, continually excoriated Chief Moose, and attacked the police effort as "disjointed and disorganized" and dependent on too many officers, all at the same time. Likewise, an ABC report on October 21 about the stakeout in Richmond concluded by clearly showing disappointment with police efforts, noting that it had all ended where the day had started—in fear. In an earlier report, on October 17, Greta Van Susteren openly questioned the optimism expressed by police and criticized, somewhat tepidly, their efforts.

Yet, guests, and then Van Susteren herself, also provided far more positive views of the police. In a telling exchange on October 10 with Brian Wilson,[18] a FOX correspondent in the field, Van Susteren repeated Wilson's earlier report that police morale was high. Was it high,

18. Brian Wilson joined the FOX News Channel in 1998 and is a former anchor of the network's *Weekend Live* program. Prior to joining FOX News, Wilson was an anchor for FOX5 in Washington, and a Capitol Hill correspondent. He is currently vice-president and Washington, D.C., bureau chief at FOX News. (Source: FoxNews website, http://www.foxnews.com/story/0,2933,1238,00.html.)

she questioned, because they knew something, or simply because they were dedicated? Wilson replied:

> I think these guys have got their game faces on. I think they real-ize that this is a once-in-a-lifetime event, that they need to rise to the challenge of trying to solve this crime, that there's a lot on them. I think these people are more dedicated and more focused than probably they've ever been at any time in their careers, but they are probably more frustrated by the fact that this guy keeps striking and [they] can't bring him to justice.

And, in response, the host noted—in total contradiction to what Jimmy Breslin argued on a competitor's show—that one could not blame the authorities if there were no clues. Though viewers would have seen more critique than praise on these television shows, Van Susteren was not alone in sometimes offering support. The October 15 *Today Show* ran a largely positive report on the police, and also concluded op-timistically several days later, on October 18, that the lie told by the Home Depot witness had not undermined the investigation.

Oddly, another staple of television news—interviews with criminal profilers—also reinforced negative reporting about the police. Circum-stances and the police practice of tightly controlling information and dispensing it only at formal news conferences had combined to lead the press to rely on profilers. The police understood the voracious needs of television for information, a demand that was only worsened by the frequent deadlines, which occurred far more often than those of print outlets. Yet a lack of information hampered the police, who often had little to report. Secondly, Chief Moose's pronouncement early during the crisis that the schools were safe had been followed by a school shooting at Benjamin Tasker the next day it was open. Officials deduced what in fact proved to be the case—that those responsible were watching and responding to what the police said and did. Accordingly, for the rest of the period, the police carefully measured their words. This left a huge news void to be filled. Unfortunately for the reputation of the law enforcement officials, the partial filling of the void, with profilers as a substitute for police analysis, inadvertently and indirectly tended to undermine the police. Even though these profilers occasionally praised the police investigators, this was not their usual approach. More im-portantly, their very presence suggested the absence—and thus the weakness—of the authorities. In addition, their presence suggested on-going evaluation and even criticism of the police for not knowing what the profilers were able to know.

Interviews with profilers often conformed to a pattern. Whether the guests were academic analysts or retired law enforcement officers, they were asked to use the limited evidence that was available to identify the sniper. Some profilers believed their subject very capable; others only perceived a diabolical nature. A brief synopsis of part of a *Nightline* show of October 8 gives a sense of the contour of the appearance of profilers. With Chris Bury[19] as host, the show received insights from N. G. Berrill, a forensic psychologist and John Jay College professor, and from Clint Van Zandt, an FBI veteran, who appeared in this crisis in the media as much as any other expert. Berrill believed the sniper's motive to be self-empowerment: "This is a fellow that's [feeling] inadequate, and these crimes really make him [feel] very powerful right now, he's [feeling] very powerful." Calling him possibly "prior military," Berrill speculated that the shooter had perhaps been a marksman. Agreeing that power was the motive, Van Zandt called the shooter a "man with a mission," and added that the shooter would continue his acts until he was caught. In Van Zandt's view, this formed the first case of "interactive terrorism," in which the sniper watched the media and responded to the actions of the police. But Berrill suggested that the Son of Sam had behaved similarly. Then, to the question of stopping the sniper, Van Zandt called the episode the high point of the shooter's life and argued he would not quit until apprehended. In the profile the experts put together, Berrill suggested a Caucasian male in his thirties. Adding that the sniper "doesn't understand or care about the pain that he's causing," Van Zandt noted, "If he has a significant other, it would be a one-way relationship." Both profilers agreed that capture would be difficult as long as the shooter continued his rampage. Berrill expected it to end quickly with a slip-up, while Van Zandt thought a combination of science, detective work, tips from the public, and good luck would rapidly solve the case. In these last predictions, they both proved generally correct.

One small sidelight of this matter worth mentioning was the ama-

19. Chris Bury has been a reporter for ABC News since 1982, when he joined the network as a general assignment correspondent. He has reported for numerous news shows, including *World News with Charles Gibson, Nightline,* and *Good Morning America.* Bury was also the anchor of *Up Close* for eight months. He has covered various military and political stories over his career, and has won five national Emmy Awards and numerous additional journalism accolades. He is currently a national correspondent for ABC News. (Source: ABC News website, http://abcnews.go.com/Nightline/News/story?id=128635.)

teur profiling attempted by political figures—almost always those representing affected areas—who reached judgments very similar to those of some of the experienced experts. So irresistible were such comments about the possible identity and character of the shooter that, on October 16, Lynne Cheney, spouse of Vice President Richard Cheney, appeared on the Van Susteren show to discuss the fear gripping the area and suggested that the killer was deranged. Further, she declared, no one had disputed the shootings as an act of terrorism.

While attention to identifying such a shooter might raise doubts about police competence, the other main focus of coverage was describing the community, which usually was depicted as being gripped by fear. Of course, exceptions existed. Following broadcasts that heavily focused on social anxiety, *Nightline* ran a show that balanced its previous emphasis on fear. In fact, producer Tom Bettag[20] speculated about a possible latent desire for the show to move in an opposite direction. In the October 11 show, which, without ignoring fearfulness, provided a more optimistic approach, founding anchor Ted Koppel[21] interviewed a panel of experts who were members of societies that experienced trauma—Ariel Shaler, a psychiatrist from Israel; Denis Murray, a BBC correspondent for Ireland; and Gayle Porter, a clinical psychologist who studied violence and families. The discussion focused

20. Tom Bettag joined ABC News in 1991. He joined CBS News in 1969, as a news writer, and spent twenty-two years there. During his tenure at the network, Bettag was the executive producer of the *CBS Evening News with Dan Rather,* senior broadcast producer of the *CBS Evening News,* and an associate producer for the *CBS Morning News,* among other roles. After moving to ABC, Bettag became senior executive producer of *Nightline* in 2002, and the executive producer of *This Week with George Stephanopoulos.* A graduate of the Columbia University Graduate School of Journalism, Bettag has taught film production and editing at the school. He was a Fulbright Scholar in 1977 and has received numerous awards for his work, including six Alfred I. duPont–Columbia University Silver Batons. (Source: ABC Media Net website, http://www.abcmedianet.com/shows05/news/producers/bettag.shtml.)

21. Ted Koppel worked for ABC News for forty-two years. When the late-night news show *Nightline* debuted in 1980, Koppel was named the anchor. As anchor, he submitted reports, performed interviews, and served as managing editor. He resigned from the show in 2005. Koppel has received many accolades for his decades of news gathering, including the first Goldsmith Lifetime Achievement Award for Excellence in Journalism by the Joan Shorenstein Barone Center on the Press, Politics and Public Policy at Harvard University. (Sources: ABC News website, http://abcnews.go.com/Nightline/News/story?id=128629; Wikipedia: The Free Encyclopedia, http://en.wikipedia.org/wiki/Ted_Koppel.)

on coping mechanisms. Shaler and Murray advised that while individuals might choose to limit activities, it would be unhealthy to avoid pursuing life. Murray stated: "If you change your life radically, you're letting the bad group win everything." Porter went further, declaring that "actually, more children are hit everyday crossing the street than have been shot. So, first, [is] to acknowledge the fear. But then [it is necessary] to put it in a context that the child and the parent can understand." Porter concluded further that parents should emphasize to older children the likelihood of the perpetrators' being caught. She concluded in a rather upbeat way: "Most people are very good. Most people are loving and there is a whole network of people wanting to support us, to protect us, and to try to help us to live the lives we have a right to expect." While acknowledging fears as legitimate, this *Nightline* program encouraged a particularly brave face and certainly the avoidance of panic. Other programs urged efforts to recognize but mitigate fear. Even in the aftermath of the shooting of the bus driver, which really shocked the Washington area, PBS's *NewsHour,* on October 23, interviewed an eyewitness who asserted that most people are good, and we have to keep going. In a like manner, many outlets (including ABC's *World News Tonight* and CNN's *American Morning*) gave significant publicity to Montgomery County Executive Douglas Duncan's statement on October 10 in connection with the Brown shooting that strength could overcome fear.

Overwhelmingly, however, what generally differentiated these television shows from those on CBS was the other stations' inclination to air stories that expressed fear. The normally sober Aaron Brown launched his *NewsHour* coverage of the initial five murders on October 4 with this introduction:

We begin with a story of terror. Terror is a word we've used a lot over the last twelve months. But this is a reminder that terror isn't always spelled with a capital "T." Sometimes terror is as simple as a guy with a gun.

And that terror is what we begin with tonight, or at least it so appears. If you think we are overstating, here are the words of a mother . . . "My kids are scared now more than on September 11."

Although the rest of Brown's report did not exactly follow from the introduction, it overwhelmingly told of panicked reactions and of how those who went home boarded the door and tried to freeze the world out. The even more measured Ted Koppel remarked on October 11:

Folks are afraid to go food shopping, to gas up their cars. Schools are canceling football games. One of our videotape editors is getting married this weekend, and some of his out-of-town guests are staying home rather than come to Washington. My wife spoke earlier today to a woman in our dentist's office; she's driving to Delaware this weekend to do her food shopping and to gas up the car. And I must admit, my first reaction was, come on. But how do you react sensibly to an unseen, unpredictable danger, except to take comfort in the odds?

Here Ted Koppel seemed to accept retreat, or at least evacuation, as a normal response. This was the communication of fear.

Much other evidence of such references can be found scattered throughout this sample of the media. On October 9, ABC reported that "tensions are high." On its October 11 show, *20/20* noted that it was "normal to be afraid." On October 14, Greta Van Susteren referred to the Home Depot incident as "terror." And in Van Susteren's interview with Lynne Cheney, the Vice President's wife, while affirming her belief that Americans could get through this time, stated that the situation was "really terrifying." The randomness of attacks caused anxiety, resulting in kids in "lockdown," unable to go outside any longer. Fear was the staple of this medium, though many reporters tempered their reports of anxiety by referring to coping behaviors. Many reports, however, seemed closer to retreat than a determined cautiousness.

While viewers all over the country saw the horrible pictures accompanied by a message describing fear, did newspapers outside the region temper this? To sample this opinion, I looked at a group of large dailies that were geographically dispersed: the *New York Times,* the *San Francisco Chronicle,* the *Houston Chronicle,* and the *Chicago Sun-Times.* Obviously, these are all large-circulation dailies and they do not represent a cross-section of the print media, but they may be said to represent the daily papers in large American cities and adjacent suburbs. Though they represent a subset of the press, it is one serving many people, and these papers thus constitute an important part of the printed media.

The best way to grasp the coverage in these papers is first to consider the two *Chronicles* and the *Sun-Times,* and then turn to the *New York Times,* whose treatment of the sniper case varied somewhat from that of the other papers. The pattern already discussed above generally applied to these other large dailies. First, the expectations of the audience were already conditioned by national television shows. Second, as we shall see, much of the copy in these pages came from other news services and major papers, which most likely followed in the wake of the *Post.* Through its extraordinarily aggressive coverage of the story, the *Post* apparently influenced other reporters. Nonetheless, the *Sun-Times* and the two *Chronicles* did not follow the *Post.* Instead, they stayed closer to the national electronic news media.

Readers in Chicago, San Francisco, and Houston were easily able to follow the story because of the large amount of newsprint dedicated to it. Because of variations among editions and my reliance on the electronic version, which did not post every article, as well as on articles that do not fit categories perfectly, it is impossible to sum up the precise number of articles on the sniper case. However, in the three weeks of this incident, the *Sun-Times* provided approximately forty-five articles, the *San Francisco Chronicle,* twenty-nine, and the *Houston Chronicle,* forty-nine. Articles appeared almost every day, with few links one to another. As in other print media, the most powerful message was not the narrated story but its themes. In this case, the papers focused on the level of fear in the Washington metropolitan area. The community existed as the locus of fear, and the papers' evaluation of the authorities and the opinions of profilers were largely in the background. Of course, the police and the shooter appeared as cat-and-mouse protagonists, elevating the former and denigrating the latter, as characters in a story mainly about community anxiety.

Any effort to tailor this story to the paper's home city was limited. As noted above, a large amount of the copy originated elsewhere. For the *Sun-Times* this was 44 percent, for the San Francisco paper, 49 percent, and for Houston, 70 percent. The *San Francisco Chronicle* relied on several papers, but mainly the *Post,* while the Houston daily depended substantially on the Associated Press. The *Sun-Times* exclusively used Associated Press articles. While the other two papers consistently used outside sources, the *Sun-Times* basically depended on its own reporters through October 15, then turned almost exclusively to the Associated Press until October 21, and after that used both sources evenly for its news. Relying so heavily on other sources practically guaranteed that these newspapers would produce a limited local spin on the story.

Despite this dependency, these dailies somewhat structured the story, as they concentrated on the fear pervading the area. The *Houston Chronicle* spilled somewhat less ink than did the other two papers but still left enough evident tracing to point readers to fear as the most solvent characteristic of the story. Apparently, beyond the borders of the Washington metro area, print outlets mostly presented a community gripped by fear.

Considering how little these papers shaped the story, it is interesting to note that all three editorial pages took a swipe at the media's emphasis on fear. In the entire period of the sniper episode, the *Houston Chronicle* only devoted two editorials to the event, one noting the failure of the police to reach out to the public and the other discussing the fear that gripped the D.C. area. Yet, in that editorial, which ran on October 10, the writer commented that the "saturation coverage of bizarre and terrifying murders amplified their impact." On October 23, the op-ed writer Richard Roeper[22] conceded that the cable news channels had overdone their concentration, but he defended the mainstream media as covering the story appropriately. He excused even the excesses, writing, "Given the choice between too much coverage or none at all, I'll take excess every time, and rely on the intelligence of the news consumer to figure it out." Such justifications of media behavior still raised the question of impropriety. The *San Francisco Chronicle* also once encouraged minimizing the coverage of terror. An October 15 editorial attacked the media for playing into the shooter's hands by emphasizing what would make the public most fearful. In addition, the same editorial criticized the emphasis on fear itself: "The national climate of fear, energized by this psycho sniper, demands that the media examine its decisions more carefully than ever. What kind of coverage serves the public interest? What information helps, and more important what harms?" This same set of criticisms found their way into an article on media published on October 25, just after the apprehension of the snipers.

While the Houston paper hewed very closely to the details of the case, the other two papers developed stories that seemed like excursions from the main path. Both the *Sun-Times* (October 8) and the *San Francisco Chronicle* (October 15), used the high-profile shootings as an opportunity to endorse further gun-control, positions popular in those

22. Richard Roeper is a syndicated columnist and film critic. He has been a columnist for the *Chicago Sun-Times* since 1987, and co-hosted *At the Movies with Ebert & Roeper* from 2000 to 2008. In his columns, Roeper explores a wide range of issues, including politics and the media. The author of several books, Roeper started his career as a radio host. He has received several awards for his columns, which appear in newspapers worldwide. In 1992, he was named the top newspaper columnist in the United States, with a National Headliner Award. (Source: Wikipedia: The Free Encyclopedia, http://en.wikipedia.org/wiki/Richard_Roeper.)

cities. The papers also focused on one aspect of the shootings. One of the frustrations of the police was the problem of matching. Although one bullet could easily be matched to another, little possibility existed of using that information to track a gun unless authorities had possession of the weapon. However, a limited database existed, and could be expanded, of ballistics "fingerprints," so that analyzing a bullet could lead to a gun, its registration, and ultimately to its owner. Although the National Rifle Association and other gun rights groups resisted this as a useless intrusion, the *San Francisco Chronicle* supported the database, on October 15. Likewise, both the *Chronicle* and the *Sun-Times* also published articles, on October 22 and October 11, respectively, that were much like one in the *Post* which asserted that suburbanites were now experiencing the danger of inner cities. Such stories clearly used the sniper to point out class differences in America. Indeed, these stories projected a number of critiques, but they all seemed to indicate that more attention should be given to those people whose neighborhoods inspired fear every single day—and perhaps less should be paid to those whose comfort was assured in the long run. For example, a story published in the *Sun-Times* on October 22 argued:

> The sniper fear that has gripped an entire region of the country is a microcosm of that urban terror. But while lawmen from around the country hunt for a brazen shooter, the casualties from the quiet war mount.
>
> For instance, where is the outrage over what happened to a Baltimore mother of five who was killed (along with her children) last week for allegedly calling the police to report drug deals and other crimes in her neighborhood?

So, concluded the article, while the sniper victims received great support, "victims of the other war desperately need the same." On that same day, two thousand miles to the west, the *San Francisco Chronicle* noticed the difference between the treatment of the sniper case and that for the eighty-nine victims of violence in Oakland in 2002. In fact, the paper noted, inner cities were already places filled with random murders, multiple snipers, and innocent victims who were no different from the Washington-area casualties. Much like its Chicago peer, this article concluded: "At some point the sniper will be caught. The nation must then turn its attention to ending murder in the inner city as an American way of life."

Detours such as these, interesting as they are, should not draw attention from the actuality that large national dailies did little to muffle the fear projected in other news media. Although the *New York Times* did not dramatically challenge this picture, it differed enough to change somewhat the overall impression. Certainly, the paper was sufficiently obsessed with the subject that it published some ninety articles (all penned by staff reporters and editorialists), along with a dozen or so letters to the editor. Much more than the other papers, the *Times* chronicled the progress of the police case. Nonetheless, like the other dailies, the crime story did not create a sharp focus. The paper concentrated on the complex proceedings of the previous day so that even everyday readers would have found it hard to develop a clear picture of an advancing story. Rather, these were disjointed episodes. Moreover, the stories contained little criticism or analysis of the police effort, so that facet of the news did not create a gripping story.

The focus of the *Times* also gave little attention at all to the impact of the sniper on the New York metropolitan area, either by covering the local reaction or by considering stories of special interest to New Yorkers. Several stories on October 17 and 18, about White House resistance to a national program of the ballistic marking of bullets and reporting some scattered remarks regarding federal indifference to the case, can be related to the editorial policy of liberalism and the strength of public support in New York for the Democrats. On the whole, the coverage focused more on the case than on community, in either the area surrounding the District of Columbia or that of New York City.

Most important, here, for the argument of this book, is that fear did not receive the same kind of coverage as it did in the other dailies. Still, the difference remains subtle, since all the other papers did substantially report on the details of the case. Their relatively less emphasis on the police and crime, and greater attention to fear, allowed the coverage of anxiety to stand out more significantly than it did in the *Times*. The significant difference thus lies in the context of the other reporting on the case. All that said, fear still remained the most evident theme in the *Times*.

How the New York paper actually dealt with fear–still its most pointed coverage–shows great similarities with other papers, and occasional departures. In fact, one of the most compelling nuggets from all media that urged less worry appeared in the *Times*. Although the article, published in the October 12 edition, described the fear overwhelming Greater Washington, basically it advocated an accommodation with fear. The initial drift of this piece, while providing evidence of coping, tended to show fear and the severely limited lifestyle available to Washingtonians. Midway through the article, the journalist began to provide examples of a more positive nature. Howard Smith, a representative of the sheriff's office of Spotsylvania County, Virginia, described the local reaction: "I'm sure there are a lot of people afraid to do anything right now. . . . We [still] need to go on with our lives. We can't stop living because of these incidents." The *Times* piece also noted those who, despite the fear, adopted "less restrictive measures" and carried on their daily activities through minimizing the odds of danger. For example: "Congested city areas were suddenly considered more desirable than wide-open suburban shopping strips with ample parking." The irony of Americans "suddenly" finding urban areas more comforting than the suburbs–a total reversal in attitude at least–indicated appropriate risk-calculation at work.

Still, most of this article illustrated very fearful approaches to daily chores. For example, at a gas station in Virginia, customers asked the proprietor to pump gas for them. Such a request suggests extreme panic in which people do not stop to consider the possible results of their fearfulness. Furthermore, the station's owner narrated his clientele's actions: "The people come inside while their car is filling, they pick up things like they're going to buy them, but they're not buying. . . . They just want to wait inside." This antisocial behavior indicated to thoughtful readers the customers' terror.

Many articles showed little ambivalence on the subject of fear. In the coverage of the sniper case, most issues dedicated one story to an overview of the police investigation and the activities of the sniper. Although these articles seldom focused on community reaction, they usually included a short paragraph to this matter. Inevitably, these paragraphs focused on the area's anxiety; several pieces paid greater attention to this subject, and some were entirely devoted to it. A story in the "Week in Review," section of October 20 was headlined "The Nation: Beltway Anxieties; When Risk Ruptures Life." As in the case of the article of October 12, the people interviewed for this article considered the risk of being shot by the sniper. Unlike those who determined that such a calculation would lead to action, here almost all found such exercises created feelings of impending doom. The story began with Massachusetts Institute of Technology statistics professor Arnold Barnett reassuring himself that his own probability for encountering disaster was "statistically low." Yet, despite advocating in principle this rather reasonable idea, he averred he could only conclude that he did not know if "this sniper's next idea won't be to shoot people at the Metro station of Washington Reagan airport." Then, as the story moved on to other issues, it quoted Barnett again: "I'm going to come down, and I'm going to try not to think about it. It will completely fail, of course." Much of the remainder of the story considered why such analytic considerations would not work–largely because such predictability could not provide enough assurance in the face of the seemingly random actions of the sniper. In the concluding paragraphs, the article turned to psychology professor Melvin J. Lerner, who advised that residents should obtain as much information to calculate "true" probability. But in response to a question about the inexactitude of such measurements, he answered, "only half in jest, 'You just raised my anxiety enormously.' " Such interviews, of course, tended to suggest that trepidations were the only reasonable response to the circumstance.

Such examples of reporting about fear in the *Times* could be easily multiplied to show that, even though this theme was more muffled than in the other dailies surveyed here, the reporting of the papers carried a strong dose of doom and gloom. Furthermore, just as the other dailies did not report on community solidarity to mute the message of panic, the *Times* similarly remained largely silent on this subject. A couple of laudatory articles on individual victims and some occasional favorable mentions of the police did not amount to a vision of social harmony. However, the *Times* refrained from castigating the actions of the snipers and thus symbolically expelling them and purifying the public.

Reasons for the reticence of the *Times* deserve further analysis in general, and at least some speculation here. The *Times* encounters considerably greater local competition than do the Houston, San Francisco, and Chicago papers used for this analysis. In particular, the *New York Post, Newsday,* and the *New York Daily News* generally take a very shrill tone. In contrast, the *Times* has positioned itself as the "grey lady" of journalism, trying hard to avoid sensational approaches. While critics have accused it of failing in this regard in numerous ways, and it has also endeavored to become more sprightly, it still projects greater calm than almost any other U.S. daily identified as a local newspaper. Included in this is, it seems to me, a news orientation that remained more focused on political and official police sources. Perhaps this posture explains why the *Times* stuck more with the police investigations and ventured less into the murky and uncertain evaluation of public emotions.

Thus, despite some exceptions, overall the national print and television news, including the *Times,* like most of Washington's local media, still told the sniper story as a narrative about high levels of fear. Perhaps the most surprising part of this conclusion is that cable news operators did not stand out as substantively different from print or local television news.

• • •

Television opinion shows must be added to the mix. This category is difficult to define with precision because the "hardest" news shows contained elements of opinion, and vice versa. Even the evening news half-hour telecasts might involve opinion or summaries of debates. PBS's *NewsHour* and Ted Koppel's *Nightline* mixed a news summary with panel discussion. Yet some programs, in my view, feature opinion and discussion. Although not used in this survey, *Larry King Live*[23] relies almost exclusively on debate or discussion. Yet others, like Chris Matthews's[24] *Hardball*, which include reporting, primarily feature debate. This genre deserves special treatment because much of the public ire directed at cable television really is targeted at those shows. While the contours of this category remain debatable, the value of looking at these broadcasts as a group outweighs the definitional problems. Of the many shows of this ilk, this study utilizes CNN's *Crossfire*, FOX's *O'Reilly Factor*, MSNBC's *Abrams Report*, MSNBC's *Hardball*, MSNBC's *Donohue*, and FOX's *Hannity & Colmes*. Reasonably prominent at the time of the sniper shooting, the shows represented a political range, from FOX's conservative programs to Phil Donohue's[25] liberalism. The other shows

23. Larry King has been in broadcasting for over fifty years. He has been the host of *Larry King Live* on CNN since June 1985. The first phone-in television talk show broadcast worldwide, *Larry King Live* has earned King an Emmy Award and is CNN's highest-rated program. (Source: CNN website, http://www.cnn.com/CNN/anchors_reporters/king.larry.html.)

24. Chris Matthews began his career in politics, holding several positions, including speechwriter for President Jimmy Carter. He then moved to print journalism, working for fifteen years at the *San Francisco Examiner* and the *San Francisco Chronicle*. He frequently appears on NBC's *Today* show, and hosts the MSNBC program *Hardball with Chris Matthews*. (Source: CNBC website, http://www.cnbc.com/id/15838038/.)

25. In 1967 Donohue began hosting *The Phil Donohue Show*, for what became the longest continuous run of any syndicated talk show in U.S. television history, at twenty-nine years. He also hosted a news program on MSNBC called *Donohue* from 2002 to 2003. On his firing from MSNBC, he said, "We had to have two conservatives on for every liberal. I was counted as two liberals." (Sources: Wikipedia: The Free Encyclopedia, http://en.wikipedia.org/wiki/Phil_Donohue; Media Matters website, http://mediamatters.org/items/200410290004.)

were politically more centrist, largely because of a desire to appear even-handed.

In a way, the sniper case was difficult for these shows to cover, because they preferred an exchange, and even confrontation, between the host and the guests, or simply among the guests. Such a debate was more difficult in this case because no one seriously disagreed about the evil of the sniper. In the only situation I discovered in which someone tried to defend the sniper, that person found himself quickly ushered off the air. When, on the morning of October 24, the media were trying to learn all they could about John Muhammad, Connie Chung,[26] anchoring for CNN, took a live call from someone claiming to be a friend of the sniper. Addressing the question of why the sniper carried out the shootings, the caller claimed it was because of the anger and dissatisfaction Muhammad felt about the poor treatment of veterans. A reason that sounded like a justification was far too much for Chung, who was clearly shocked, recovered her aplomb, thanked him for his opinion, and rapidly moved to the next caller. Her approach was, no doubt, shared by almost everyone, but it did undermine the most obvious, though too unseemly to pursue, debate line–John Muhammad, devil or bedeviled?

This problem of framing debate still did not dissuade most programs–a decision which, given the public's fascination for this subject, as shown by the ratings surge–would have been quite surprising. In fact, when one caller questioned Bill O'Reilly's[27] interest in the show and called for ratings not to rule all, O'Reilly dismissed this view as totally unrealistic (October 22). So, follow the story they did, and follow them we shall. And, of course, other issues than the sniper's abominable actions could inform the debate format.

26. Connie Chung has worked for NBC, CBS, ABC, CNN, and MSNBC. In the early 1970s, she covered the Watergate scandal for the *CBS Evening News with Walter Cronkite.* She became a co-anchor of *CBS News* in 1993, becoming the second woman ever to hold such a position. In 2006, Chung premiered *Weekends with Maury and Connie,* an MSNBC show she co-hosted with her husband, Maury Povich. It was canceled after less than six months. (Source: Wikipedia: The Free Encyclopedia, http://en.wikipedia.org/wiki/Connie_Chung.)

27. Political commentator Bill O'Reilly is the host of FOX News's *The O'Reilly Factor* and the syndicated talk radio program *The Radio Factor.* He has held several positions in broadcasting throughout his career, including anchor of *Inside Edition,* correspondent for *ABC World News Tonight,* and reporting and anchoring positions for local news. He is also the author of seven books. (Source: Wikipedia: The Free Encyclopedia, http://en.wikipedia.org/wiki/Bill_O%27Reilly_%28commentator%29.)

To disabuse readers who might find this media category fundamentally outside the definition of the "press," at least in regard to historical analysis, I should begin with an absolutely prescient interchange which occurred on the October 4 show of *Hardball.* In a conversation with profilers, Chris Matthews, whose show was one of those paying the least attention to the sniper story and whose host seemed fairly uninterested in the subject, offered: "There's been some discussion that the guy's got a truck, and he's getting there–there's somebody driving the truck and there's somebody in the back of the truck with a duck-line kind of–you know–situation here . . . where he can actually bring the truck right up in a parking lot or on the street and shoot. Nobody will see the rifle. Nobody will see the guy get out of position." To this suggestion, profiler Clint Van Zandt replied that although Matthews might be right, it was more likely that the vehicle had a driver on one side and a passenger on the other who used the window frame to steady the rifle. Thus did Matthews' explanation seemingly perish, apparently never to appear again. Had police officers considered this a possibility, they might have viewed Muhammad's automobile quite differently, given the many times they encountered it during the search for the sniper. In short, even idle talk from a host, an amateur to the area, was not lacking in insight. It is best to examine seriously these broadcasts to determine their themes and their relation to the rest of the national press.

Like the remainder of the press, opinion programs documented the fear penetrating the Washington metropolitan area, but with the exception of *Donohue,* did not spend a great deal of time on this. Donohue, on the other hand, perhaps because of his longevity as a talk show host concerned with social issues, repeatedly focused on this issue. For example, after the shooting at Bowie's Benjamin Tasker Middle School, Donohue, on October 8, interviewed two parents, including Regina Tucker. After hearing how this mother learned a shooting had occurred at the school, Donohue asked her to continue, "so we can understand your immediate terror." She then replied: "Yes, we [she and her husband] jumped in the car immediately, praying all the way to the school. We were able to be let into the school. As they were locking the doors, we just made it in and had to wait to hear if it was our child. It was so nerve wracking." Donohue encouraged her: "I bet. I can imagine your heart racing." She then responded that thirteen-year-old Benjamin finally came down, and "It seemed like an eternity before we actually saw him. And . . . I almost cried." On the day the show taped, she reported, all three children were at home because the youngest, a seven-year-old, was crying, "saying that he was scared."

The interview then progressed to Steve Thaler, a second parent. Even though Donohue prompted him to explain his fears, some resolution and limits on fear became apparent. Despite the fear, and because of confidence in the police and school authorities, Thaler said that his child had returned to school as soon as possible. Seemingly sympathetically plumbing the actual level of anxiety, Donohue returned to Regina Tucker, "Well, Mrs. Tucker wishes she had your confidence. But we understand you, too. Madam, what are you going to do tomorrow?" She replied that the children were going back. They just needed a day to recover. Pushing one final time, Donohue asked how long it would be before they could walk to school. "Have you thought about that?" Tucker replied that they take the bus, and that would be nerve-wracking, but he added that people have to live, continue to have faith, and pray. Despite the resolve of his interlocutors, Donohue concluded, "You've got to wonder who's losing sleep, who's tossing and turning, who's getting paranoid, who hears a noise, [sees] a white truck."

Despite Donohue's efforts to elicit descriptions of fear, generally the probing of fear ran into a desire to limit the impact of anxiety. And on other occasions when he returned to this theme—for example, his October 22 show, devoted to children's fears—fear was balanced by resolution. Likewise, most of the other shows in this genre took a similar tack. Some even voiced the notion that the terror in the D.C. area was an overreaction. In his October 11 show, Dan Abrams[28] held a debate on whether the area's response constituted an "overreaction." His own answer was that while he was afraid for his family in the area, he believed the frightened response was sending the wrong message—attack and the people shall cower. One of his guests, radio talk show host Victoria Jones,[29] agreed with him, but went further. Canceling events

28. Dan Abrams, a graduate of the Columbia University School of Law, hosted *Verdict with Dan Abrams* on MSNBC and is the chief legal correspondent for NBC News. Abrams has published articles in the *New York Times* and *USA Today,* and has worked for Court TV as reporter, where he covered such high-profile cases as the O.J. Simpson trial and the assisted suicide trials of Dr. Kevorkian. (Source: Wikipedia: The Free Encyclopedia, http://en.wikipedia.org/wiki/Dan_Abrams.)

29. Victoria Jones began her broadcasting career in her home country of England, then worked in Australia before moving to the United States in 1987. The host of *The Victoria Jones Show* for the last fifteen years, she covers the hot-button issues of the day from news to entertainment and has appeared on CNN, FOX News, MSNBC, and the BBC. Prior to her radio show, Jones worked for Talk Radio News

"isn't the answer. It's a complete overreaction. If anything, we need to be prudent, in the way we probably should have been after 9/11 but weren't. We don't need to change all our habits because of this guy. We don't need to cancel all outdoor events. If necessary, increase the security around them." Likewise, in his October 21 program, Sean Hannity[30] made the case that Washingtonians and their neighbors were "overreacting," and he received an affirmative response from a former New York City police chief and a retired FBI investigator. The *Crossfire* debates of October 16 further toyed with this idea.

In yet another way, cable opinion shows tended to dismiss anxiety by almost uniformly rejecting the notion that the shootings might be linked to foreign terrorists. The one exception, Sean Hannity, deserves scrutiny because of his insights into the management of his own show, and perhaps the rest of them, in regard to other issues. On October 13, Hannity introduced the notion that the sniper was a terrorist and asked why this idea had been discarded so early. His guest, Mark Fuhrman, well known as the lead detective in the O.J. Simpson case, immediately dismissed the idea. On the very next broadcast, on October 16, Hannity again raised this possibility, but again without any agreement from the profiler being hosted. A few minutes later, Hannity pressed this point, and this time both of his guests disagreed. Co-host Alan Colmes[31] managed to change the subject. On the next show, on October 17, Hannity

---

Service in Washington, D.C., as a managing editor. She has received many accolades for her career, including being named seven times to the "Most Important Talk Show Hosts in America" list by *Talkers Magazine* (Source: 3WT Radio website, http://www.3wtradio.com/?nid=22&sid=1392002.)

30. Sean Hannity served as the co-host of *Hannity & Colmes* on FOX News Channel, which became *Hannity* after Alan Colmes's departure in January of 2009. A political commentator, he was the conservative member of the duo. He also hosts *Hannity's America* on FOX News and the radio program *The Sean Hannity Show.* Hannity began his career as a radio talk show host in 1989 at a college station and worked at several stations before moving to television. He is the author of two books: *Let Freedom Ring: Winning the War of Ideas in Politics, Media, and Life* and *Deliver Us from Evil: Defeating Terrorism, Despotism, and Liberalism.* (Source: Wikipedia: The Free Encyclopedia, http://en.wikipedia.org/wiki/Sean_Hannity.)

31. Alan Colmes was the co-host of *Hannity & Colmes* on FOX News Channel, with Sean Hannity, until January of 2009, presenting liberal viewpoints that offset Hannity's conservatism. Colmes is the host of the radio show *The Alan Colmes Show* on FOX News Radio. His first career was as a stand-up comedian before he moved to radio, working at several radio stations prior to joining FOX. Colmes is also the author of *Red, White & Liberal: How Left Is Right and Right Is Wrong* (Source: Wikipedia: The Free Encyclopedia, http://en.wikipedia.org/wiki/Alan_Colmes.)

resumed the same tack, and this time the guest admitted the possibility, along with several other theories. The next show, on October 18, saw Hannity return to this possibility, and the guest somewhat acknowledged the possibility. On the next discussion of the sniper case, October 21, forensic psychologist Jack Kitaeff admitted that he was considering that foreign terrorism might be possible. Hannity jumped on this assertion, agreeing and asking Kitaeff to lay out his argument, which depended on the timing of these shootings with the world situation. He also asserted that the slaying of out-of-towners was part of inflicting a national wound. Hannity replied, "You make a compelling argument." Although another guest disputed this logic by using much more evidence, Hannity did not concede the point. However, this issue did not come up in subsequent shows. Interesting here was the ability of Hannity—and this occurrence likely has been common in this genre of shows—to continue to raise a position that was largely unsupported by the opinion of experts, even those who were invited to his show. However, fairness requires noting that alternative views were also thoroughly aired at those times.

The overall inclination of cable programming to dismiss foreign terrorism as a motive, combined with its limited coverage of either the community or its fears, restrained the reporting focused on anxiety that was so common elsewhere in the media. But they compensated in other ways. Characterizations of the shooter or shooters were usually very negative. The only divergence among commentators and guests was whether they chose to emphasize the clever and intelligent designs of the shooters or their mental and psychological pathology. Everyone agreed on the essential evil. Typical were Clint Van Zandt's remarks on *Hardball* on October 4: "When you get a psychopath like this, they don't care about your pain . . . all they want to do is to be entertained and do something. You can't say, 'Hey my friend, you know how much pain you are causing? Knock this off.' He's going to sit there, thumb his nose." Or Geraldo Rivera,[32] never known for his understatement, on

32. Gerald Michael Rivera, known to many by simply Geraldo, is the host of FOX News's *Geraldo at Large* and is also a commentator for the network. In 1969 he earned a J.D. from Brooklyn Law School and began his career by serving briefly as an investigator for the New York Police Department before becoming a television reporter. He has appeared on myriad networks and television shows throughout his career and is known for pursuing high-profile stories. He joined FOX News as a war correspondent following the September 11 terrorist attacks. (Source: Wikipedia: The Free Encyclopedia, http://en.wikipedia.org/wiki/Geraldo_Rivera.)

*Hannity & Colmes* on October 11, calling the sniper, "this pervert, this creep." On the eve of the capture, on the *Abrams Show*, October 23, opinions sounded much the same, as one guest said: "But I agree . . . he's a maniac. He's not going to stop for money, and I don't think it's about money. I think it's the thrill, it's the publicity, and he wants recognition and right now he's reveling in that recognition." The behavior of the sniper could only be condemned, and yet this focus indicated the public should be fearful of such a monster. This contradicted the discussants' tendency to belittle the fear felt in the Washington area.

While, elsewhere, writers suggested that Washington was a community driven together, these opinion-bound television shows spent so little time on the sense of community that it is difficult to believe this image of the sniper might have helped to construct the scarcely mentioned society. And, in fact, these opinion shows, whenever they argued that the area had overreacted, tended to belittle any idea of social coherence born of opposition to evil. Moreover, these shows' treatment of both the police and the media also did nothing to suggest a societal opposition to fear.

While the other media contained much criticism as well as support for the police, opinion television differed by its complete lack of sympathy for the authorities. With the exception of *O'Reilly Factor,* which occasionally praised the police (e.g., on the October 22 show), it is difficult to find a positive word. Instead, *Crossfire* host Tucker Carlson,[33] on October 9, characterized Montgomery County Police Chief Charles Moose as a man who had lost emotional control and was "nasty and sarcastic." In a similar vein, on *Donohue,* one guest, Laura Flanders,[34] a radio talk show host, on October 11 criticized the chief and

33. Tucker Carlson is a political news correspondent and commentator for the Fox News Channel. He has hosted CNN's political program *Crossfire* and MSNBC's *Tucker.* He began his career as an editorial writer for the conservative journal *Policy Review.* He was the youngest anchor in the history of CNN. Carlson's work has appeared in *Esquire,* the *Weekly Standard,* the *New Republic,* and the *New York Times Magazine.* He is the author of one book, an autobiography, titled *Politicians, Partisans, and Parasites: My Adventures in Cable News.* (Source: Wikipedia: The Free Encyclopedia, http://en.wikipedia.org/wiki/Tucker_Carlson.)

34. Journalist Laura Flanders has appeared on numerous television programs, including *O'Reilly Factor* and *Hannity & Colmes,* and her work has appeared in publications such as *The Nation, In These Times, The Progressive,* and *Ms. Magazine,* among others. She has spent many years working in radio and has written several books. Flanders hosted the radio program *CounterSpin* for more than ten years and was the initial director of the women's desk at Fairness and Accuracy

argued that the police were no better than the media at handling evidence. She characterized them as in "disarray" in their dealings with the press. Likewise, a week later, on October 18, on the same show, Donohue, in reaction to the perjuring Home Depot witness, seemed to associate himself with a *New York Daily News* story that called the police "clueless."

What deepened this attack on the police was the general defense of the media that was put forth during the episode. As events first unfolded, the police were successfully able to cast themselves as the representatives of the community. As the rancor between Moose and the media accelerated, praise for the press came to mean criticism of law enforcement. In order to protect society, the police, by necessity, stood outside it. Interestingly, these cable shows, even though they did not back the press at every turn, were far more vocal in this defense than was any other media outlet. It is difficult to ascertain why these shows seemed more adamant than other media, except that, perhaps because of their outspokenness, they depended most on First Amendment rights of press freedom to do what they did on most of their broadcasts. In any case, these programs provided a solid block of support. Most strident was Dan Abrams in his "closing argument" for October 16. Responding to those who criticized the press, Abrams provided a defense. In an aside to those who deprecated the press for publicizing details that might frustrate the investigation, Abrams assured them that the media did hold back official material. Secondly, he argued that the public's learning the authorities were carrying out more investigations than they reported might help calm fears. Moreover, were the media to report nothing, he continued, the Internet would be full of rumors, which would lead to greater panic. Also, he argued, the police might be wrong. Were they correct about not realizing the message sent with the tarot card? Abrams then continued, " Remember, it was the officers working the case who provided the information. . . . More information is often the only way you can assess that the authorities are doing a good job." Furthermore, he pointed out that such information had led to arrests. Abrams closed by reassuring his listeners that he realized that the press made mistakes, and he was listening to complaints. "But I assure you, I want this coward caught as much as you do." Others supported Abrams, including Bill O'Reilly, who justified the report

---

in Reporting, a media watch group. (Source: Wikipedia: The Free Encyclopedia, http://en.wikipedia.org/wiki/Laura_Flanders.)

made by Mike Buchanan, the reporter who broke the story on the tarot card on October 14. On October 22, Sean Hannity opined to an acquiescing Ed Meese, who served as attorney general during Ronald Reagan's presidency, "I believe that the press, ultimately, are going to help in the apprehension of this man because the widespread coverage creates an incredible awareness." Although not using the broader, fourth-estate rationale put forward by Abrams, that without the press the public would not be able to judge police work, Hannity nonetheless defended the media. As such, he and others inadvertently added to the criticism of police forces already battered by other reports. This support for the media indirectly damaged the notion of a coherent community. In this crisis, with solidarity at such a high premium, the outsider position of the press seemed to threaten society's strength.

Thus, the opinion media contributed to the climate of fear, though they did so using quite a different pattern. Although not emphasizing public anxiety so much, they did little to bolster any sense of community. Instead, their reports portrayed the evil of the sniper and cast doubt on the competency of the authorities. To some extent, the positions adopted by these cable opinion shows earned them enmity as well as higher ratings. As the rather defensive tone of Abrams indicated, the press, as well as the police, were under the scrutiny of the public. Apparently, this genre of show received specific criticism, as some believed them to be purely speculative. O'Reilly defended his own show from that charge twice, on October 16 and 21, by saying that the opinions presented there represented consensus views. This would have hardly stayed any doubts, since the essence of such programs was then, and remains, disagreement.

• • •

This chapter, which has mainly presented the area and national media's treatment of the sniper case, needs to consider a related question before closing: the reporting effort of the international media. This vast subject can provide comprehension of how the foreign press treated American issues. In addition, a considerable portion of the press corps covering the event were, in fact, from abroad. That said, the problems of defining these media are enormous. With so many different types of media, so many press regimes, so many different traditions–in short, so many different variables–constructing a representative sample becomes a gigantic enterprise. To begin consideration of this question, this study chose several different newspapers, ignoring magazines because the essence of this story required daily circulation, and ignoring electronic media because I could not access them. Thus, considered here are two British papers, the *Daily Mail* and *The Guardian;* Paris's *Le Monde;* the *Indian Express* and the *Times of India;* the *Johannesburg Star* and the *National Witness,* in South Africa; and the *Sydney Morning Herald* and the *Australia.*

Insofar as this small group can represent thousands of outlets, they show that readers outside the United States could easily follow the story episode by episode–even if no overarching narrative was provided. Moreover, the main elements delivered are very familiar–fear in the Washington area and criticism of the police. Most other elements– profiles and profilers, as well as the emphasis on community–appeared only infrequently or not at all. Perhaps most interesting was the general focus, which carried little emphasis on a meaning of this event for the home readers. Those who consumed these periodicals mainly carried away the crime story.

Instructive for comparative studies is the way that these newspapers portrayed the case and the fear it created. On some occasions, the media envisioned the sniper as an extension of American character. The *Daily Mail,* on October 16, equated this shooter with Oklahoma bomber Timothy McVeigh, who was intelligent and resourceful. The writer continued the comparison: "I suspect the Washington sniper shares with him a self-regarding seriousness, a lone-wolf arrogance, which he himself would regard as central to the American character. . . . It is possible, therefore, that we have here the most frightening kind of patriotic show-off." As a finale, the *Daily Mail* author stated that such arrogant guys had twisted American pride into contempt for American decency. From a different tack, the *Times of India,* on October 25, as it was chronicling the climax of the case, argued that the race of the suspect meant that "the killings can't be part of the domestic climate of latent violence which sporadically erupts into psychotic rage." Because the author believed African Americans were excluded from mainstream American society, they could not reveal American traits. In *The Guardian,* on October 17, the famed commentator Timothy Garton Ash argued that the climate of fear emanated from an atmosphere of "menace" that emerged from the government's rhetoric.

More often, the international papers, when they wanted to make the sniper story promote their own concerns, restricted the focus. In particular, in many cases they saw the shootings as the emanation of gun culture rather than anything as broad and endemic as violence or arrogant pride. For its October 21 issue, the *Daily Mail* printed thriller writer Philip Kerr's reaction to gun culture in America. Under the headline that asserted that "Americans have only themselves to blame for claiming the Godlike power to carry guns," Kerr announced: "The only really astonishing thing about the Washington sniper . . . is that this sort of thing does not happen more often in the United States." Proceeding further on his theme, Kerr noted that ten times as many Americans died from gunshot wounds each year than had been killed in the attack on the World Trade Center towers. Although the president stated the series of shootings was not American, "it's the America that everyone else in the world knows." In fact, continued Kerr, shooting someone with a high-powered rifle is common in America. In his conclusion, in which he sought the identity and purpose of the sniper, Kerr noted:

> If the Washington sniper is taken alive, it is more likely that he will be not some Al Qaeda terrorist, or even a cackling nutcase like Scorpio [a character in Clint Eastwood movies], but a quiet, white skinned man, aged 40–55, who is a stalwart member of the National Rifle Association.

Future scholarship may reveal further appropriation of the sniper story by the international press, but my sample mainly stuck to the details of the case and the themes of terror and police incompetence. For example, this was the approach of *Le Monde*, which carried a rich description of events but nothing more. Thus, the focus on fear apparently captivated the media outside as well as within the borders of the United States. While CBS News and the *Washington Times* constituted important exceptions, and many different approaches existed, the overwhelming theme emphasized worry, anxiety, and outright fear. A little leavening from cable broadcasts encouraged courage and coping, but the onslaught of information and opinion mainly conveyed the same strong message of fear, with little attention to a strong alternate community. Outside of this leavening, coverage was more fear-laden than that of the *Post,* which documented coping but still showed a deep pessimism. Only the schools, which will be treated in chapter 5, would take a more optimistic view.

# The Journalists' Ordeal

About 6 o'clock on the morning of October 24, 2002, *Washington Post* reporter Jamie Stockwell received a call at home from her editor. She had left the police task force headquarters only four hours earlier with information that included the names of two suspects. Now, she learned the two men had been apprehended. Stockwell both breathed a sigh of relief and set to work. The morning's beautiful colors excited her, a sense that was heightened as she assumed those charged were the snipers. Although she still had work to do, it would be as a wrap-up. A long, exciting, tiring, and nerve-wracking reporting assignment had come to an end.

How Jamie Stockwell and her thousands of journalist colleagues, hailing from many nations, arrived at this point provides the central thread for this chapter. Following Stockwell, who was assigned to the case from its inception until the end, allows an extended examination that gives insight into the mind-set and the processes involved in reporting. Even though her experience by no means encompasses the full panoply of the events, as she was mainly located in Maryland, she encountered all of the general situations that confronted the press, an understanding of which are central to understanding the journalistic challenges. Thus, her story serves as a springboard for discussing what I understand to be the basic parameters of reporting during the sniper episode. In addition, using interviews from some thirty-five other journalists, as well as several profilers and anchors, this chapter traces the actions of some of the journalists in the region from October 2 to October 24. Most of the journalists came from the *Post,* the *Richmond Times-Dispatch,* the local ABC News affiliate WJLA, *Nightline,* and Washington's all-news radio channel WTOP. The most important omission is a representative of the print media from outside the region, but the Richmond paper can at least partly fill that category because at first it treated the event as not impinging on its local area. Also supplementing the national electronic media in this sample were two cable journalists. And bolstering all this data are interviews that were, on the whole, long and detailed.

Still, such a sample is small compared to the two thousand or so journalists estimated to have covered this event. So this chapter will offer less of what the preceding ones have. It will not examine the press as a variegated body that reacted in different ways during different circumstances, and instead it will offer an indication of the aggregate experience of the journalists who underwent this experience. Because it was an experience and because this chapter more than others must rely on the self-reporting of these journalists as its major primary source, one other caveat is necessary. Plaguing all history, and oral history in particular, are fading memories as well as post facto rationalizations. I have tried to grapple with this weakness of evaluating sources by subjecting them to as much cross-checking as possible, as well as to my own judgment of their veracity.

Nonetheless, despite such limits, valuable information and insights emerge regarding how the news media responded in this era. Although some excellent studies exist on journalistic behavior, this precise period has not received attention (see the bibliographic essay). Further, other investigators of the contemporary press have not examined the actions of the press forged in the crucible of a large social crisis. Finally, comprehending the media context will help explain the pattern of reporting described in the preceding chapters, but this last synthetic subject must await the conclusion.

For now, this chapter will allow an understanding of the general principles of reporters, as well as the mutations in their application of those principles. Further, this chapter describes the complex initial decisions to report on these murders and how to do so—a combination of uncertainty, alacrity, and hesitation. It also discusses the press's battle and accommodations with the police in general and, in particular, with Charles Moose, chief of the Montgomery County police and the nominal leader of the investigation. It also reveals how, throughout the sniper events, the journalists covering them felt a mixture of personal fear broken by the dreary boredom they felt when they languished at the headquarters of the investigation in Rockville, Maryland, waiting for developments to occur. It also explores the news media's reliance on profilers to fill in around the gaps of information they were given by the police. And, finally, it chronicles the excitement even the journalists felt at the capture of the snipers.

• • •

By following journalists' experiences chronologically, this chapter concludes with a summation of their activities, thus framing the overall reporting, and it then points to the following chapters for resolution of the questions raised. Let us begin by returning to the *Post*'s Jamie Stockwell and explore her experiences before the events of October unfolded. Her experience is more than a little bit typical of newspaper reporters working in the field at the time of the sniper events. Her interest in journalism had begun early, with a visit from a reporter to interview her mother who, ill from cancer, was taking an experimental drug. The twelve-year-old found the process of news gathering fascinating. Moreover, her mother had herself wished to be a journalist. The profession appeared as a great way to know about people and their stories. In high school Stockwell joined a "journalism team" that competed every weekend, and she wrote news stories and features. Better at features than news, she won trophies, eventually becoming editor of her high school paper and then working on the student newspaper at the University of Texas. Majoring in journalism along with her work on the *Daily Texan,* she came back to news, which, as writers were paid by the article, offered better remuneration. Newly graduated in 1999, she interned at the *Post.* Beginning on the financial desk, she quickly moved to metro and then to the Virginia desk, covering city government in Prince William County. By April 2000 she was covering criminal justice stories in Prince George's County, later serving as criminal justice editor, until she left the paper in 2007 to become deputy metro editor of the *San Antonio Express News.*

Although relatively new to the profession, Stockwell had a well-worked-out definition of journalists, whose role she saw as being to inform, educate, and entertain. A good reporter must ask the obvious questions, such as "why something occurred or what sort of impact the incident might have on the public." Reporters should probe and not accept official statements at face value, she reasoned. They must question the source rigorously. Best practices include skepticism, even if it means criticizing one's own sources. Stockwell averred: "My first responsibility is to the public, and disseminating to them the news that matters. Sources cannot stand in the way of good, important journalism, even if they are great fountains of information." In her view, poor

The *Washington Post*'s Jamie Stockwell.

reporters become an extension of officialdom, rather than represen-tatives of the public. And sensational information that unnecessarily frightens ought to be eschewed, she believes. In our interview, Stock-well found it more difficult to answer how certain stories are selected for priority attention by reporters and editors while others are not. In the end, she believed it a gut reaction.

Interestingly, Stockwell viewed her work as providing relevant infor-mation to the public, whether authorities liked it or not. This approach, long used to justify the press's independence, often has been framed more aggressively through the concept of the fourth estate. This notion casts reporters as defenders of society's interests and as providing an in-dependent, rational position that separates them from official decision-makers as much as it does from the passions of the people, while they deliver to the public information and an independent judgment. Stock-well assumed a more moderate position, and her answer indicated a strong empiricist bent. While pursuing a story, the reporter seeks the facts wherever that search may lead, Stockwell reasoned. Empiricism has often been perceived philosophically as the inverse of theory and abstraction. In this case, empiricism appears in such a guise because, despite all the reflection over how to cover a story, the rational selection of the story remains instinctive and unexamined. The strength of this approach lies in the lack of any preconceived political or ideological agenda; its weaknesses may be the omissions in coverage that emerge.

Among both journalists and editors, Stockwell's attitudes and ten-dencies put her in broad company. Repeatedly, news reporters have described their method for choosing a story as using their instincts, or "gut," to know when the subject is worth tackling. The only exceptions to this were those journalists who specifically wanted to eschew the salacious or the gruesome. Matt Ackland,[1] a reporter for FOX News in Washington, especially decried the tendency to choose stories according to the slogan "If it bleeds, it leads." Also interesting was the hostility among journalists, expressed by *Post* executive editor Leonard Downie, to covering a person or event only because it would build sales or ratings. Yet these admirable dicta do not go very far in differentiating among serious stories that may involve some of the same aspects as the less serious ones do. Making the reportorial instinct somewhat more problematic is the journalistic embrace by many of notions of entertaining or interesting the audience. While it is necessary to do just that, the conflict also explains how news can slide into territory many reporters overtly wish to avoid, such as the salacious, tawdry, or macabre.

Stockwell's emphasis on a questioning empiricism possibly raises the value of the journalistic judgment. And her approach surely leads to her using her own powers of discernment. While this is seldom mentioned, members of the press clearly do not support reporting that offers an opinion. They draw a very firm line between judging stories and informing those same stories with their own views. Mark Holmberg, a writer for the Richmond paper, explained the role of the reporter as that of defining the story. He noted that his own approach charted a plan: to discover who, what, when, where, and why of the story. Beyond these basic facts, he searched for unusual angles. Avoiding the spokesperson, he sought out sources outside the limelight. But even in using these powers of discernment and judgment, he nonetheless does not refer to providing an opinion.

Holmberg's approach, of course, stressed novelty, which he overtly championed as he noted that he constantly looked around for the information that others did not have. For police reporting, he loved to listen

1. Matt Ackland always wanted to be in journalism. From the time he was a child watching television with his dad, he was drawn to television. For Ackland, it was more than a job; it was a way to learn something new each and every day. In addition, he felt that it was a way to give back to society by providing a service and helping people. Ackland knew from high school that he was going to be a journalist. He went to the University of Florida and worked in Gainesville until graduation. Afterward, he worked in Fort Myers, Fla., for about four years and then moved to Milwaukee, Wis., as a general assignment reporter, where he remained for three years. He is currently a general assignment reporter for FOX5 in Washington. (Source: Ackland interview.)

**Richmond reporter
Mark Holmberg.**

to the scanner, so that he could arrive on the scene not only before rival reporters but also the police as well. In fact, this ethos of the scoop—the reporting of something different or reporting a story before one's rivals do—informed the views and the work of every journalist. They also customarily expressed this as the goal of having the lead story, or being on the front page because of the scoop and its high news value.

Evaluating the views of several other newsmen and women illuminates and expands on Stockwell's journalistic creed. Yet, interestingly, they say little abstract about the press as a conscious bulwark against authority. As has been apparent and will be further examined, the press certainly resisted authority during the sniper events, but generally reporters tended to see themselves as the eyes of the public, without any reference to those for whom they were observing. At the extreme end of this perspective was Rebecca Miller,[2] a WJLA producer, who asserted

2. Rebecca Miller became interested in journalism in high school, when a local news anchor visited on Career Day. As a junior in high school, she interned at the local NBC affiliate. She majored in art and later went to graduate school for a communications degree. When she was in graduate school, working on her thesis, she moved to Atlanta and worked with the investigative unit of CNN first as an unpaid intern. Another unit then hired her on as a production assistant. Working at CNN taught her that to learn the ins and outs of news, the best way was to experience the daily grind of local stations and work your way up. From CNN she went to Birmingham, Ala., for a year; New Haven, Conn., for two years; and Houston for a year and a half before moving to WJLA. She had been at WJLA three and a half years

that reporters find and show what the public wants to know, and in doing so inform society of its wants and needs. In this view, the journalist's agenda, eschewing personal opinion, directly derives from the public. Likewise, a Richmond editor, Tom Kapsidelis,[3] averred that the press should rely on the news judgment of the public. Jeremy Redmon[4] of the *Richmond Times-Dispatch* stands out for his assertion that the journalist, in informing the public, becomes the vigilant guardian of open government. Serge Kovaleski, an experienced and noted investigative reporter for the *Post,* reflected a view similar to Redmon's edict

---

at the time of my interview with her. (Sources: Miller interview; NATAS website, http://www.capitalemmys.tv/nominations/nominations_2001.html.)

3. Tom Kapsidelis grew up always wanting to work for a newspaper, although no one in his family had ever worked at one, because he "grew up in a house full of newspapers." He loved to read as a child and was always fascinated by newspapers. When he was nine, his family moved from a small town in Virginia to Silver Spring, Md., and subscribed to the *Post.* The paper stimulated an interest. He worked at his school's newspaper, the University of Maryland's *Diamondback.* In college he also worked two summers at the morning newspaper in Columbia, S.C., *The State,* where he went after graduation. He also worked at *News America,* in Baltimore, for a semester, and at the *Prince George's Journal* for a semester. *The Diamondback,* he noted, was an extremely competitive environment and he worked harder because it "lit the fire in him" to keep up. He was a reporter for *The State* from 1978 to 1981, covering local government, higher education, and politics. In 1981, he moved to Richmond and got a job at United Press International, where he was employed until the end of 1987, and rose to bureau chief. He started at the *Richmond Times-Dispatch* in 1988. Tom Kapsidelis is currently the deputy editor of the Metro-State News desk for the *Richmond Times-Dispatch.* He was an in-the-field editor for the newspaper's 2007 Virginia Tech shooting coverage, directing more than twenty reporters and editors who were on the scene. (Sources: Kapsidelis interview; http://www.leadershipprofiles.com/preview.asp?docid=30511&t=0; Virginia AP Managing Editors website, http://vapme.org/events.htm; PRSA Richmond website, http://www.prsarichmond.org/en/cev/?45.)

4. Jeremy Redmon, a reporter for the *Richmond Times-Dispatch* during the D.C. sniper case, is currently an enterprise reporter for the *Atlanta Journal Constitution.* He held an internship with the *Prince William Journal* in 1994, right after graduating with his bachelor's degree in English/Writing from George Mason University. "I wanted to write for a living, and I studied creative writing but didn't think I could make a living out of it," he said. He worked at the *Richmond Times-Dispatch* from 1999 to 2005 covering military affairs, Richmond City Hall, and Henrico County government. He was embedded with U.S. soldiers and Marines for about four months during two tours in Iraq. Redmon has been a reporter at the *Atlanta Journal Constitution* since 2005, covering enterprise, state politics, and military affairs for the National and Metro desks. (Sources: AJC website, http://www.ajc.com/search/content/metro/cobb/staff.html; Redmon interviews.)

in an attack on cable discussion shows, which he defined as "not de-liberate." In contrast, Kovaleski held that print outlets had sufficient space to cover business and government in depth and to create the conditions demanding accountability. In this, he joined Redmon and Stockwell, who cast the press as being in opposition to authority. Still, in all these cases, the tones of the reporters' views suggest that opinion and conclusions always are left to the audience of readers and watchers.

Of course, this assessment of the journalistic temperament is lim-ited by the failure of this sample to include either editorial writers or sufficient numbers of representatives of the more aggressive television talk shows. However, the former contributed relatively little to the ac-tual coverage of the sniper story, and the latter refused my requests for interviews. Nonetheless, even though the views of some journalists might lie outside the parameters of those of the reporters interviewed here, this analysis offers representative coverage of most of the press corps members who covered the sniper story.

Even though staff reporters have their philosophy about what to cover, they work within a system that most often has at its heart a routine for finding and developing stories about the news of the day. Jamie Stockwell described her basic task as working within her "beat," which at the time was criminal justice in Prince George's County, Mary-land, pursuing a combination of self-generated story ideas and breaking news events. Essentially, she found interesting stories, whether sched-uled or impromptu, whose importance was self-evident to her. Again, the method for this selection remains hard to penetrate. Once she had a story, she called the editor to provide an outline of the material, and also created a list of those she wanted to interview. Although she mainly worked alone, she sometimes teamed up with a colleague. As Stockwell began to write, her stories could be read by the editors through the single, central computer system used to compose, file, and edit news reports. Generally, she submitted a forecast of the story that could be discussed with the editors, so they could settle on its length as well as on the lead–the opening paragraph plus the next two or three paragraphs that supported the opening. Once the story had been submitted, editors at the *Post* had latitude to edit stories as they saw fit, but they generally consulted the writer if they contemplated large changes. Of course, above Stockwell stood a network of assistant editors who had subject and geographical specialties and who served as gatekeepers to the pages of the paper. All of these lines of authority led up to Jo-Ann

Armao,[5] who headed the Metro section of the paper. At noon, after she surveyed the electronic competition and saw the stories available, Armao set a template for the day. Later that day, she jousted with other editors for the placement of stories on the front page. The managing editor participated in these meetings as well.

As Katherine Graham's richly documented autobiography, *Personal History* (A. A. Knopf, 1997), has revealed, the executive editor, the publisher, and even the legal office, in exceptional circumstances, all weighed in with their opinions on stories during editorial discussions at the paper. The *Post* has had a hierarchical system that gave to editors the final say on a piece, and ranking editors could change language in a story without consultation or contradiction. Reporters generally allowed that it was up to the editors to decide and strike material deemed out-of-bounds for the paper. All this comes into play for big stories, where coordination is more important or the stakes are higher. Clearly, later in this chapter, some of these aspects of the newspaper will play a part in the organization of the reporting on the sniper.

Nonetheless, the reporters and those editors who deal with stories at the point of initiation–the assistant metro section editors, for example–clearly control daily impact on the specific context in the *Post*. Since it is the reporter who mainly evaluates the reliability of sources, more authority remains in his or her hands. Furthermore, under the stewardship of the Grahams, and even more so when Katherine's son, Donald, has been publisher, less intervention from on top has occurred. In general, the editors prefer to be informed about problems rather than be involved on a daily basis. The main power of the editors would seem to lie in whom they hire, more than over the actual content. According to one of my anonymous print sources, such a situation certainly was the case at the *Richmond Times-Dispatch,* perhaps to an even greater extent because both reporters and editors consider the paper to be a writer-oriented outlet. Seemingly, reporters felt more autonomous and this status resulted from design.

5. Jo-Ann Armao has been with the *Post* since 1984. Her career in journalism began in 1973 at the *Buffalo Courier Express.* Upon joining the *Post,* Armao was an assignment editor, becoming a reporter two years later. She covered government and politics in Montgomery County, Md., before becoming Virginia editor in 1992. She was then named deputy metro editor in 1993, city editor in 1994, and an editorial board member in 2006. She is currently an editorial writer for the paper. (Source: *Washington Post* website, http://projects.washingtonpost.com/staff/articles/jo-ann+armao/.)

However, substantially more top-down involvement could be found in the electronic media. Perhaps because the amount of copy is more limited, the producers authorized most of the stories in advance. In addition, the heightened technological aspects of electronic journalism affected the financial side of this business. Because there are so few reporters, the producers have to marshal their efforts just to produce a show. Another reason for more hierarchical management has been that the electronic program is much more linear. People change channels or turn off the set if they get bored. Thus, the pressure and responsibility for meaningful and engaging journalism is much higher, and supervisory personnel seek to guarantee meaningful and engaging journalism. This does not mean that television and radio reporters have been reduced to mere conduits. They clearly have not. Their bosses, however, clearly have a larger role to play than do those in print media.

Take as a first example the local electronic news shows. On a normal day, WTOP radio begins the day with an early morning meeting during which the news director, assisted by the early morning editor, makes assignments to the ten or so reporters available. (This contrasts with a staff of two hundred available to the *Post*'s Metro editor.) These reporters are very mobile and can transmit back their reports, which commonly are thirty-five seconds in length, without having to return to the station. Likewise, WJLA news begins its day with an early morning meeting given by the news director, the vice-president for news. At this point in the day, the news director, Steve Hammel,[6] already would have watched morning television, read the *Post,* listened to WTOP, and glanced at the *New York Times, Wall Street Journal,* and *USA Today*, even though a common goal for television stations is to make use of their ability to break into regular programming. He always hoped that his station would find a way during the course of the day to scoop the printed press. The morning meeting was well attended by producers and directors. Their collective goal was to cover news that reflected the community. All participants were supposed to come to the table with a story that was not self-evident and that might lead the news. From this meeting stories were assigned. Basic segments were one minute and fifteen seconds in length (along with thirty seconds for introduction and conclusion), and these were adjusted as conditions warranted throughout the course of the day.

6. For Steve Hammel's bio, see note 4 to chapter 3.

The practice of morning meetings followed by additional ones was common throughout the news business. The impact of this practice can be seen by examining a day in Matt Ackland's life as a reporter for FOX News in Washington. By morning, the stories the reporters were to cover would be available, along with the direction they were supposed to take. Reporters were generally allowed to choose what stories they wanted to work on, and if a reporter's choice was not available, the reporter would get a preferred story another day. With the assignments made, Ackland would work with a cameraman to find out as much as possible, making certain to obtain both sides of the story if that fit the sort of story he was given. Assisting him were researchers paid to listen to police scanners while at home. Editors made calls and supplied information to reporters. Usually, Ackland tried to have two or three interviews backing up each story, and would discuss the story's development with his supervising editor. Once a supervisor approved the story, he would send a camera truck to the reporter. With this equipment and crew, the reporter would conduct his interviews and mix the narration and video. In Ackland's case, he customarily worked with blocks of a minute and a half or a minute and fifteen seconds, with twenty seconds on each end for an introduction and conclusion. His station wanted to increase the number of live interviews, so he altered his approach to accommodate this goal. In such circumstances, the news managers would be prompting him through a speaker in his ear. They had ultimate authority. News anchors were given greater latitude than reporters, but even their opportunity to speak remained somewhat limited by the supervision of producers.

Although television and radio journalists certainly had their own sources, and many also had their routine territory, or "beats," from which they report, in these media compared to print much more authority customarily resided in the managerial group. One can see a similar arrangement in other parts of the electronic news. For ABC's *Nightline,* CNN's *Crossfire,* NBC's *Today,* and PBS's *NewsHour,* the top-down structure has been as tight as the structure for local news, largely because these programs focused mainly on a single part of the news (although this was somewhat less the case for *Today* and *News-Hour*) and presented a clear package of information. For example, according to Tom Bettag, the executive producer of *Nightline,* the evening before a show, *Nightline* employees left the studio with a very loose plan. At eight the next morning, they seriously discussed the coming evening's show. At eleven, *Nightline* held a very democratic meeting to prepare an outline of the show. After much discussion, Bettag and managing editor Ted Koppel then made final decisions. A senior producer worked through each element of the show with the remainder of the staff, and recording customarily began at 5:30 p.m. Breaking news sometimes changed all that. In the end, Bettag and Koppel checked off the show before air time. Clearly, this show featured live interviews, and they could be managed only up to a point. Bookers interviewed the talent, but those guests could say what they wished. Overall, though, in this show, reporters had a great deal of influence, but the top manager governed final access to the air.

According to my interview with an anonymous cable executive, *Crossfire,* a purely discussion show that thrived on vigorous debates and sometimes even confrontations, differed markedly from the dispassionate and reflective *Nightline,* but the two were structured somewhat the same. Even so, their preparation processes were similar. *Crossfire* also began with a meeting, this one at nine in the morning, and including at least the executive producer, the producer, and the hosts. With the staff in D.C. at one table, the Atlanta staff similarly positioned, and the hosts at their homes, agreement was reached, usually within an hour, about the topics for the day. Three different segments might be decided upon, and the responsibility passed to producers and bookers to find guests whose views would balance one another. As a live show, it depended on the hosts to ask good questions. Producers helped by suggesting questions through an ear speaker. The only scripts, written by the producer, were those that introduced the show. Here, the hosts played a significant role. Still, the producers, through their participation in selecting both the topic and the guests, as well as their promptings during the show itself, would seem to have taken the preponderant role in all this. In any case, the hosts and the senior staff cooperated with each other to produce shows where the autonomous decisions mainly occurred at meetings of the top personnel of each program.

Without continuing to multiply examples, it seems reasonable to conclude that on a usual day, electronic and print newspeople shared values, but as their media differed so did the place of reporters. This difference will loom larger as we move to an examination of the methods used by the journalistic community to cover the sniper event.

Some readers may by this point wonder whether this book will discuss two of the main controversies surrounding modern journalism: those of liberal bias and a general inclination to sensationalism. The preceding analysis characterized journalists as empiricists. Interviews turned up dogged empiricists who followed stories of interest. Only a few saw themselves as congenitally opposed to authority. Mainly they associated themselves with discovering news of interest and importance to their community. This obviously is not the stuff of liberal bias. Surveys of journalists suggest that those interviewed for this book were predominantly liberal in political orientation. At the same time, my interviews turned up no evidence that this political leaning penetrated their conscious understanding of their jobs. As shown later in this chapter, journalists also sought to screen out their own elemental fears, a more pervasive sentiment certainly in this case than were any particular political leanings. That this analysis depends on self-reporting makes it somewhat liable to cynical manipulation. However, this would also demand that these reporters be able and willing to suppress their views, even in the face of probing. Instead, it seems more likely that a subtle bias emerges, because of reporters' identification with the public and their tendency to wish to expose elites who had proved undeserving. This inclination, though, could lead the journalists to attack the "big government" of liberals as much as business and the military interests beloved by conservatives. In yet another way, this information might still overlook the existence of a liberally dominated press. Perhaps this study, by interviewing reporters who covered a crime story, ends up with a less politically engaged group than would have emerged in a study of those who cover, say, the White House. Or had this survey been taken in the context of a political story, such sentiments might have been closer to the surface. On the other hand, had I been able to speak with more cable news journalists, this study might have discovered a conservative bias in the press.

As we have seen, the sniper coverage could be termed sensationalistic, yet there is little in the description of the representative media that would seem to account for that. In fact, the general omission of cable talk show personnel eliminates the most likely place to find causes for this. However, as mentioned in the preceding chapter, such shows were not particularly sensationalistic. Further analysis will suggest that the sensationalism mainly emerged for reasons other than the newspeople's general attitudes or news-gathering processes.

Let us turn to the actions of journalists as events unfolded, first at 5:20 p.m. on October 2, 2002, when someone shot through the window at a Michael's craft store in Aspen Hill, Maryland. No one was injured. About forty minutes later, however, a man named James Martin was gunned down in a nearby parking lot. The press treated this as it presented itself, as a single murder. However, the next day four more people were killed, between 7:41 a.m. and 9:58 a.m. Yet another person was killed later that evening. It became apparent to the police and then to the media that a sniper (or snipers) was shooting people.

According to Jamie Stockwell, her becoming involved in covering these events started somewhat slowly. On the morning of October 3, listening to WTOP, she heard of the shootings as she was driving to a dental appointment in Bethesda, Montgomery County, not far from the shootings. Phoning her editor, she learned that the editors had it covered. This was not unexpected, because Stockwell was assigned to neighboring Prince George's County. After her dental appointment, she returned to her normal office. No one seemed certain what was happening.

The *Post* was consumed with activity. On the morning of October 3, reports of shootings started to filter into the *Post* newsroom. Confusion was intense. At first, newspeople heard that the second shooting was a murder-suicide. By the third shooting, according to assistant editor Paul Duggan,[7] he began to see something of a geographical pattern. Reporters were sent out, so that by the afternoon the *Post* had between thirty and forty reporters on the scene. For the simple sake of comparison, if the *Richmond Times-Dispatch* wished to cover a local event with this number of reporters, it would have to send everyone on both its metro and state desks. But the *New York Times* could potentially put twice as many reporters on a story in its hometown.

According to Jo-Ann Armao, when the *Post* committed that many reporters to that day's murders, the paper had committed itself. The paper's editors had set up a process that would allow the *Post* to dominate and master the story. Even this early in the development of the

7. Paul Duggan is currently a metro and regional reporter for the *Washington Post*. Duggan had no idea what he wanted to do after high school and joined the Marine Corps with a friend. Eventually, he attended college in Boston. He bounced around, going to a series of schools and never finding anything in which he was really interested. He discovered that he enjoyed writing and began to write for a newspaper at Suffolk University in Boston. He enjoyed it, and soon changed his major to journalism, taking a summer internship in Providence. He remained in Providence for six years as a reporter before moving to the *Philadelphia Inquirer*, also as a reporter. He moved to the *Washington City Paper* in 1987 and worked as a metro reporter and national correspondent, then spent five years in the Austin, Tx., bureau, returning to Washington just prior to the sniper shootings. (Sources: *Washington Post* website, http://projects.washingtonpost.com/staff/articles/paul+duggan/; Duggan interview.)

sniper episode, the *Post* editors believed it must be the paper of record for this story. The events were unfolding in the paper's back yard, in an area where it dominated news coverage and circulation both. So the *Post* editors decided to "flood the zone," using football slang popularized previously within the media by the *New York Times.* They also evolved a standard procedure, based around the pervasive morning news meeting. Over the course of the events, staff met daily in Armao's tiny, windowless and cluttered office. Two to three hours earlier than usual, with many more people than usual in attendance, often including Executive Editor Leonard Downie,[8] the editor, deputies, and graphics people discussed the day's coverage. They commonly hoped for six to eight stories each day, along with the "lead-in," which was a 40-inch story of some twenty-five hundred words gracing the front page. Michael Ruane[9] composed quite a few of the lead-in stories. According to Ruane, journalists working all over the metro area were constantly sending him bits of information that he then crafted into a major story that framed the day's coverage.

The morning meetings were frantic, as ideas seemed to fly. Assistant Editor Paul Duggan recalled some common questions: Can these events be compared to any other? What was the state of the investigation? How were other publications reacting? What was happening on the street? Armao was responsible for the final decision, but so much was underway that occasionally even the editors were unsure just what had been decided with regard to the main story's ingredients and the sidebars, or related stories, that would be in the package. But they had a direction, and the discussion in general and the specific decisions

8. Leonard Downie Jr. was the executive editor of the *Post* from 1991 to 2008. He began at the *Post* as an intern in 1964, worked on the Metro desk as a reporter and editor, and was an assistant managing editor, deputy metropolitan editor, national editor, and managing editor. After retiring in 2008, Downie became Vice President at Large of the Washington Post Company. He is the author of four books. (Source: *Washington Post* website, http://www.washpost.com/news_ed/news/edit_bio.shtml.)

9. Michael E. Ruane is a metro and regional reporter for the *Post.* He began his career as a crime reporter at the *Philadelphia Evening Bulletin* in 1976. He then moved to the *Philadelphia Inquirer,* working as a general assignment reporter in the city and in rural Pennsylvania. From 1991 to 1992, Ruane was a Nieman Fellow at Harvard University. He then covered the Pentagon for the Knight-Ridder newspaper chain. He joined the *Post* in 1997. (Sources: *Washington Post* website, http://projects.washingtonpost.com/staff/articles/michael+e.+ruane/; Ruane interview [Price].)

guided the editors, as they in turn directed the reporters through the course of the day. As developments unfolded, of course, story ideas changed, as some material the reporters sought might not be available, or at least not at that time, or as the deeds of the snipers and their investigators might interrupt an attempt to interview an expert and present reporters and editors instead with an event that had to be covered, and flooded with personnel. Thus was each day's coverage a combination of focused energy and fluid responsiveness to developments beyond the control of the reporters or editors. *Post* reporters and editors found covering these events the most intense story on which they ever had worked. The September 11, 2001, attack on the Pentagon, while shocking, had been both a discrete event and a less uncertain one, because the culprit was immediately identified. In the case of the sniper, evidently, the anxiety and uncertainty eroded the customary reportorial autonomy. The extent to which it did so remains to be evaluated as the effort by the *Post* and other papers over the three weeks is chronicled.

Difficulties plagued the paper's coverage. A major problem was the uncertainty of much information. First, other outlets were publishing news that the *Post* either did not have or could not promulgate. Armao insisted that before information was printed, as with any other news in the *Post,* reporters had to find two sources for the item, unless it was an officially released piece of information. This protected the paper from many errors but increased the reporters' workload. According to Armao, another major factor making this job so exhausting was that the *Post* came to treat every shooting murder as possibly related to the sniper and sent a reporter to investigate. At first there was little way to test whether the incident actually was connected to the sniper. Although ballistic tests and other common indicators of the sniper emerged, editors and writers found their stamina tested.

Just a few miles to the north and east of the *Post*'s main building in downtown Washington, the editors of WTOP radio confronted the same decisions in sorting out the events of that first day. His first reaction, according to Mike McMearty,[10] news director, was that this was crazy. The murders produced a "mad scramble" to figure out what was going on and try to cover all the bases with reporters. The staff pulled out a map to try to figure out what to do, as they simultaneously dispatched reporters to the scenes while detailing others to grill sources.

10. For Mike McMearty's bio, see note 13 to chapter 3.

By the third murder, newspeople at WTOP thought they saw a pattern. The rest of the day, WTOP mainly covered the killings in Montgomery County.

Confusion was not alleviated when reporters showed up. According to Steve Eldridge, he had been expecting to show up at the radio station at 10 a.m., but instead he was sent to the Shell service station where Lori Lewis-Rivera had been shot at 9:58. Posted to the crime scene, Eldridge had no knowledge that Lewis-Rivera's murder was the fourth shooting of the day, and was linked to others. As he arrived some thirty to forty minutes after the murder, he ran into a very wide police perimeter and could not discern what was happening. Although he could see the van that proved to belong to the victim, he really did not understand what was transpiring. However, police officers, far more lenient than they later would be, allowed him to cross the tape, and Eldridge was able to interview one of the employees. Sending back frequent reports, Eldridge remained at the gas station the better part of three hours. He talked with witnesses who recalled the shooting quite well. Speaking over a year after this incident, Eldridge still painfully recalled seeing Lewis-Rivera's abandoned van with its baby seats just sitting on the pavement. Unlike later killings, where the press was held at a great distance, reporters gained access to witnesses who told what they knew. Authorities remained uncertain about the direction from which the shots had been fired.

Over the next three weeks, WTOP stayed on top of the events, sending a reporter to every single shooting, even as they began to occur deeper into Virginia, far from the station's listening area. The radio station continuously posted a reporter at Task Force headquarters as well. When no breaking news occurred, WTOP worked the personal side of the story. Using a different sports metaphor than the *Post*, this radio channel's news director, Michael McMearty, labeled their work a "full-court press." He wanted to get it right and get it first, envisioning WTOP's coverage as the basis for that of everyone else. With relatively simple technology, radio reporters could arrive easily and report immediately. And in keeping with McMearty's goals, WTOP developed a suitable approach that made it a prime source of information for both the press and public.

Just across from Georgetown, in Rosslyn, Virginia, sat the studios of the local ABC affiliate, WJLA-TV. According to Steve Hammel, the initial shooting occurred before the news editors' daily meeting, but the assignment editor sent out a crew and reported the shooting at the meeting when it started. As the meeting continued, other news of fatalities reached the station. Because the day still was early, the producers had crews there to be dispatched. Eventually, the noon newscast morphed into continuous coverage as the station dropped its regular programming for the afternoon. Although this decision, and others like it, cost tens of thousands of dollars, the producers argued the public's need to know required it.

In this frantic, impromptu situation, producers orchestrated the coverage and assigned the reporters' work as well as that of the camera crews. While the assignment desk used the phones to recruit neighbors to speak to reporters and generated other shots, the producers paced the anchors, available experts, reporters, and press conferences. Juggling these pieces produced by the assignment desk working with reporters, the news staff worked on uninterruptedly. Anchors could provide auxiliary materials and reflections to paper over gaps in information. The station tried to rent a helicopter to provide better video recordings but was unable to do so. At WJLA, newspeople were creative, and when no direct camera feed was possible, they made a map do its work.

Each day produced a large amount of coverage of the sniper story, including frequent returns to continuous coverage. Producer Rebecca Miller groaned under the weight of this coverage, feeling as though she was in the midst of a tornado. She later recalled that it felt like being in a really bad movie that could not be turned off. Even when one left the studio, the fear associated with daily tasks such as pumping gas, buying groceries, or driving children to school–some of which had proved fatal for some of the sniper's victims–took its toll.

Although it immediately was clear to the news outlets that served the D.C. metro area that they would cover the random shootings, national and international organizations, and even media in neighboring areas, were faced with a more difficult decision. While CNN turned quickly to the shootings, the *Richmond Times-Dispatch* and ABC's *Nightline* took some time. The contrast between CNN and those other outlets that delayed joining the coverage is instructive.

CNN immediately embraced the story. Already geared up to track a hurricane predicted to hit land, the network had a news hole when the storm suddenly weakened. This opening was quickly filled with the sniper shootings, which, although a local story, commanded attention.

According to Keith McCallister,[11] senior vice-president for news, he believed it was a local story, but with national resonance. He posited that it was genuinely fascinating, with the randomness of the shootings making them compelling and fearful to all. That it took place near the nation's capital brought it home to many. Finally, on a personal level, the staff at CNN in Atlanta had many friends and colleagues in the Washington area.

Once CNN had committed to cover the story, it threw in tremendous time and resources. Already in the Washington area was a four-hundred-person bureau, with a news staff of one hundred and sixty. As many as twenty-four reporters worked together on this story. During this period, the network shifted its focus from the federal government to this story, creating an around-the-clock assignment desk. In addition to the two satellite trucks it owned, CNN rented more. Furthermore, to supplement the D.C. staff, CNN sent extra people, including top anchors to work from Rockville.

*Nightline* was far more hesitant than CNN or, for that matter, NBC's *Today,* which took largely the same tack as did cable news. *Nightline* executive producers saw the difference between its approach and that of others as a difference in purpose. The program staff hesitated. Even when they took up the story after the shooting of middle-school student Iran Brown on October 3, they were still somewhat reluctant to jump in with more resources because so little information was actually available. Also, many news media were covering this story and part of the intended purpose of *Nightline* was to take a tack different than those of other outlets. Although the story was clearly a national one, according to producer Tom Bettag it was seen more as a cable TV story because it was a violent crime story. Hungry for news because of the tremendous amount of air time to fill, cable TV stations saw the events as national for them. The *Nightline* staff reiterated many of these same views, but emphasized that they generally avoided Washington stories because they did not want personal concerns to overwhelm the national perspective that they endeavored to offer. While all these reasons explain why

11. Keith McAllister spent almost eighteen years at CNN in a variety of roles. At the network, McAllister was vice-president and New York bureau chief, New York managing editor, field producer, assignment editor, writer, production assistant, and executive vice-president and managing editor of national news gathering. He left CNN in 2003 and is a global editor at Thompson Reuters and a member of the board of directors at Mochila. (Source: Mochila: The Media Marketplace website, http://www.mochila.com/company_management.html.)

the producers hung back, the staff averred that in the end it was the apparent link to September 11, as the capital again seemed under siege, that finally pushed the show to invest significant effort in covering the story. Reasonably, one might conclude that *Nightline*'s decision sprang from a strong sense of the kind of stories it covered and a wish to be different and avoid associating itself with other media widely viewed as more attuned to sensationalist tastes. Interestingly, PBS followed the same approach, for some of the same reasons. Taken together, the generally cautious and highly reflective styles of these shows made their producers hesitate before leaping into coverage of the sniper. Nonetheless, once the dam had been breached, both programs made a considerable effort.

The *Richmond Times-Dispatch* also proved to be reticent in committing resources to the story, but for entirely different reasons. After the shootings of October 3 in Montgomery County, Paul Bradley,[12] who staffed the nearby Alexandria desk for the Richmond paper, called state editor Tom Kapsidelis to ask whether they should report on the story. Kapsidelis decided to wait and see whether any shootings would occur in Virginia, a decision which relieved Bradley, as his sources were stronger in Virginia. He thought to himself that this crisis would come to Virginia, and the very next day it did, with the wounding of Caroline Seawell in front of a Michael's in Fredericksburg, some fifty miles south of the earlier attacks. This story fell into the bailiwick of Kiran Krishnamurthy,[13] who was in charge of the *Times-Dispatch* office in that city.

12. Paul Bradley's father was a long-time photographer for the Associated Press and several newspapers in Boston. As a child, Bradley visited his father at work and thought journalism seemed like a way to have fun and get paid doing it. He pursued it in high school and became the managing editor of his college newspaper at the University of Massachusetts. He got his first job, in 1977, at a local newspaper as a police reporter after getting a tip from a college professor. He stayed there for five years and then moved to Phoenix, working at the *Phoenix Gazette*. Bradley remained in Arizona for about five years before taking a job at the *Hartford Courant* doing general assignment work—he started as an editor before getting back into reporting, covering city hall and public housing. He joined the *Richmond News-Leader* in 1987, which eventually became the *Richmond Times-Dispatch*. He worked for the *Times-Dispatch*'s Northern Virginia bureau until May 2006, when he was dismissed for allegedly fabricating facts in a story. According to his paper, the fabrications included an interview that did not occur and a misrepresentation of an onsite visit for the story in question. (Sources: Bradley interview; *Roanoke Times* website, http://www.roanoke.com/news/roanoke/wb/67100.)

13. Kiran Krishnamurthy has been a reporter for the *Richmond Times-Dispatch* since 1999. His interest in journalism began with his work for his high school

According to him, everyone on the staff immediately perceived that it had become their story, as the paper quickly turned from relying on Associated Press reports to producing its own copy. For his part, Krishnamurthy monitored the press conferences late that afternoon and turned up at Michael's at 7 a.m. the next morning to obtain information that would aid in questioning the police. Back in Richmond, Andy Taylor,[14] the city editor, joined the scramble by offering his reporters to help those assigned to the state desk. He believed that the story was definitely headed his way.

As the *Times-Dispatch* generally focused on breaking news, Taylor and Kapsidelis had no trouble orchestrating an all-out effort that ceased only after the capture of John Muhammad and Lee Boyd Malvo. Despite the depressing context, the work energized the newsroom because it was an exciting story to cover. The day after the shooting at Ashland (fifteen miles north of Richmond), the staff worked from 8 a.m. until 2 the following morning trying to discover as much information as they could. In retrospect, Kapsidelis said he believed his staff had done a good job providing a coherent narration of the event, and had managed to break a number of important stories about it.

Evidently, in this atmosphere even the Richmond paper moved to direct its writers, yet room still remained for writer initiative, as

---

newspaper, where he worked for about two years. He was also the editor of his school's yearbook. He applied to college as a business major, considering advertising as a good financial career choice, but was soon drawn back to journalism. After earning his degree in journalism from James Madison University, he began to write for the *Petersburg Progress Index* in Virginia. He remained there for about three years before moving to the *Freelance Star* in Fredericksburg, where he worked for four-and-a-half years. During his time at the *Times-Dispatch,* Krishnamurthy has covered a variety of human-interest stories, including survivors of the September 11 attack on the Pentagon, a profile of the Washington postal worker infected with anthrax, and the growing prevalence of suburban sprawl. (Sources: Krishnamurthy interview; SAJA website, http://www.saja.org/krishnamurthy.html.)

14. Andy Taylor was the *Richmond Times-Dispatch* news editor of the combined State and Metro desks until his retirement in January of 2009. A native of Richmond, Taylor originally planned a career as a history teacher. Encouragement from teachers and a job writing for the school newspaper drew him into journalism. His position after college was with the *Petersburg Progress Index* for about a year before going to the *Tampa Tribune,* where he worked for about two years. Moving back to Richmond in 1988 with his family, he began working for the *Richmond News-Leader,* an afternoon paper that merged with the *Richmond Times-Dispatch* in 1999. (Sources: Taylor interview; AJR website, http://www.ajr.org/article_printable.asp?id=4267.)

Mark Holmberg's experiences indicate. One of the most admired reporters on the staff, Holmberg found the sniper case gripping, and
often worked on it eighteen hours a day. Like many at the Richmond
paper, Holmberg believed the sniper was in the area. In fact, he scouted
locations, mainly near Interstates, where he figured the sniper might
strike again. He even kept an eye out for people–people comfortable
with rifles–who might be, vigilante-style, hoping to kill the assailant.
Holmberg thought creatively, not only about subjects, but about how he
might use his stories to unsettle hasty conclusions. In particular, the
reporter was convinced that the sniper was no longer in the white van, if
ever he had been, and, in a subtle manner, he wrote that this assertion
should be questioned. Furthermore, in his own search for the suspect,
Holmberg drew on a strong belief from his time as a crime reporter that
killers return to the scene of the crime to admire their handiwork. In
this, he was challenging the police's search for a vehicle fleeing the
scene. And, as it later turned out, Holmberg was correct, at least twice.

In sum, even when media operations were slow to begin to follow
the sniper story, they stayed focused on the subject. The hesitancy can
be reasonably explained in terms of their goals. In the case of *Nightline*
and the *NewsHour,* it was mainly a desire not to follow the herd instinct
and not to cater overtly to their home base in Washington, D.C. For the
Richmond paper, the focus was Virginia; the story would have to involve that state. And, of course, the arrival of the sniper at the door
explains why the Richmond paper never gave it up. In the end, for
*Nightline,* and the *NewsHour* as well, perhaps CNN's fascination with
wide-scale vulnerability provides the best explanation for why this story
claimed so much attention and so many resources. Ratings soared and
only confirmed these decisions by major electronic media.

• • •

At the same time as many media outlets were deciding to join the sniper
story, Jamie Stockwell's own involvement greatly increased. Her story
provides an intense and detailed look at several of the problems that
bedeviled coverage.

On Saturday, October 5, the day after Caroline Seawell was shot,
Jamie Stockwell was far from that story. Another paper had named a
suspect, who was living in Montgomery County. She located his house,
in a cul-de-sac near where Sarah Ramos was gunned down, but the
potential suspect was not there. After additional driving to survey the
geography of some of the local crime scenes, Stockwell returned and
spoke to his family and friends. While Stockwell turned up another tip

on this person, everyone else with whom she spoke could not imagine he could be the shooter. Without more evidence, the *Post* decided not to run her account. Stockwell went home and spent the rest of the weekend there. After hearing about the Seawell shooting, she had been "itching" to be a part of the story.

On October 7, Monday morning, Stockwell got her chance. Planning to go to Montgomery County to check on another crime scene, she called the police very early to learn about any news. She found out about the Tasker shooting, heard it was unconnected, and consigned it to the category "regular old" shootings. Around 8 a.m., the *Post* called and told her that this assault was part of the story. To avoid the tremendous traffic jams that had quickly built up on the roads leading to the scene, Stockwell took the back roads. She immediately saw someone who had been a good source for her, and he told her the shot had come from about 140 yards from the victim. Speaking with the Prince George's County school superintendent and the county police chief Gerald M. Wilson, Stockwell learned that they thought this shooting was connected to the sniper but were being careful to avoid causing a panic. She also spoke to both Iran Brown's mother and the aunt who had dropped him at school. All these interviews meant that Stockwell returned home quite late.

The next day passed uneventfully for Stockwell, who was at Montgomery County police headquarters, but the night was full of surprises. At home that evening she received a call from the night editor at the *Post*, who informed her that CBS affiliate WUSA had reported that a tarot card had been found at the scene with the message, "I am God." Stockwell's first reaction was utter disappointment that no source had told her. She was also "creeped out" about a criminal who could send such a message.

Stockwell's second reaction was to call Chief Wilson, whom she could not reach immediately. Within a minute or two, he returned her call. She informed him that it was reported that his detectives had found a card at the scene. He was surprised, and responded that he could not believe WUSA had reported that. When she told him that the paper was going to go with this news, he said he understood.

Then Stockwell called up a Prince George's County detective who similarly expressed surprise. He noted that the *Post* had gained this information before the authorities told Montgomery County about it; now it was out. On the following day, the same source added, "If I was a leak, you would have the real words." He then told Stockwell that the phrase on the card had been, "Call me God." Further, he said that the card specifically warned them not to leak this to the press. The authorities had hoped this message would start a conversation and that it would be a code that could be used to ensnare the killer. The officer added that it seemed as though the chase was as exciting as sex to this murderer. Further, he emphasized, he was telling her because he liked her, but that the information remained "totally off the record," meaning it "totally" could not be used. Perhaps, offered her source, the police might prove to be the next target. Stockwell was thinking that maybe a reporter would be the prey instead. In fact, the police would erect a tarp the next day at the press conferences to shield reporters.

The next day arrived. Although Montgomery Police Chief Moose did not know the extent of Stockwell's knowledge, nor, of course, how much more she would learn that day, he did know that WUSA had reported the existence of the tarot card and a version of its language. With the confirmation supplied by Stockwell, the *Post* had done the same. Arriving in Rockville, Stockwell witnessed the chief really blasting the *Post* and WUSA and ordering them to stay out of the investigation. Several thoughts passed through her mind. First, she believed that Moose's tantrum was meant to establish bona fides with the killer and to show that he had not willfully disobeyed the demand of the tarot card. At the same time, she was proud that she had pulled off this scoop. She called her mother to say that it was because of her that the chief was upset and attacking the *Post*. On the other hand, after a while, Stockwell walked around the area. Always there is a little part of you, she offered, that does not want to be hated. "I thought for a moment, did I really want to be thought a scum."

While October 8 and 9 were frightening, intimidating, tumultuous, and disappointing days, as well as successful ones, for Stockwell, this account of her actions then poses some very interesting questions. First, how did the press seek to structure its relationship with the police? Overall, it might seem that this can be only an adversarial relationship, as the police generally think that sharing information jeopardizes investigations. They believed this all the more strongly in the sniper case because they were convinced that the shooter was watching the media and acting in response to it. Thus, for public safety, the police wished to control media content as much as possible. Equally strong was the press's belief that the public has a right to know and, indeed, protect itself with the best knowledge available. Furthermore, a knowledgeable public can help bring a criminal to justice. Finally, the newspeople also averred that holding back material could endanger public safety. Over-all, many would later justify this latter position by reminding their critics that all that publicity generated by press initiative led to the identification of Muhammad and Malvo as the suspects, and then, in separate but related events, to their arrest.

Journalists are generally quick to elaborate their views about in-forming the public. In our interview, Mark Holmberg was characteris-tically forceful. Recalling the situation in October, he later noted that the relationship between the newspeople and the police is a constant cat-and-mouse game as officials withhold information and the press tries to get it. But, averred Holmberg, journalists need to do their job, and their job is to present the news, which usually concerns problems. Without this knowledge, solutions cannot emerge. In the sniper case, it was necessary for the public to get the best information that would not be dangerous to them. Then he gave an example. He was the first to hear about the phone call connection between the police and the sniper on the heels of the shooting in Ashland. At that point, posited the jour-nalist, the snipers were beyond the police about "90 miles an hour." Thus, he had no hesitation releasing these details. In his view, the Task Force was hurting the investigation, and he should correct the informa-tion Moose was giving out.

In his interview with me, Michael Ruane of the *Post*, who wrote many stories as well as a book on the incident, concurred with Holm-berg. On this same subject he argued that the obligation of the press is to the readers, who, in the sniper case, were terrified and desperate for information. To a certain extent, he believed the *Post* had to ignore the authorities. While granting them a role, he differentiated it from that of the press. Indeed, in his view, not reporting on the snipers would not diminish them as a factor. He concluded by pointing out that many police were not at all perturbed by what the paper had published. Proof for this evidently comes from the fact that someone among the police was the source of the information, providing the information used by the press. Sari Horwitz,[15] Pulitzer Prize–winning journalist and co-

---

15. Sari Horwitz, a graduate of Bryn Mawr, moved to Washington, D.C., in 1979 to become a reporter. She worked for *Congressional Quarterly* magazine for three years before attending graduate school in Oxford, England. She became an intern at the *Post* in 1984. At the *Post*, Horwitz started on the Business page before moving to Metro staff. She wanted to be a police reporter and began by covering cops and courts in Montgomery County, Md. She then moved to D.C. and did the night police beat, which she cites as her greatest challenge. In 2006, Horwitz joined

author with Ruane of *Sniper: Inside the Hunt for the Killers Who Terrorized the Nation*, generally held the same views, and asserted that the controversy over press independence is deeply rooted. Fellow *Post* reporter and highly experienced investigative reporter Serge Kovaleski held a similar view and noted that he had repeatedly seen the same controversy. Unsurprisingly, according to one cable executive, *Crossfire* personnel, whose show specializes in confrontation, also agreed with the notion of the press's opposition.

If the general principles of the press seemed reasonably clear and consistent enough, this situation produced additional thoughts that many journalists shared. Modifying the viewpoint was that this case involved questions of public safety for individuals who might become targets. With safety at stake, many reporters painstakingly explained how they considered holding back news, especially if the authorities had requested that they do so. No one was more on the hot seat than WUSA's Mike Buchanan, who had first reported the existence of the tarot card and its scrawled messages. Reflecting upon the incident, Buchanan allowed that he had never heard an outburst quite as vociferous as that of Chief Moose at the press conference following his broadcast about the card. Although he has since had second thoughts about this ("let me tell you"), he remains certain that the television station would not have run this scoop had the police objected. When he called to clear release of this information, the Prince George's police public affairs officer obviously knew Buchanan had the scoop, because he had a prepared statement that the police would not comment on any evidence. Why would he have a prepared statement had he not known of the leak? Further, the official averred that because he had the prepared statement, the chief would not need to be called. It was the decision of police in Prince George's not to send the query to Montgomery County and thus to the Task Force and Chief Moose. Thus did Buchanan believe that he and the station had not been denied use of the item about the card, and that they had hardly just blundered ahead, but actually proceeded with caution and careful adherence to the unspoken rules for confirming source information with officials in such a situation. Furthermore, since the words were wrong, the code had not been broken.

---

the investigations unit of the paper. She has won two Pulitzer Prizes, one for investigative reporting and one for public service. She is the co-author of the book *Sniper: Inside the Hunt for the Killers Who Terrorized the Nation*. (Sources: Horwitz interview; *Washington Post* website, http://projects.washingtonpost.com/staff/articles/sari+horwitz/.)

In this view, Moose's intemperate remarks had been created by those police officers who studied the sniper's psychological profile and worried that the sniper might react badly if he believed the police had broken faith. Nonetheless, the public did not see it this way, as over one thousand phone calls of protest flooded into the station. Buchanan stated that some people wished to lynch them. Nonetheless, there was no discussion of an apology, although the station's management did become nervous.

Others also believed that the freedom to publish had to be balanced by public safety. Despite her pride over confirming the tarot card story, Jamie Stockwell was also concerned. She wondered if the *Post* had been the first to get the story, would the paper have run it. "We discussed this at the paper and concluded that we were going to put out the most information possible," she said. Upon further reflection, she added that in her view this airing of information could only do good, "for the most part, at least." Doubts plagued her as she realized that she did not want to be responsible for something evil. She concluded this discussion of conflicting pressures by noting that to put out a "nugget" could overwhelm the desire to hold back. Still, if it might be important for the police to assert that only the killer know a certain detail, she always held back. And so in fact she did in this case, for until the capture of the snipers she did not share the precise wording on the tarot card.

Many other journalists argued that they would have held back if danger to the public accompanied the scoop. Richmond editor Andy Taylor said that they decided to pursue information aggressively, but would not publish it if it put someone at risk. Matt Ackland at FOX TV news felt the same way. Steve Eldridge, of WTOP, said that they often held back when it might "burn" the source or impede the investigation. Likewise, according to Keith McAllister at CNN, they knew but held back all the details of the aerial surveillance because these could have provided the assailants with too much useful information. Restraint was commonplace among those covering the sniper story.

Restraint might blend into active cooperation with the police, as it did in the case of WTOP reporter Kristi King. On the night of the Home Depot shooting, she broadcast an interview with a woman who had seen a white van zipping down the road. An hour later, the Task Force called the station wanting her tape. King met them on the scene but did not know the specific address of the person she had taped. As King recalled, the agents were serious and grave, peppering her with questions. She was worried that she was in trouble. They became less upset when she gave them the tape. After the Conrad Johnson shooting on October 22, she also provided information to the police.

Reinforcing these recollections of deference to authority was an account of cooperation provided by Fairfax County Public Schools' public information officer, Kitty Porterfield.[16] When the shootings first broke out, Porterfield immediately believed that the best defense was to keep the schools out of the paper as much as possible. Even though she believed that Fairfax County's schools had an excellent reputation for cooperating with the press, they made it a policy not to discuss their response to the sniper. She called the ten or so reporters whose beat was the school system and asked them not to discuss the school system in relation to the sniper. While they continued to telephone her to see if the ban would be lifted, that was the limit of their entire response. When the press covered the effort to move athletic contests out of the region for safety purposes, the decision was amended because sports reporters had not been included in the request, and they were given direct access to athletic directors, who told them the news. According to Colin McNamara of the Marshall Road Elementary School, only one photographer managed to slip into a school and stoutly resisted Porterfield's request not to publish the pictures. But when later asked if the agreement had held, Porterfield believed that the press essentially decided to hold off coverage because the school system had argued on the grounds of safety.

Another factor that emerged that may have reinforced boldness, even as the continuing shootings caused reporters to question their actions, was a general hostility to Chief Moose for his management of the Task Force and its relationship with the media. WJLA reporter Gail Pennybacker, judicious in her opinions, tried to excuse Moose by pointing out the difficult task he faced, but she nonetheless noted that he was

16. Kitty Porterfield was a director for community relations programs in public school districts in Northern Virginia for almost thirty years before establishing her company, Porterfield & Carnes Communications. She was with the Fairfax County Public Schools at the time of the sniper incident. Porterfield, a graduate of Radcliffe College with a government degree, has received several awards for her work. In addition to being recognized by the U.S. Departments of Education and Homeland Security, she is the recipient of the 2004 Gold Medallion and the 2007 Mariner Award for Exceptional Leadership. Porterfield has written articles about education and has presented at numerous conferences. She is co-author of the book *Why School Communication Matters: Strategies from PR Professionals.* (Source: Porterfield & Carnes Communications website, http://porterfieldandcarnes.com/?page_id=2.)

among those police officials who neither understood nor liked the media. He was predisposed not to appreciate the press. According to Pennybacker, even other police officers felt he had hurt himself by appearing too often and saying too little. Editor Andy Taylor also believed that police in his town of Richmond felt that Moose, along with the FBI in Rockville, were handling the investigation poorly. WTOP news director Mike McMearty likewise faulted Moose for his inaccessibility.

Most critical was the *Times-Dispatch*'s Mark Holmberg, who deemed Moose exceptionally weak. Witness to much detective work, Holmberg reacted strongly to Moose: "This ain't getting it." He blamed Moose, as well as the Task Force, for the intense damage done to the investigation by focusing for too long and too exclusively on the white panel truck. Not far behind in disdain for the chief was Holmberg's Northern Virginia colleague Paul Bradley. Bradley insisted that people rolled their eyes when Moose spoke because he appeared as a public face who probably did not know what was going on. The press was skeptical about him, not so much because of his manner, but because he refused to share so much as a "tidbit" with reporters. Perhaps he did not know anything. He failed miserably to understand that the press had a job to do but its members could be mollified by a little information, without showing all the cards. While Mike McMearty suggested that Moose was either a "genius" or a "buffoon," he noted that most all newspeople had concluded it was the latter.

An exception to this hostile reception was the reaction of WJLA producer Rebecca Miller. She had a completely different interpretation of the news conferences, focusing on their frequency rather than their vacuous nature. By coming before the press so often, Moose kept the story alive. In Miller's estimation, this was a good move. Further, she took an opposite approach from that of her peers by saying that the press should not solve the crime. A reporter who discovers a piece of evidence should tell the police, not the audience, she said. Because the sniper case was a major crime, public safety should come first.

Even if one sees Miller's opinion as an outlying one, the different impulses regarding the relationship between the media and police created a swirl of competing values around which each news outlet had to navigate. Summarizing the most commonly held viewpoint–the advocacy of journalistic independence in publishing as long as it does not directly raise safety issues, and the conviction that Chief Moose's performance was unimpressive–raises questions: Did journalists follow behaviors during the sniper case that were different from the media's abstract stand about defending but not endangering the public? Were their actions closer to the harsher views expressed by a few, of their being consciously opposed to authorities? While it may be likely that they did go toward this more challenging direction, it probably did not change their overall position regarding public safety and their not acting to endanger anyone. It seems that it was their lack of confidence in Moose that influenced this shift, rather than any systematic repositioning of them as antiestablishment. As Andy Taylor said, a lot of police agreed with the journalists.

• • •

Stockwell's activities during and after the Tasker shooting also reveal the role of leaks from the police, which should be considered to explain what the media were doing. And these leaks additionally require examination because they provide another perspective on the relationship between the press and the police. The relative silence of the press conferences in Rockville, as Moose sought to tightly control the outflow of any information, virtually guaranteed that if newsworthy items were to be published or broadcast they would have to come from leaks. But why did the police talk to the media? After all, people in the media were themselves wondering how far to go in publishing confidential information. And, in principle, the police, far more hierarchical than the press, should be following their own commander's rules about the nondisclosure of evidence.

Leaks of this nature are a vexed question. Many reporters who wrote stories did not depend on leaks to inform them. Instead, they used information available to the public or they simply interviewed witnesses. But it is true that the larger number of reporters relied upon "sources." The goal here is uncovering why some sources became "leakers" of information that the Task Force wanted to keep secret. Most insiders gave the same general answer. First, some police leak "forbidden" information either because they want it to circulate or because they want to elevate their own significance. They give it to the specific reporters who receive it for a number of reasons, but those of trust, respect, or friendship predominate. Perhaps the best way to illustrate and illuminate the circumstances in which this interaction occurs is to follow several examples.

The *Post*'s Jamie Stockwell gave excellent examples. According to Stockwell, whose family has worked in law enforcement as well, sources talk because they have information and they know that knowledge is power. In part, she sees it as an exercise in masculinity, as she has described their attitude: "I am the man. I have information and can make your day." This is an extension of the power they exercise every day. Seeing a story they inspired makes them feel great.

Yet, according to Stockwell, convincing the source to speak requires, at bottom, a level of trust between the reporter and the source. She hung out at the police lodge and drank beers with the officers. Relating to them was very important in creating that trust. Also important was how the reporter asked the questions: "So what's going on up there? What kind of stuff do you have that no one is interested in?" Seemingly, for Stockwell, equal association, being a confidante, is important. Indeed, the officer who was forthcoming on the tarot card explicitly told her that friendship with her was the reason for his divulging that detail.

Sari Horwitz stressed some of the same themes in her description of how she relied on sources. Horwitz, a long-time investigative reporter for the *Post,* started as a D.C. reporter. A very early experience taught her the need for being "thoroughly sourced." When she was sent out to cover a drowning, the officer on the scene announced to her that he did not speak with reporters. Returning to the paper, she had to tell her editor that she had learned nothing. Simultaneously, she vowed that that would never happen again.

Horwitz first got to know every part of the D.C. police department. She, like Stockwell, hung out at the Fraternal Order of Police and took officers to lunch and dinner. She asked them about their work, attended funerals, actually went through the course work at the Police Academy, and hung around the courthouse while officers were waiting to be called to testify. She accompanied them on police patrols. Although she consciously made every attempt to avoid flirtation, she described getting a source to talk as a "seduction" of a source. The source talks and the journalist promises to do right by the source. This bargain can take time, and Horwitz avoided pressure. In her view, the journalist has to accept that some sources won't talk.

All such groundwork paid off when reporters ran into the stone wall erected by Chief Moose and the Task Force. The basis for leaks in part was that many police officers did not like the way the investigation was going and were looking for reporters to whom they could express themselves. Although Horwitz was assigned to the case only after it was far along, she threw herself into finding out about the letter left at Ashland by the snipers. She put out feelers to many police officers that she knew and met them in out-of-the-way places, so they would be more comfortable. Horwitz worked the phones relentlessly, "groveling" and "begging," as she put it. Finally, one source called and gave her some points that the letter covered. This source provided the information because he trusted her from the past and knew that she would not reveal his identity. Also, both he and she knew that the information she was receiving would not hurt the investigation in any way, so the *Post* published it. Once she had these opening details, more information could be gleaned from others.

Horwitz found one more big leak on the day of the arrest. Metro editor Jo-Ann Armao wanted a copy of the Ashland letter. Horwitz thought this impossible but asked her major source, who late that evening replied that this was unlikely. Since Horwitz was leaving town the next day, she told her source that she needed the letter by that morning or it would be too late. Caving completely, her source agreed to meet her, but warned there would be no conversation, and no hug either.

Horwitz's description parallels that of Stockwell's: police want to talk to reporters with whom they have a relationship and whom they believe they can trust not to betray them. The next two cases, both involving male reporters, show a similar but slightly different pattern, with gender as an important factor. Reporters Serge Kovaleski (the *Post*) and Mark Holmberg (*Richmond Times-Dispatch*) agreed with Stockwell and Horwitz about why sources talk, but how they went about obtaining information varied considerably.

Holmberg believes that wandering the city and learning its street people, including drug dealers, have been central to his success. At times, he has arrived at crime scenes even before the police. The police like, respect, and fear him, but he emphasizes the last two points. In his

Sari Horwitz covered the story and later co-wrote, with Michael Ruane, a book-length account of the Sniper event. (Photo taken by the *Washington Post*)

words, they fear him because they know they cannot "snowball me." He said he knows more about crimes than the police do because many in poor black neighborhoods are willing to talk to him but not to the police. In the fairly clean-cut news world of Richmond, Holmberg stands out for his six-foot-seven frame and his unkempt long hair and casual dress. Appearing to be a "renegade" can earn credibility. He said he thinks that the police trust him because he tells the truth and that he is not out just to get a "pelt" for the good of the story. Likewise, like Kovaleski, a personal relationship is not very important and is at best implicit. Rather, sources talk because they believe in the reporter's ability to use the material. In particular, he believes they have to believe that the journalist will be true to the information.

The similarities among these four journalists clearly indicate motives for leaking and the important role of the journalist. Trust comes first and foremost. The one disagreement is the nature of the connection between the source and the journalist, with the two women emphasizing a personal relationship, while the men focus on some version of the reporter's credibility. Horwitz's view that a man in her position would behave differently somewhat supports this notion of difference. Also, FOX TV reporter Matt Ackland argued that some options are open to women only. This difference seems somewhat plausible, as it might signal gender differences in relating to sources, which in this case and many others were predominantly male.

Still this is a very sensitive area for some, because it can be twisted into the traditional charges that women use feminine wiles to advance their work or themselves. It is worth scrutinizing more closely how it is that the situation itself is sexist. Women may act differently because of different options open to men and women. Put another way, they may have to conform to the situation that presents itself. In this case, in particular, the sources were male. Their trusting a male reporter might depend on his embodying competence, while their trusting a woman journalist might require her to show friendliness. Thus it is that circumstances can dictate women's options more than the other way around. Furthermore, these differences may in large part reflect how male and female reporters viewed themselves more so than what they actually did. Thus, the male reporters' view of the authority they exuded may not have been a view that was shared by those leaking items to them. That these are merely the observations of a small group of reporters makes these assertions extremely tenuous. Yet the difficulty of convincing anyone to discuss in detail these methods makes these observations worth pondering. Essentially, these are secret strategies to get secrets. Yet with such limited conclusions, this section must point to the need for further inquiry.

Yet another element of Stockwell's experiences during the shooting at Tasker demands examination. It was there that she began to experience a substantial level of fear, a feeling that engulfed most of the journalistic community. To witness and at least partly understand the source of this fear is important because it may well relate to the important role that fear played in the press. Nonetheless, this question needs to be fully considered in the final chapter along with other factors. In part, such scrutiny seems necessary because in almost every case frightened journalists claimed they were successful in filtering out their own fear from the accounts they presented. The connection thus between personal sentiment and media content cannot be understood in any easy, one-to-one connection.

Striking in its intensity, however, was the reaction of radio reporter Kristi King when she journeyed to the October 3 shooting of cab driver Premkumar Walekar, who had been struck down while pumping gas at a Mobil station in Aspen Hill. When King arrived, having been diverted from another story, it was unclear what was transpiring. Detained on the other side of the street along with a group of bystanders, King depended on the police to tell her what was happening. Approaching a female officer who was "practically sobbing," King learned that the victim was dead and that another murder had occurred elsewhere. This was the first time that King learned the event included multiple shootings, and the "horror" of it fell like a "rock in my stomach." Simultaneously, her husband sent her a text message that he had seen her on CNN, and he told her to get her head down. Although she was able to move closer to the crime scene, and could have taken some pictures, the splattered blood there deterred her. She knew she must remain calm on the air. While she thought that sometimes journalists disassociated themselves from victims to retain some composure, King found this amazingly hard on that day. All that anxiety inflected her reporting of the suspected white van as she mentioned it on the air. People might feel safe when they did not see a white van. Such a report might help when people were feeling so powerless.

Thus, right from the beginning, King witnessed and reacted to both the disaster visiting the community and families as well as to her own personal vulnerability. Elements of both these views emerged for many journalists, with Mark Holmberg as the exception. He said he saw relatively little fear in the public or in himself. Nonetheless, some reporters connected their anxiety to their personal place in the community. For example, seeing people go inside the station as their gas was being pumped gave Paul Bradley considerable pause. And members of the *Nightline* staff (Chris Bury, John Donvan, Lisa Koenig, Elissa Rubin, and Madhulika Sikka) seriously discussed how not to become paralyzed by the situation. Their concern also focused on the daily problems of picking up children and the effects on the neighborhood. They hated to tell their children about their own personal worry. Although he felt no personal fear, Mike Buchanan anguished about people hiding behind cars and kids running into their houses. He believed that with all that had happened in the Washington area during the preceding year, in 2001, children had seen too much. Tom Kapsidelis also sympathized with the anxieties that the Richmond area experienced.

Many journalists felt considerable personal fear. Investigative reporter Serge Kovaleski, even though steeled by having interviewed Colombian drug lords in their lairs, still worried. As he noted, his spouse (also a *Post* reporter) and he took an alternate, less vulnerable, walk home when going to and from work. Sometimes they hailed a cab. Smoking in front of the *Post* building came to be seen as dangerous. And he was also concerned for his parents, who had just moved into the area. He simply felt that, given the gaze of the killer, writing on the story made one more vulnerable. And Stockwell worried to herself what a great coup it would be for the sniper to drive by Task Force headquarters and gun down a bevy of journalists. Likewise, Kiran Krishnamurthy tried to avoid standing under bright neon lights when it was not absolutely necessary. While he did not feel that the crime scene itself was a particular target, because the police were all around, Matt Ackland certainly found the scenes disquieting. Finally, Gail Pennybacker was upset and felt more exposed to the shooter when an announcer made clear where Gail's neighborhood was.

Underlying these fears was, according to Michael Ruane, a general atmosphere that reinforced them. That was the usually unspoken truth of journalism, that reporters work in dangerous neighborhoods and in circumstances in which they must ask difficult questions. For example, mourners at funerals sometimes become angry, feeling that reporters are intruders. Once Ruane was escorted out of a funeral parlor in just such circumstances. Such frequently fraught circumstances may have helped to set off alarm bells whenever a journalist confronted particularly problematic situations.

•  •  •

For nearly two weeks after Chief Moose's eventful press conference about the revelation of the tarot card, Jamie Stockwell endured being a part of the backwater of the story. Assigned to police headquarters, or "Camp Rockville," as it came to be known, she was far from the shootings that occurred in Virginia and close to many, many press conferences in which very little of importance was said. Indeed, stationed there with another colleague, she found they tended to duplicate each other's work. Essentially, Stockwell's job was to attend the news conferences, which she recorded. But so did her colleague, as well as the reporters from television and radio. Beyond this, newspeople elsewhere, including other *Post* reporters, unearthed information, and she tried to use her sources to confirm or deny it.

The press conferences in particular proved exercises in frustration. Because of the large number of journalists there (around thirteen hundred press badges were issued), a carnival-like quality reigned. Only the louder questioners got answers. Whenever the famous television personalities, such as Wolf Blitzer and Katie Couric,[17] were in attendance, a huge team accompanied them that could dominate the session. Moose, however, would not say anything of substance during the question-and-answer periods, and reporters found this frightening as well as problematic. Stockwell believed that these news conferences were designed to reassure viewers. The best channel for her was to speak with the retinue that stood behind Chief Moose, including people from the FBI, the Alcohol, Tobacco and Firearms Bureau, and the offices of local government leaders. She found that, at the least, they might confirm material that she had already learned.

Still, Stockwell was working her sources. The only bathrooms available were actually in the building where the Task Force was housed.

17. Katie Couric, the first female solo anchor of a weekday network evening news broadcast, joined CBS in 2006. She is currently the anchor and managing editor of the *CBS Evening News with Katie Couric*. She is also a correspondent for *60 Minutes* and anchors primetime specials for CBS News. Prior to moving to CBS, Couric spent fifteen years as a co-anchor of *Today* on NBC. (Source: CBS News website, http://www.cbsnews.com/stories/2006/07/06/eveningnews/bios/main17 81520.shtml.)

Using those visits as an excuse, she sometimes milled about inside hoping for information. And, not surprisingly, she used her cell phone and spoke as often as possible with those who might be able to assist her. She also met sources, customarily just down the road, away from the teeming press corps. However, despite her best efforts, she became, in her own words, "a bit player."

Press conferences and contacting sources did not fill up the many hours spent at Camp Rockville. In bad weather, she had to sit in her car. When the weather was good, Stockwell had a chair and would spend time reading and talking with local television and print reporters as well as a few out-of-town journalists. Although they certainly did not share scoops, they did help each other write background information, especially if the other reporter was not "too rude." They also spent time speculating about the case. And, as a group, they had dismissed the white van theory.

Paul Bradley remembered Camp Rockville similarly in many respects, but not completely. Like Stockwell, he found information difficult to obtain, and he described it as being in a bubble outside the information loop. Every question Moose took he could not discuss. Unlike Stockwell, Bradley had no Maryland sources, and many of his Virginia sources were far from the action. The only way an outsider could break out of this, in his opinion, was to be from a prestigious outlet such as the *New York Times*, the *Post*, or the television networks. Bradley thought that the calls from their reporters were returned when his were not. This differed from Stockwell's perception, and it also suggests that leakers may have responded simply to the status of the publication rather than to the particular reporters, as most of my evidence indicates. Bradley's social experiences resembled Stockwell's in that both found an amiable community of journalists.

But the atmosphere of Camp Rockville and the Task Force did produce another result: a substantial reliance on criminal profilers. The paucity of information and the reluctance of officials led journalists and editors to turn to outside experts to throw light on the subject. *Today, Nightline,* and the *Richmond Times-Dispatch* all used profilers in order to try to understand the shooter's actions, and in particular, his silence.

Every journalist interviewed for this study attempted to use screening in order to find the most responsible and capable profiler. *Nightline* producer Tom Bettag stated that his show sought the most conservative and cautious. In particular, it searched for those who would not cast the story in shades of black and white: they looked for those who preferred ambiguity and who would admit to ignorance on some subjects. The *Post*'s Serge Kovaleski carefully evaluated profilers by comparing what was known to their pronouncements and eschewing the most flamboyant. He also searched for those with large case experience with excellent credentials, including work with the police. Likewise, Kiran Krishnamurthy of the *Times-Dispatch,* who was very careful, tended to interview profilers over the phone. Relying more on those who had helped him in the past, perhaps those who had been generous with their own time, the reporter sought help with understanding the case.

Even allowing that many or most journalists generally tried to vet profilers thoughtfully, this proved to be a somewhat risky enterprise. First, the net often had to be cast fairly indiscriminately. Krishnamurthy and the *Post*'s Michael Ruane used the Internet service "Prof.net" to gather such experts. After putting in search criteria, the journalists received a list of possibilities. They could call experts from this list and use the ones who could be reached. Like the other journalists cited above, they had to decide about using the information they received. Ruane noted that this was no perfect science; one chose based on a "gut feeling." Thus, at times, possibly many times, the press relied on experts with whom they were scarcely familiar.

Complicating this entire problem of dealing with profilers was a shortage of them. One of the most prolific of all, James Alan Fox, a professor at Northeastern University, noted that he worked for NBC. Because of the shortage of individuals specializing in that kind of serial murder, the networks tried to buy up all "the talent." And only a few could present their views well. Indeed, as Serge Kovaleski noted, he used profiler Clint Van Zandt because the latter could be pithy without sensationalizing. Surely, this lack of choice strained the system.

While Clint Van Zandt and James Alan Fox reported that they prepared themselves thoroughly for such presentations, working with the media is very difficult. Experts mostly answered a lot of questions in a short period. Krishnamurthy noted that he usually spoke with his respondents for fifteen minutes. For television, this situation became even more problematic because, in most cases, profilers were either live or "live to tape," which, though recorded and replayed, still relied on impromptu remarks from the experts. In this situation even the most conscientious profilers cannot be at their best. Clint Van Zandt regretted such circumstances and the general media use of profilers. In particular, he believed there was too much coverage, and that the white van theory was wrong. He even called analyst Jerry Nachman to say that he was going to quit commenting on this case. As Van Zandt recalled, "Jerry told me that you can get out if you want, but worse people will be doing it. I had to think about that." And so Van Zandt continued to participate fully. Yet one additional factor may have made using profilers especially problematic. Although NBC was evidently paying Fox, profilers in general spoke without compensation to media, in order to publicize their skills to private, paying clients. Such a system might well give incentive to say something splashy and memorable.

However, one might counter these concerns about profilers by noting that their relationship to reporters parallels that which journalists have with all their sources. In dealing with experts under these circumstances, reporters become more dependent on profiler availability and their special information. In this way, profilers had greater access to print than did most criminal experts. And perhaps because of the silence of the police, some profilers overstayed their welcome.

For Stockwell, outside experts were neither her opportunity nor her problem. Instead, it was boredom, and she recalls the days at Camp Rockville as decidedly dull. Poignantly punctuating her long stretch of days at Camp Rockville was the evening shooting of Linda Franklin at Home Depot in Falls Church, Virginia. It coincided with Stockwell's own birthday. She felt depressed that this horrible event was linked to her birthday. Also, she called a friend who had family members in the Washington area to make sure everyone was alright. This entire incident reinforced for Stockwell that she was not the "invincible journalist" she had imagined herself to be. She found it all "scary." And the resultant activity kept her at Task Force headquarters, so she did not return home until 2 a.m. Still, for her, the basic routine continued to grind on for several more days. Because her editors were calling every half-hour to check on various items, she found concentration difficult. She dug out a few little nuggets from the Task Force about its functioning and its pursuit of various suspects, but she mainly found herself waiting for the end of the ordeal. On reflection, she found it more stressful than the attack on the Pentagon a year earlier had been.

Others, well away from Stockwell, were checking out the crime scenes from the Tasker shooting right up to the endgame. On the night of October 19, the night of the Ashland shooting, FOX News reporter Matt Ackland covered the police as traffic was stopped and people were pulled out of their cars to face officers with guns drawn. Days earlier, Jeremy Redmon of the Richmond paper had traveled from Richmond up Interstate 95 interviewing people at gas stations near the highway about their level of fear. And, according to Andy Taylor, it was the *Times-Dispatch* that broke the news of a telephone communication between one of the snipers and a Catholic priest as Muhammad and Malvo sought to open channels between themselves and officials. Although Paul Bradley, like Stockwell, was in Rockville, he often was responsible for working with the paper's team of reporters and writing the general story for the paper. And there also was WJLA's Gail Pennybacker, rushing to the scene of the October 11 Kenneth Bridges shooting in a Massaponax gas station just off Interstate 95. On the way down, she was talking on two phones—on one, delivering the news she was witnessing about the traffic stops conducted by police, and on the other, calling sources to find out what was happening elsewhere. Other reporters were feeding her information. Meanwhile, her cameraman, Marty Doane, was cutting through back roads to arrive at the same scene. For an hour he taped the scene, before a satellite truck arrived to send the tapes.

Left out of the action on some occasions, Stockwell exemplified what occurred to every journalist interviewed for this account—they did not constantly remain in the bull's eye of activity. It was tedious or frustrating that the story just became too big and frenetic for one individual to take it all in. Someone had to cover unpromising leads. However, as the trail of activity returned to Maryland with the last shooting and the capture of the snipers, Stockwell was abruptly shaken out of her routine.

Early in the morning of October 22 Stockwell's phone rang. Bus driver Conrad Johnson had been shot. Her editors wanted her to interview some firefighters around the scene, and gave her directions on how to avoid the roadblocks and arrive as quickly as possible. Showing up at 7:15, she spent the day knocking on doors and doggedly digging up details. Her big success lay in speaking to a source who described the turmoil within the Task Force, which became the basis for a story that she completed. By 10:30 p.m., when she requested additional directions, the editors sent her home.

The next morning at Camp Rockville dawned just the same, but Jamie Stockwell was wondering all the more when this ordeal would end. Although not a religious person, she found herself praying for an arrest. Was it some "guy" or just a "kid on a bike"? But nothing occurred to answer her prayers until the late afternoon. When the late afternoon press conference was cancelled because of new developments in the case, Stockwell, along with the rest of the press corps, began to worry about what was happening. Shortly thereafter, the reporters began to receive tips that Malvo and Muhammad were the snipers and that a monitor showed federal agents pursuing clues in Seattle. But no news was immediately to be had and Stockwell accompanied colleagues to a barbecue restaurant. Later that evening, Chief Moose presented a cryptic news conference. Reporters then discovered, and released, the license plate numbers heard over the police radio. Stockwell went home at 2 a.m.

In the middle of the night, acting on a sighting of the car by the public, the police arrested the snipers near Frederick, Maryland. The *Post* editors decided to send Chris Davenport,[18] Stockwell's partner at Camp Rockville, to the scene. Later, when she learned of this posting, Stockwell felt jealous that she had not received the assignment. At 6 in the morning, however, Stockwell received a call which directed her to Rockville to gather all the information they would need. She rapidly took down the list of what she would need: a reconstruction of the sequence of events; the way they had identified Muhammad; the context of the letter; what happened during the two hours it took for the arrest; the issue of what vehicle had been involved in the shootings; run-ins in Baltimore; Muhammad's motivation; and more. At the same time, she was "so happy." She assumed that they had the right people, and, somewhat relieved, she reflected on the beautiful colors of autumn. It was over.

Stockwell spent most of October 24 wrapping up the details. She was working in a madhouse, as the electronic media were frantically trying to learn whether the two men arrested were merely suspects or the actual culprits. Gradually, they all decided the latter. A *Times-Dispatch* reporter was amazed at the resources that the network people could bring to dig up information and finalize a story. Because Frank Green and the print journalists had a later deadline, they were trying to put together the kind of comprehensive account that Stockwell had previously outlined. In fact, she was busy working the scene and talking

18. Chris Davenport graduated from Colby College in 1995. He was a staff writer for the *Post* and won a 2007 Alicia Patterson Journalism Fellowship for his piece "Soldier-Citizens: How the Army National Guard and Reserves are Adjusting to Life after the War." (Sources: Alicia Patterson Foundation website, http://www.aliciapatterson.org/APF_Fellows/2007/APF_Fellows2007.html; Colby University website, http://www.colby.edu/colby.mag/issues/win03/alumni/9599.shtml.)

to all the sources that she could. She was "disgusted" by the press conference, where all the officials turned up to take the credit and pat themselves on the back. Finally, though, it was over, and Jamie Stockwell went back to her beat at Prince George's County, where lots of stories needed to be written up. Interestingly, many murders had occurred while she was away.

Following Jamie Stockwell for three weeks permits a close view of the experience of one journalist. In the end, it also indicates that the *Post* editors gave much more direction than usual during this period. Interpreting the instructions that she had been given, she found herself with assignments more often than not. And, through her, we see many of the general issues raised as this investigation was pursued through a number of outlets. Moreover, one must conclude that a more comprehensive look might illuminate complexities that this initial survey of this topic could not. With thirteen hundred reporters registered with the police, and possibly two thousand altogether, it escapes the ability of any one researcher to understand this enormous "beast," as many refer to journalists working in packs. A close study doubtless would produce more nuances and further divisions within the press than this analysis, which has tended to reveal its overall contours. Nonetheless, however tentatively, this chapter has laid a background for understanding why the press reported as it did–a subject to be further addressed in the concluding chapter.

In short, then, the sniper coverage of fear seems not to have come from any political views or any conscious embrace of sensationalism, as their self-reporting of motives points repeatedly to the desire to seek out information. Routinization and tedium may have dampened enthusiasm, but, in this story, news organizations' high focus probably encouraged activity. One should look more to their passion for reporting and to the competitiveness which Stockwell and others exhibited. Getting leaks and scoops were very important. Plus scorn for the police emboldened some. Overall, the press's view of its task overwhelmingly motivates staff but does not lead directly to deliberate, intentional sensationalism. Only the fear of being a target seems directly and indubitably related to this type of reporting. Further reflections in the conclusion will help us see the connection between the journalists' attitudes and their reporting.

## The Schools and the Sniper

Other than law enforcement and the media, no institution within the affected area had to deal more with the impact of the snipers than did the public school systems. Because schools are entrusted with the safety and security of students, the officials who manage them had to, in these circumstances, consider the shootings and all their implications for the safety and well-being of the students and the school employees. Moreover, from the beginning, the Montgomery County authorities noted the safety of the schools as a bellwether of the general climate of the area. Further pushing educational institutions to the forefront were the actions of the snipers. Their action on October 7, still fairly early in the episode, to target thirteen-year-old Iran Brown as he entered Benjamin Tasker Middle School focused attention on area schools. Also, the messages left at the Ponderosa on October 19 and in the days after contained specific threats against children.

What role can a study of the school system and the sniper play in a book on the media? In understanding how schools operated in these times, one may discern somewhat independently of the press how an important segment of society functioned in this period. If one considers the school system to include the staff, parents, and students, the schools can be seen as a significant institution during this period.

Moreover, the schools supply this study a much-needed alternate vision of the sniper. This allows us to begin to evaluate comparatively the viewpoint taken by the media. For example, if the press's construction of the story emphasized fear and panic but the schools adopted a less-anxious attitude, that would provide a comparison with the rhetorical stance adopted by the media. If the chronological frameworks of important events vary, that may also help us understand the activities of the press.

In addition, the schools offer a particularly interesting alternate vision beyond their mere size. First, it is reasonable to conjecture that they would be among the most conservative of organizations when it comes to exposing individuals to dangerous situations or putting safety in jeopardy. Schools both act and are seen as a safe haven in our society, so one might hypothesize that these systems would take the snipers' threats and actions very seriously and act in the most cautious manner.

Reasonably, one might object that the schools, while having to deal with the sniper, did not need to–and, in fact, very seldom did–explicitly formulate an image of the shootings and the attendant set of events. While this is true, school administrators, in reacting to the crises, had to evaluate the threat posed by the sniper. Estimating the schools' viewpoint by using their actions is not easy and is speculative, but it has the advantage that this view can emerge even without the schools responding to questions specifically about the shootings. When a researcher queries a subject, the answer is always conditioned by the relationship between researcher and responder. In the case of the sniper, questions answered after the events are often erroneously inflected by the spate of information that has come out since the arrest, including several trials. By focusing not on the sniper but on the actions in the schools during that time of crisis, this project can avoid a picture unduly influenced by emotions and discussions subsequent to the event. Thus, we can learn more about how educators behaved and reacted than about what they thought of the sniper. That information allows a circumstantial, and somewhat believable, depiction of the sniper as perceived by the schools.

One last question must be considered, and that is whether, as the vast majority of administrators, teachers, and parents read or watched the media coverage of the sniper events, could the views they formed about the sniper in the arena of the schools be really separated from those views expressed by the media. First, the schools relied on a wide range of sources beyond newspapers and television–the police, school security, plus their own independent connections to the community. Second, as will become apparent in the account that follows, much of what schools did was related to their own internal procedures and mechanics of crisis management. It would seem that, while never distant from the press, schools were hardly transparent conduits for information gleaned from daily and weekly publications.

To track the schools' activities, I selected three very large districts which felt first-hand the impact of the shootings–Fairfax (Va.), Montgomery (Md.), and Prince George's (Md.), the school systems of the counties that ring the District of Columbia. All three are among the top-twenty in size in the nation, collectively serving over 430,000 students. Furthermore, the Montgomery County Public Schools were the first and most heavily impacted, while the Prince George's system was the only one in which a student was shot. Fairfax County, Virginia, also was the scene of a shooting, and the Fairfax County Public Schools thus also became very much caught up in the difficulties that gripped the region. Press reports of the actions of the schools allowed me to supplement their own reports to see how these three systems reacted.

The first and most obvious thing about studying these three systems was the general similarities in their responses. While teleconferences and close personal relationships worked to keep these three systems in harmony, it was, I would contend, shared principles that created coherence, even though some differences did emerge. This general unity permits a more streamlined narrative, as this study does not have to pursue three entirely different stories.

Surveying these largely shared approaches, this chapter focuses mainly on the Montgomery County Public Schools (MCPS), and adds information from the other systems either to amplify or to show differences between the positions taken by the schools in Montgomery County and those taken in Fairfax and Prince George's counties. That both the first and last shootings occurred in Montgomery County further allows us to privilege its experience. Also of importance is the fact that the MCPS school system has retained an extraordinary written record of its activities. In particular, Superintendent Jerry Weast, as a management tool to understand and thus improve the decision-making process, added a "scribe" to the crisis team, who kept the minutes of that group's daily morning meetings. Although not verbatim, these reports appear to summarize substantially what occurred, and I have used them extensively, along with my interviews of the principle actors, to create my narrative here.

Essentially, the sources show school systems balancing between fear and coping. This chapter examines elements that impinged on this balance. First, after the first few attacks began to recede, pressure began to build to put activities, especially athletics, back on track. This effort succeeded to the point that Fairfax County took some risks to start up even outdoor sports and Montgomery was on the verge of doing so. Continued shootings disrupted these plans, and the slaying of bus driver Conrad Johnson set off a new powerful day of jitters. Still, the ambivalence between fear and coping survived. Finally, the balance between high anxiety and a commitment to performance varied according to the risk one faced. As the likelihood rose that an incident would occur in one's domain, caution and concern escalated. Schools with many students and proximity to shootings were a lot more wary than others lacking problematic locations or statistical odds of disaster. The evaluation of all these findings about the schools, in reference to the media, remains the subject of the book's concluding chapter.

On October 3, the day that the rampage became evident to all, Montgomery superintendent Jerry Weast[1] was in a meeting at 9:40 a.m. when one of his security team interrupted to tell him that a shooting, perhaps even two, had occurred. In fact, three shootings had taken place that day, and one had occurred the preceding evening, although it would not be linked to the others until later. Although such violence was unusual in a county where homicide was rare, Weast cautioned himself not to overreact. Already, the residents had lived through the attacks on the World Trade Center and the Pentagon, not to mention the anthrax scare that followed. However, when he heard a rifle had been involved in the shooting, he felt it was time to get going, and get

1. Dr. Jerry Weast has been the superintendent of the Montgomery County Public Schools in Maryland since 1999. He holds two education degrees, one in general administration from Pittsburg State University in Kansas and one in educational administration from Oklahoma State University. Weast has presented at numerous education conferences and seminars over the years, on topics including school reform, early childhood education, community collaboration, and crisis management. He has also presented at international education forums and is the author of myriad articles and reports on education. He is a member of various boards, including the Committee for Economic Development and the Junior Achievement Worldwide Education Group. Weast has received many awards for his work in education. In addition to being named the Maryland Superintendent of the Year in 2003, under his management Montgomery County Public Schools in 2005 received the U.S. Senate / Maryland Productivity Award, and in 2006 were a finalist for the Malcolm Baldrige National Quality Award. Weast has been a superintendent for eight school districts spanning five states for the last thirty years. (Source: MCPS website, http://www.montgomeryschoolsmd.org/departments/ superintendent/ about/biography.shtm.)

going he did. In the next few hours, he assembled a crisis team and began to study the situation. Others brought information on transportation, traffic, and logistics, as he believed coordination with other agencies would be essential. After notification of the third shooting that day, Weast decided to call for Code Blue, or lockdown, as other systems would term it. While there were different versions of what a lockdown included, Weast explained that the initial plan distributed to the schools called for stringent measures: no after-school activities, indoor or out; cancellation of outside recess; and cancellation of transportation to other extracurricular programs. Yet, according to an October 3 e-mail from Brian Porter to the MCPS principals, on that same day, the superintendent also announced that school would open the next day, although under Code Blue restrictions.

Brian Porter, the MCPS press information officer, recalled that, from the first moment, the schools were considering the safety of the students. This thinking clearly governed the cautious actions of the system's leaders, which had been first developed as a response to the Columbine shootings, in Colorado, and had later been honed after the events of September 11, 2001. Nonetheless, the Montgomery administrators kept the schools open at this point, because they did not expect the shootings to continue. Furthermore, the county had a good record of "catching the perps." In addition, according to Porter, the Montgomery system believed it was important for both staff and students to keep a sense of normalcy and routine.

This latter impulse toward normalcy evidently inclined the Montgomery administrators by mid-morning of the next day to allow sports and other activities to resume. In fact, a full slate of sporting events took place Friday night and Saturday. The *Post* thoroughly covered important contests, as the fall season was well underway.

At the same time, the Montgomery schools showed considerable caution. Maryland State Police identified twenty-eight schools in Montgomery County whose locations made them vulnerable to the type of attacks that had transpired. Police officers were detailed to cover all these schools for one hour prior to each school's opening and one hour after its closing. Other school systems likewise were wary. On October 3, the security chief of Benjamin Tasker Middle School in neighboring Prince George's County asked the principal to put that school on Code Blue. Believing a shooting would never happen there, the principal ruled against the recommendation. Across the Potomac, in Fairfax, school officials were concerned by some of the language used by the Maryland authorities. Although the superintendent, Dan Domenech,[2] believed the shootings were still a Maryland problem, he recalled that others were concerned. Most notably, Charles Moose, Montgomery County chief of police, had assured citizens that the schools were safe. Doubtless the chief was well-intentioned, but school administrators in Virginia worried that the shooters might respond to what they saw as a challenge. After subsequent events, many people—and seemingly everyone responsible for schools—came to believe that the snipers' attack on a child was a direct response to Moose's earlier guarantee of school and student safety. Those prescient administrators who made the connection fretted.

There would be plenty to fret about. On Monday morning, October 7, Iran Brown was dropped off by his aunt at Benjamin Tasker at 8:09. As he approached the building, only a few steps from the car, the sniper shot him. As she pulled away, Brown's aunt, a nurse, heard the shot, and she returned for her wounded nephew, who climbed into the car. She sped to nearby Bowie Medical Center, where he was treated and medevaced to Children's Hospital in the District, where he recovered.

Meanwhile, back at Tasker, a teacher who had been arriving at the school had heard the shot and seen the boy fall and then get into the car. Without really knowing exactly what had occurred, she raced to the principal's office, where he was in a staff meeting that had been going on for some time. The group that heard the news was momentarily stunned,

2. Dan Domenech, senior vice-president and head of the Urban Advisory Resource for McGraw-Hill Education, has worked in public education for more than thirty-six years. His most recent position was as superintendent of Fairfax County Public Schools, which he held for six years. Prior to that job, Domenech was district superintendent of the Second Supervisory District of Suffolk County, N.Y., and chief executive officer of the Western Suffolk Board of Cooperative Educational Services. He has held additional superintendent positions in Long Island, N.Y. Domenech earned a PhD from Hofstra University. His first job in education was as a sixth-grade teacher in Queens, N.Y. He has served on several boards for the U.S. Department of Education National Assessment, the Department of Defense schools, the Association for the Advancement of International Education, and the National Urban Alliance. Domenech has also served as president of several organizations, including the New York State Council of School Superintendents and the Suffolk County Superintendents Association, as well as being the original president of the New York State Association for Bilingual Education. He is currently the executive director of the American Association of School Administrators. (Source: AASA website, http://www.aasa.org/content.cfm?ItemNumber=10296.)

and then ran out—all seven of them—to see what had happened. Finding only a book bag with neither victim nor blood, principal John Lloyd recalled that he had called 911 and that a group of police cars had arrived almost immediately. The crime scene quickly was cordoned off.

With the police occupying the front of the building, the school then confronted the first of several problems. Buses and students started arriving but had to be rerouted to another entrance. Lloyd explained that the authorities had to control the situation. Although the students knew something was amiss, because of the altered bus stop and the police presence, the principal kept them in the dark. He arranged the "normal" day as much as possible: sending the children to their customary staging area and then, at 8:45 a.m., on to their first-period classes—except that those in trailers were assigned to the cafeteria.

Both the news media and parents—the latter alerted by the former—started to show up. Administrators turned aside reporters and focused on uniting kids with their parents. Unfortunately, this was not easy. Because the staff meeting had concerned overcrowding and reworking the schedule, at that exact moment the current schedule, with the precise whereabouts of each student, had been deleted. Nonetheless, teachers who had no first-period class acted as runners, and the school delivered the children to worried parents. Many children learned what was happening from teachers or televisions in the classrooms. At ten o'clock that morning, the entire school learned over the public address system that a fellow student had been attacked. Children remained calm, and the pick-up system was orderly. By noon, half were gone. At dismissal, only twenty-one of over thirteen hundred students remained.

Even though John Lloyd and the students sought a kind of eerie calm, the virtually unanimous decision of parents to retrieve their children revealed high anxiety. Such concerns were also felt in neighboring Montgomery County. According to an October 7 e-mail from Brian Porter in the MCPS archive, at first, administrators in Montgomery County did not believe the Tasker shooting to be related to the shootings of the preceding week, but by 9:12 in the morning outdoor activities had been canceled, seemingly as a precaution. Within the hour, however, the system had reverted to the stringent policies of the previous week. Student safety patrols were also withdrawn because of fears about the exposure of these children. Ed Clarke,[3] security chief for

3. Ed Clarke served for more than twenty-four years as a police captain in Montgomery County, Md., and is the former director of the Department of School

Montgomery County, remembers that day as one in which efforts were ratcheted upwards.

New on that day was a significant effort to address the palpable worry that parents were showing. MCPS issued a series of advisories to help students, parents, and staff deal with anxiety. These materials advised everyone to allow the expression of fear, but, most important, they emphasized learning how to cope and helping others cope. Children need reassurance, the circulars reminded adults. The administrators advised the staff that it was up to the police to solve this crime. The schools' job was to attend to academic matters and provide a safe and secure environment.

MCPS superintendent Jerry Weast also became quite exercised as he communicated with his principals. At the 12:30 p.m. staff meeting, he wanted to judge their state of mind to ensure that they followed central directions. As the scribe recorded, Dr. Weast "doesn't want something happening tomorrow and principals not using good judgment or there being inconsistency. He wants everyone to hear everything at the same time—no variances in what people are told." According to the MCPS Timeline of Events, dated October 7, out of this staff meeting came a gathering with the principals in the late afternoon. Although clearly, according to the MCPS minutes, the impetus for this emergency meeting was the fear that permeated the county, Weast and other executives emphasized security. Weast himself concentrated on making it through the ordeal. He promised that he was working on finding out the best way to do this. Then, as the scribe recorded: "The reason we have not closed schools is that we do not want to close down based on fear or for an indefinite period of time, making life more stressful for parents, students, and staff. Schools in this county to date have been very safe." He concluded, "All of you affect the lives of thousands of kids. You must take care of yourselves. A lot of people are looking to you to help them get through this crisis. Think about what you say and how you say it, and carry yourself as a leader and role model to our employees and parents."

A similar balance between fear and coping also characterized the reactions in Fairfax. After the shooting at Benjamin Tasker, Super-

Safety and Security at MCPS. In 2002, during the D.C. sniper case, he was the MCPS liaison to county police and government. He is currently on the School Security Officials Committee for the U.S. Department of Education's Office of Safe and Drug-Free Schools. (Sources: Clarke interview; U.S. Department of Education website, http://www.connectlive.com/events/edschoolsafety/.)

intendent Domenech felt that matters had taken a grave turn. Before, the incidents appeared isolated, but this shooting meant the violence clearly was continuing and this time had involved a student. He felt that a considerable danger existed, and that the shooting announced to his security chief, Fred Ellis,[4] a willingness on the part of the sniper to shoot again. Yet, Fairfax also took action to keep schools open. Profiling the schools, authorities identified thirty-eight that would need extra protection and were to receive additional security. Interestingly, they did not notify principals, so that this news would not be leaked out. In fact, Fairfax was already using the principle, eventually shared by all the systems, that they were in an unwilling dialogue with the shooter or shooters. Anything revealed might be exploited or avenged. Thus, they consciously sought to stay out of the press. And, Ellis later noted that Fairfax County never considered closing schools, because that would have put too great a strain on society. As long as the schools could "reasonably" provide protection, they believed that they had to go forward.

Over the next two weeks, the ambivalent balancing between showing fear and maintaining a cautious pursuit of normal operations continued. Inside the MCPS headquarters, both attitudes were visible. Fear evidenced itself in a number of ways. Within the crisis group, the conversation on October 11, dutifully recorded by Jerry Weast's scribe, turned to the escalation of fear and its possible spread, as well as the almost continuous commitment to some form of Code Blue. The stress on staff and other support personnel seemed, from the point of view of top administrators, to be increasing. Also, according to an MCPS document dated October 15, the system made a deliberate attempt to cut off the news media's access because they feared any publicity would lead the snipers to another attack. Even this strategy could prove problematic. Security chief Ed Clarke had opined in an October 14 meeting in Montgomery County that the schools might need to be represented at press conferences. "If the shooter doesn't see enough press coverage,

4. Fred Ellis served the Fairfax Police Department in Virginia for twenty-three years and was a Major upon his retirement. He has been with the Fairfax County Public Schools since 2000 as the Director of Safety and Security Operations. In this position Ellis has helped to create an Emergency Response Plan for the district, to encompass any possible crisis situation such as a fire or tornado. Ellis, a graduate of the FBI National Academy, received his bachelor's degree in psychology and sociology from Radford College. (Sources: White House "Briefing Room" website, http://www.whitehouse.gov/news/releases/2006/10/20061009-3.html; National Institute of Justice website, http://www.ojp.usdoj.gov/nij/events/nij_conference/2005/biographies.pdf.)

he may step up his activity. I think it is clear that the next time he strikes, the roadways will be slowed down and vehicles checked. I agree that he is still in control and will strike again." Such difficulty in determining a consistent press policy clearly was related to the uncertainty felt by the officials in their current circumstances.

Yet, in spite of such concerns, MCPS affirmed its decision to keep the schools open. Jerry Weast's open letter on October 8 embraced a stoical approach by noting that the schools would remain open but that parents should "remain vigilant and well informed." He encouraged parents to be very attentive to their children. Two days later, the crisis team found the attitude in the system "amazingly good," even beginning to return to normal. Although shootings occurred in Virginia on October 9 and 11, by Monday, October 14, the team was planning for a "step-down" that would return students to a normal schedule by the following Friday. The shooting at the Home Depot on October 14 upset that plan, but at a 7:30 a.m. team meeting the next day, the assessment remained that the students were in good shape, at the expense of staff and principals. In our interview, Weast characterized the mix of policies and practices as "grace under pressure."

Nothing better expressed this contradiction in approaches than an October 10 e-mail broadcast by Fairfax County Public Schools (FCPS) superintendent Dan Domenech regarding plans for keeping the schools open. Noting the recent shootings, including one in Manassas the preceding evening, the superintendent canceled all outdoor events that could not be moved inside. Field trips within the Washington metropolitan area also were called off. Domenech noted that these actions would lead to safety, which could be enhanced by parental involvement in taking children to school and helping them cope with the circumstances. He concluded: "There is no question that we are living in a paradox. We are determined to keep our lives as normal as possible, but, to feel safe, we find we must postpone events that are important to our children and us. It is not comfortable." But treading uneasily between normality and a suspension of activity was the schools' course.

Even though this dichotomy remained throughout the two weeks following the Tasker shooting, over time a change took place toward a greater emphasis on normality. The main way in which this shift can be seen concerned the scheduling of outdoor athletic events. Encouraging this development were some activities directors, coaches, players, and parents, all of whom did not want the season destroyed. For some students, earning a college scholarship depended on a return to action. Doubtless, some administrators and other members of the scholastic community had other motives for supporting this resumption of sporting events. In fact, on October 10, the *Post* ran an article, "High Schools are Adjusting Plans," which focused on high school teams returning to action. Prince George's County supervisor of athletics Earl Hawkins[5] said that his schools wanted to "return to some of the normalcy we had before." To facilitate this, games would take place at three central sites, to allow for increased security. After the shooting in Manassas, games were pushed back from Saturday to Monday. First FCPS, and a little later MCPS, both of which had planned for weekend games, postponed any plans for a significant period.

But this hiatus did not last long, and new efforts resumed a few days after the sniper-free and sports-free weekend of October 12–13. First, however, the effect of the previous week's shootings and that on the evening of October 14 had to be absorbed. October 16 proved to be the crucial day.

The break really occurred in Fairfax County. As the county's public information officer, Kitty Porterfield, recalled, activities directors and the superintendent's staff strategized that the press would not know their new plans. However, on October 16, the *Post* reported that the Northern Virginia schools were considering playing games at remote locations to the south in Virginia. That same Tuesday morning, the FCPS official position was that games were canceled. Yet at 1:27 p.m. on October 16, Francis Dall,[6] Westfield High School's activities director, e-mailed a specific plan to Alan Leis,[7] the chief administrative officer of FCPS–a plan for football that awaited his approval. At 3:34 p.m., Leis

5. Earl Hawkins is currently the director of interscholastic athletics for Prince George's County Public Schools. (Source: Prince George's County Public Schools website, http://www1.pgcps.org/athletics/.)

6. Francis Dall is currently the director of student activities for Westfield High School in Fairfax County. (Source: Westfield High School website, http://www.fcps .edu/WestfieldHS/faculty_staff/admin.htm.)

7. Alan Leis served the Fairfax County Public Schools for thirty years as a teacher, coordinator of instruction, executive assistant, assistant superintendent for the Department of Human Resources, interim superintendent, and deputy superintendent. He was named deputy superintendent in 1996, a position he held until 2003, when he became superintendent of Naperville Community School District 203 in Illinois. Upon his departure, the Fairfax County School Board renamed the Walnut Hill Center the "Alan Leis Instructional Center" in recognition of Dr. Leis's accomplishments. (Sources: FCPS website, http://www.fcps.edu/ media pub/pressrel/3-14-03.htm; FCPS website, http://www.fcps.edu/schlbd/minutes/ 20030410R.pdf.)

told principals in an e-mail that a plan had been prepared. Twenty-one minutes later, Dall sent that plan to the activities directors. His e-mail noted that there should not be any publicity about the plan, not even on the hotlines that announced individual school events. Only public address announcements at each school would be permitted. Dall added: "We are often very critical of our southern schools because they don't have similar issues to ours. I hope all of us will realize the sacrifice being made for us—true Southern hospitality at its best. Please make sure we treat their facilities and people with the utmost respect." With a lot of cooperation from the many fellow high schools in Virginia, FCPS wagered that it could maintain security. At 4:47 p.m., in a media advisory entitled "Fairfax County Schools to Play Football Games," FCPS let it be known that games were scheduled, but it said nothing about their times or locations. Also promised was a resumption of field hockey and cross-country events. The secrecy element, however, could not be maintained, as sports writers, activities directors, and reporters learned of the new locations at a meeting of the Virginia High School League. They would be there to publicize the games.

Simultaneously, on October 16, at 5:00 p.m., the crisis team and Jerry Weast in Montgomery County announced a work group to consider sports options. Prepared also at this time was an analysis of the precise situation facing each sport and the requests to pull together a season. Only the next morning at the 7:30 a.m. meeting did the crisis team actually tackle its subject. Council member Mike Subin[8] presented the possibility of using six schools that could be secured reasonably well. Yet Subin also gave counter-arguments, including the possibility that increased visibility would create a target for the sniper. He expressed other concerns, including that of damage to the field caused by increased use and the lack of options for pre-game practices. Ed Clarke posed other security problems, but prospects for resuming sports contests seemed really to founder on the problem of holding contests but having no place to practice. Subin proposed more study,

8. Michael Subin was formerly County Council Education Committee chairman for Montgomery County Schools, serving five terms. During his time on the council, Subin worked with Montgomery County Public Schools and the Board of Education to secure funding for school programs. He has also headed the county's Criminal Justice Coordinating Committee. (Sources: *Washington Post* website, http://blog.washing tonpost.com/annapolis/2007/10/former_moco_planner_rai ses_mon.html; http://www.washingtonpost.com/wp-dyn/content/article/2006/ 09/18/AR2006091801313.html.)

which Dr. Weast endorsed. The latter concluded by indicating that he wanted a thorough study before making a decision. Furthermore, an updated report on the status of individual sports was completed. This effort went beyond the previous day's report and gave specific suggestions that could be used to restore the season. This effort could provide a blueprint for administrators, while the earlier one had simply highlighted obstacles and advantages. Nonetheless, on October 17, at 1:18 p.m., Weast e-mailed Brian Porter that he had decided that Montgomery County high schools would play no games through Monday, October 21.

The decision making intensified after the officials at MCPS learned of the FCPS plan to schedule games. At 6:27 p.m., Brian Porter notified the high school principals about the planning taking place to resume athletics in Montgomery County. The planning document was made available on public websites and a media announcement followed. Jerry Weast later recalled his reactions on that day. Feeling blindsided by Fairfax County, he also was braving the criticism of the football community. Still, he noted that he was ultimately responsible and had to use the security calculations on which he had relied earlier. Specifically, he really had to consider the probability of putting the shooter in a situation outside his preferred comfort zone. Any acceptable plan would have to deny the shooter the customary modus operandi. Weast was cognizant that this killer was sophisticated. The superintendent definitely did not believe that checking identification before allowing some to enter games would uncover this sniper. Because of the sniper's changes in location, Weast found it difficult to defend against him.

Pressure was building on the MCPS team. One participant noted that if Fairfax were successful, many would want Montgomery County to follow suit. Weast vetoed a plan for each sport's practices and games. By Monday, October 21, people might be clamoring for a resolution. Over in Prince George's County, a reaction also was occurring. Football teams would be allowed to practice inside, and volleyball and soccer teams could resume their regular season.

But Fairfax's plans soon went astray. Although football and field hockey games were played throughout Virginia, the shooting in Ashland on Saturday evening, October 19, brought into question the entire approach. Superintendent Domenech, knowing that some players had eaten only hours before at the Ponderosa, where the shooting occurred, found this juxtaposition nearly unbelievable. Although many others believed the choice of this shooting location was selected to avoid a military reconnaissance plane that the Defense Department had contributed to the investigation, Domenech thought the shooting was designed to send a message that no area was safe. On Sunday, all activities in Fairfax schools were suspended until further notice.

But the momentum to allow play was not disrupted. Fairfax immediately embarked on a new plan, and Prince George's played games, with the exception of football. According to Russ Tedesco,[9] security chief for the county, the visibility of football, the number of teams involved, and the number of spectators simply made it too dangerous to allow resumption of this sport.

Examining the efforts at MCPS headquarters illuminates this resumption of effort to schedule sports. Upset by the "flip-flop" of Fairfax, which led to canceling everything, the Montgomery crisis team harkened back to other differences that had earlier emerged regarding the appropriate level of caution. According to MCPS documents, at the team meeting on October 21 the crisis team focused on athletic sites, and Weast added: "Let's look at anything that has a large area that is fenced that we can mow and line." He also suggested gaining a senator's influence as a way to convince military authorities to let them play at military bases. Practice would begin on Thursday, with games soon following. Furthermore, a new and more precise plan to resume contests was prepared on October 21. Added was a simplified page that isolated and presented concisely all the relevant considerations.

During the two weeks following the Tasker shooting, a desire and commitment emerged to get students back on the playing fields. Sports activities weighted the ambiguity in school policy toward action instead of security and caution. In yet another way, schools were inclining more generally in that direction. This becomes evident when one examines what transpired inside school buildings.

To Superintendent Weast, attendance by staff and students constituted the vital statistics of any system. After the initial shock, and with

9. Russell Tedesco served the Prince George's County Police Department for twenty-one years, retiring as a Captain. He was then named the Director of Security Services for Prince George's County Public Schools, a position he remained in for thirteen years. He stepped down in 2007 during an investigation of his department by members of the Board of Education into the accuracy of reported security data. Also of concern was his wife's position in the same department as his own. (Sources: *Washington Post* website, http://www.washingtonpost.com/wp-dyn/content/arti cle/2007/10/05/AR2007100502270_pf.html, and http://www.washingtonpost .com/wp-dyn/content/article/2007/10/16/AR2007101602127.html.)

an exception that will be discussed, the attendance of teachers, drivers, staff, and students throughout the three systems remained strong. A closer look at some individual schools provides a more complex understanding of the dynamics of fear and confidence in the schools. Because the systems resolutely kept such discussion out of the press, our understanding of what transpired at individual institutions depends on interviews more than on contemporary documentation.

Profiling the resilience of the schools must begin with that most affected: Benjamin Tasker Middle School. At a public meeting on the night of October 7, the night of the shooting, Principal John Lloyd had a mission–get back on track. He appealed to the community to send their children to school. He described the safety plan, with business as usual the order of the day. The next morning, partial success was achieved, as two-thirds of the children attended. Teaching, which had been suspended in the mayhem of the day before, resumed. Teachers spoke about the day's events but then moved on to the new day's lessons. As Principal Lloyd and Superintendent Iris Metz[10] toured the school, it was evident that normal operations were resuming. And on the next day, there was a 94 percent attendance rate. At a PTA meeting night at Tasker, with a hundred families in attendance, a very supportive atmosphere emerged. And, according to Lloyd, from that time until capture of the snipers, students and learning prospered.

This did not mean that the school was stress-free. In fact, its staff was exhausted. Lloyd found the experience draining and emotional. According to the principal, the personnel endured on adrenaline. When the episode finally concluded, many instructors needed extra days off. Lloyd then felt that "the weight of the world had been lifted from his shoulders." An indication of the students' anxiety can be seen in the extent of their exhilaration when the snipers were captured. Entering the school that morning as news was circulating regarding the arrests, the students, in Lloyd's view, had an extra spring in their step. Many rushed to ask the principal: "Mr. Lloyd, have you heard the news?" Not

10. In 1999, Iris Metz, former superintendent of Maryland's Prince George's County Schools, was at the White House when President Bill Clinton signed the Ed-Flex Bill, which allowed school districts more flexibility when spending federal dollars. Prior to joining Prince George's County Schools, Metz worked as an assistant superintendent in Chicago. (Sources: FDCH Political Transcripts,August 19, 1999, LexisNexis, www.lexisnexis.com; http://www.cnn.com/ALLPOLITICS/ stories/1999/03/11/education/; *New York Times* website, http://query.nytimes .com/gst/fullpage.html?res=940DE6DA123CF93AA15757C0A96E948260.)

to rain on their parade, he answered, "No, what happened?" They elatedly related what was all over the news, and students and principal shared relief as they forgot anxiety.

Across the river, at Virginia's Langley High School, students and teachers were also dealing with the circumstances after the shootings began. Principal William Clendaniel[11] recalled that his own fear had increased after the Tasker shooting. He particularly worried about the woods that surrounded his school on all sides. Still, Clendaniel felt no need to have the blinds closed. The school's location, mainly tucked away in a wooded lot, might even be seen as providing some security. As most analysts assumed that the sniper required an easy getaway, access to Langley, along a busy two-lane street, seemed less than ideal. Moreover, the proximity of the school to the heavily guarded Central Intelligence Agency provided extra insurance. In fact, Clendaniel, when he joined the security guard to direct traffic in mid-street, did not seem to feel that his own risk was particularly great. Although the teachers at Langley felt much anxiety, they believed the attacks on Washington in September 2001 had toughened them. In my group interview with them, they recalled that they were united in the attitude not to let the shooters "win" through intimidation. Finally, according to Clendaniel, the students were little affected at school, since they felt safe there. As proof of the point about schools serving as comfortable havens, he pointed to increased attendance compared to the same date in the preceding year. The main problem was regret about what the school could not do. The principal believed that playing football and going ahead with homecoming were both important, to let off pressure. Thus, as they did at Tasker, fear and coping coexisted at Langley. For the students, it seems that school seemed to contain more of the latter than the former.

On the other hand, at Marshall Road Elementary, in Vienna (Fairfax County)—a school that was located near an Interstate highway and a Metro stop and also faced a major thoroughfare—the administrators felt very vulnerable. In fact, long before the sniper incident, the foot traffic

11. William Clendaniel was named interim principal of T. C. Williams High School in Alexandria, Va., on July 1, 2008. Clendaniel previously worked at Langley High School, in McLean, Va., for twelve years, eight of them as principal, before retiring. He also worked as an assistant principal at West Potomac High School in Alexandria. (Sources: Alexandria City Public Schools website, http://www.acps .k12.va.us/news2008/nr2008061901.php; http://www.alextimes.com/article.asp ?article=10206&paper=1&cat=1.)

to the Metro had raised anxieties there. Consequently, when the administrators first heard of the Montgomery County shooting—several days before the school system reacted—they immediately took action. First, the assistant principal canceled outdoor activities and went around the school telling teachers to pull their blinds. Security immediately became an issue. In the process of dealing with the danger, the administrators recognized the bus drop-off and pick-up as problematic. For example, at the end of the day, buses had customarily parked parallel in front of the school and children simply went outside and climbed onto the correct vehicle. To increase security, the buses were pulled up directly in front of the school's exit door and children were called for each bus in turn. Yet students could still be seen for a distance of fifteen to twenty feet as they crossed the sidewalk to the bus. To block a sight line, police cars were positioned at a street at one end and teachers made a line with their bodies at the other end. A similar situation existed for students being picked up by their parents' cars. And walkers were escorted home, at first by teachers and later by parent volunteers. Another incident, related to me by teachers Judith Isaacson, Jen Heigas, and Colin McNamara, reveals the tension at Marshall Road. When a photographer arrived to take pictures outside the school, the police were immediately alerted, and school officials raced outside and lectured him that he was putting the children at risk. When the police arrived, they escorted him away. According to school officials, he had seen his error. Teachers, like administrators, were worried and fretful.

Whatever the fears of the staff, and whatever the children's opinions at home, inside the school it was business as usual. As one Marshall Road Elementary teacher related, for children school is about predictability. Students allow faculty to set the tone, and they did exactly that. The youngest students were easily distracted and seemed to have no extra concerns or anxiety. Even sixth-graders saw the safety of the school. As was the case at Langley High, the worst problem for students was being pent up in school. To that end, parents sent various games to play, and the administrators made the gym and cafeteria into recreation areas. Ultimately, no change in student learning or in forms of intellectual expression took place. School administrators and teachers provided an opportunity to not think about the outside world. As one teacher put it, the daily experience was "just like being through a huge rainstorm." One other story highlights the way the staff, whatever concerns it felt, sought the semblance of normalcy at school. The custodian, at some potential personal risk, continued to mow the lawn so that Marshall Road School would look as open for business as usual.

Poised as the school systems were between dread and determined optimism, they received a shock on the morning of October 22 when the snipers struck down bus driver Conrad Johnson in the very neighborhood that had sustained the first murders on October 3. Radically increasing the impact of this incident was that, seemingly in response to the shooting at the Ponderosa on October 19, the Richmond area school systems shut down on both October 21 and 22. This reaction surely encouraged other school leaders to rethink their position and how the Richmond systems appeared to take the threat more seriously. Furthermore, by the morning of October 22, news began to leak out that a note left at the Ponderosa had threatened schoolchildren.

Such developments rocked the Montgomery County system, which of necessity perceived these new attacks as both a reprise of past horrors and a forecast of future threat by killers still in the locality. In fact, and certainly for the immediately affected area, these schools lost the self-possession that had been fostered by the drive for a normal experience in the schools.

Conrad Johnson was shot at 5:55 in the morning. Within a half an hour, roads were jammed. School buses were caught in traffic and school staff were unable to get to work. Police guarding the schools were redeployed to add personnel to the dragnet. Immediately, the Montgomery County system had to make hard decisions. As in the earlier period, it chose to have the buses deliver the children at school and to maintain the day's schedule. Part of the reason for this approach could be seen as the administration being fearful of what other alternatives promised. In a staff meeting, Superintendent Weast noted, "If we canceled schools, kids would be all over the streets and at the malls without supervision." In the letter he sent the community, as had been his practice repeatedly during the crisis, he added other reasons: students depended on the schools for after-school care and for subsidized breakfasts, and these services had to be provided. Beyond keeping the schools open to allay anxiety and protect the students, education continued. In fact, in the course of the team meetings, Weast clearly endeavored to keep the schools open and not give way to panic.

But panic seemed to surge elsewhere in the system. As recorded in the 5 p.m. team meeting on October 22, one MCPS guidance official reported about the students:

> We have been in touch with the schools and the level of fear
> is much higher than it has been, especially in the impacted
> schools. . . . The high schools and middle schools that we talked
> with said that this is the only conversation going on. Many of the
> Wheaton and Kennedy [students whose schools were located
> close to the shootings] left school today and parents were caring
> for their children.

A report prepared on the schools in the area near the shooting and released on October 22 described some students as "fine" or "ok" but argued that these were outnumbered by those who felt "scared," "frightened," and "felt the need to leave school early."

Staff members and parents clearly vocalized far greater fears than did students. In fact, as earlier evidence suggests, this difference characterized the entire event. Extra phone logs, which mainly reflected parental calls and which had previously supported the decision to keep schools open, changed direction. Just over half of the total of thirty-two calls requested that schools be closed, but others reported anxiety and requested increased security. Only five callers, of the thirty-two, seemed to support keeping the schools open. E-mail traffic also overwhelmingly endorsed shutting the schools. Both Weast and Brian Porter later recalled that the neighborhood where the shootings had earlier occurred was rocked by the reappearance of the sniper. And, not surprisingly, a stronger Code Blue was implemented, with no thought of holding any outside sporting events.

Two e-mails from a school in the most strongly affected area likely overstated the feelings of fear and frustration. Yet, they are still worth reproducing, in part because they reveal how some staff and parents reacted. These letters indicated panic–not just fright. That evening, after what had to have been a difficult day, a kindergarten teacher sent off an e-mail message to, among others, Brian Porter, several Board of Education members, and her colleagues at school. She complained of battling traffic to find only five of her students in class:

> As a kindergarten teacher I am angered at the decision that was
> made this morning to continue to send children, teachers, and
> administrators to school. I wonder if our school system has lost
> sight of what is really important. MCPS risked the lives of all of
> us and for what? I was not able to get to school until 10:00 a.m.
> and found that I had five children. No teaching was done! In addi-
> tion, I was very anxious driving to school, when I was at school,
> and when I drove home.

Asking if MCPS had "lost sight of what was important," she felt that her life had been at risk for nothing.

Likewise, according to an e-mail to Brian Porter and others, dated October 22, the attendance secretary at the same school described her experience answering phones for hours and talking with dozens of anxious parents:

> It's now after 7:00 p.m. and I still have not calmed down from the stress level many MCPS employees were subjected to today. I'm an attendance secretary and from the moment I walked into the office until 10:00 a.m. the phone never stopped ringing. I must have answered (and I was not the only person answering the phone) over 100 calls from anxious parents worried about sending their children to school, worried about leaving their children at bus stops, and questioning MCPS's decision to start school on time. I couldn't help these people; I couldn't calm their fears about their children and I couldn't explain why MCPS decided to open schools on time. It made no sense to me.
>
> We've been told that the children's safety is a priority, yet children were placed at risk waiting for buses that never arrived. We've been told that the mental health of teachers and support staff is a concern, yet staff members were trapped for hours in traffic. I would like those who made the decision to open schools on time to come to MY school and answer phones all morning and listen to frustrated and worried parents and staff members and THEN tell me that they're worried about MY mental health.
>
> Why didn't you make a thoughtful decision and at least delay opening the middle and elementary schools until you had a better grasp of the situation? As an MCPS employee but more importantly as a parent of MCPS students, I would like an answer.

Clearly, the events of October 22 had shattered the cautious optimism that had been built during the reconstruction of daily operations in the school system. The rebound on October 23 was only partial.

By all accounts, the new shootings most affected the school staff. In the areas near the recent shooting, the staff "seemed emotional, on edge and scared," as reported in the Crisis Team notes for a team meeting on October 23. Even though teacher attendance improved, Weast believed that the younger teachers were the most affected, because this was the first time that they had really had to exercise leadership in the face of a crisis of this magnitude. Also, an extensive report, prepared by school counselors, on the state of the schools in the most affected areas indicated that in the midst of a great deal of anxiety, staff members rather than students were more concerned. They felt that the cumulative load of stress was overwhelming them.

Certainly, the superintendent and his team not only were aware of the problem but also sought to visit schools to provide assurance. Weast hoped that this effort would dampen the emotions that led to hostile notes like those from staff e-mails. Whatever his success, it was far from complete, as fifty-five members of the staff from one elementary school together composed a long, blistering letter on October 23. The epistle took up issues of the preceding day. Because of roadblocks, children wandered their neighborhood searching for the school bus. Although one bus driver did get through and picked up many children, those students could have met a predator, the staff argued. In school, business as usual was impossible, they said. Continued the letter, teachers had to mask their own emotions and downplay fears. And, as attendance was well below what had been publicly announced, some felt dishonest but went ahead and reported the official numbers. Finally, concluded the note, while others did what they thought was best for their children, these people worried that they had to come to work and could not look after their own.

One good measure of the community's response, mainly that of the parents, is the school's phone log for October 23, in which concerns and worries only seemed to grow more strident. Although four callers complimented the system or urged it to remain open, sixty-nine callers expressed anxieties of one sort or another. The number-one complaint concerned the safety of the trailers, followed closely by worries about the safety of bus stops. Seven people wanted the schools closed, and five had taken matters into their own hands by telephoning in that they were keeping their children home because of safety considerations.

Thus, a vocal group continued to express the anxiety from the previous day but attendance was on its way back to normal. According to attendance records in the MCPS files for the pre-October 4 period, that is, for the period before the sniper shootings began, average daily attendance at county schools had been just under 95 percent. Table 1 indicates attendance for the last three days of the siege. The data clearly show that after a disastrous day caused by fear and intense traffic problems, students returned to schools on October 23. By the next morning, after the suspected snipers had been captured, totals neared normal. The data seem to agree with the counselors' contention that students

**Table 1.** Percentage of students attending Montgomery County Public Schools, by date and cluster

| Clusters | Oct. 22 | Oct. 23 | Oct. 24 |
|---|---|---|---|
| MOST IMPACTED BY SHOOTING | | | |
| Kennedy | 53 | 75 | 88 |
| Wheaton | 55 | 79 | 89 |
| Einstein | 52 | 87 | 93 |
| OTHER SELECTED CLUSTERS | | | |
| Magruder | 75 | 88 | 94 |
| Sherwood | 75 | 92 | 96 |
| Gaithersburg | 90 | 90 | 93 |
| Richard Montgomery | 82 | 89 | 94 |
| Churchill | 94 | 94 | 97 |
| Poolesville | 95 | 91 | 98 |
| Systemwide total | 80 | 89 | 93 |

*Source:* MCPS attendance records, October 22-24, 2002.
*Note:* Clusters represent high schools and feeder schools.

remained anxious (or at least their parents were), but significantly less so than on the day before.

According to Team Meeting minutes for October 23, the views of the members of the crisis team probably fell somewhere between those of staff and those of students. To be certain, they were concerned. Weast said, "Today (October 23) will be a critical day." One member of the team then responded that she had been personally affected: "It was the first time I have seen my grandson cry about the situation. I needed to console him—it touched home. . . . Also, I think we need to think about the impact this is having on our secretaries. They are under a great deal of stress."

Whatever the personal feelings of the team, Superintendent Weast tried to take the middle ground, showing some confidence. In "Update #12: Letter to MCPS Parents, Students, and Staff from Weast," dated October 23, the superintendent noted that the Code Blue would be continued, but that the system would continue to try to locate a secure federal facility to hold sporting events—although still more time would be needed. And Weast's letter to the school community asserted that even though the areas near the incident still showed low attendance, they also showed "resiliency," with adults really supporting the students. More generally, he noted that keeping the schools open was not easy but "reflects our determination to provide students with as much opportunity for continuity as possible." In short, October 23 was not exactly like October 22, but it was also not like October 24.

Interestingly, MCPS's colleagues in Fairfax and Prince George's counties did not undergo a similar crisis on October 22 and 23. Prince George's had managed to locate secure facilities at Patuxent Naval Air Station and NASA-Goddard and went ahead with soccer games on October 22. Even though MCPS was considering this same solution, Jerry Weast needed more time to think about it on October 22. The system even canceled an indoor tennis tournament for Thursday that Weast had initially cleared after the Conrad Johnson shooting. While FCPS referred to increased tension in public and private communications, the spokespeople always referred to the threat against children made in the note found previously at the Ponderosa. The advice offered to parents was to allay their children's fears and continue on as before. In the view of officials at FCPS, this new note found at the Ponderosa changed nothing, since a student already had been shot. Furthermore, FCPS responded to the Conrad Johnson shooting by continuing the same approach it had taken earlier. Although plans for placing games in far-flung sites had come undone, FCPS still tried to find secure sites locally. It was negotiating with several military facilities, and games and events had been scheduled. Although these games were not played as planned, the negotiations had foundered on conditions set by the military bases rather than on any increased hesitation by school officials. The October 23 edition of the *Post* quoted Domenech as quite willing to go ahead on the bases.

The capture of the snipers, announced unofficially to the media on the morning of October 24 as people awoke, and then confirmed that evening, brought relief to all three systems. This also ended the extraordinary measures that had been taken by the systems at least since October 7. In Fairfax, as early as 9:33 a.m. on the 24th, the FCPS listserv announced hope that the arrests that morning would end the tragedy that had gripped the area. At 8:00 p.m., an official announcement stated there would be a return to a normal schedule, and the superintendent sent out an informal message about half an hour later: "Thank you all for being so wonderful!!! Tomorrow, October 25, we will resume all normal activities, including outdoor practices, field trips, recess, outdoor P.E., etc., etc. HURRAY!"

Largely the same events transpired over the course of the day in Montgomery County. But the better archival materials available for MCPS trace the outlines more distinctly. At the 7:30 crisis team meeting that morning, Weast stated that euphoria was spreading and people would relax. He declared that they would need to know the precise situation and would need to prepare for deescalation. Thoughtfully, he suggested that personnel should be sensitive to the feelings of those in the schools who were named Muhammad. Still, at 11:00 that morning the team remained unsure enough that planning continued for secure athletic sites. Weast authorized the playing, without advertising, of five indoor volleyball games for six o'clock that evening. By 5 p.m., Weast was "cautiously optimistic" enough to begin to mobilize for a normal opening day, although some light form of Code Blue was envisioned. Backing this mood was a severe reduction in calls from the community and a confidence in the resumption of activities.

Throughout the day, the MCPS administrators had been issuing notes suggesting progress but caution. At 8:03 p.m. came the lifting of restrictions and a concluding paragraph in the e-mail that quoted Weast as saying everyone in the school system is "breathing a sigh of relief this evening." He thanked law enforcement personnel for capturing the assailants and assisting the schools. Interestingly, and as a footnote to the rapid developments of October 23, Bruce Romer,[12] a top county administrator, just after 5 p.m. filed a status report on secure federal facilities. The options described in this memo were not positive. Fortunately, events overtook this effort to locate playing fields. Otherwise, athletes needing outdoor facilities would have not seen action anytime soon.

Summarizing the actions of the schools indicates a continuous balance between anxiety and a desire to keep normal functions going. To some extent, this latter goal simply reflected anxiety. If, as was often stated, schools were the safest place for students, then keeping them there was just another reaction to fear. Furthermore, this confidence had limits that could be easily reached. When Conrad Johnson was shot,

12. Bruce Romer worked for Montgomery County, Md., Executive Doug Duncan for twelve years. Romer initially served as the city manager of Rockville, Md., before being named Chief Montgomery County Administrative Officer. He was removed from his position in 2006 when Isiah "Ike" Leggett replaced Duncan as County Executive. (Sources: *Washington Post* website, http://www.washingtonpost.com/wp-dyn/content/article/2006/11/28/AR2006112801449.html; Gaithersblog.net website, http://gaithersblog.net/2006/11/29/bruce-romer-fired/.)

pandemonium overturned several days of increasing normalcy, yet normalcy did begin to return again. Nonetheless, keeping the children in school also required portraying, and even asserting, some confidence. Catching a ride on the bus or walking to school constituted accepting some risk. Furthermore, as the discussion with teachers and principals indicates, schools–ever mindful of security concerns–sought to establish a routine that would freeze out fear. Moreover, other actions–for example, the desire to find playing fields–clearly represented a desire to overcome or stand up to insecurities. These cannot be seen as heroic, nor were they intended to be. But they constituted reasonable risk-taking.

Overall then, on a scale ranging from fearfulness to foolhardiness, the schools, which might have emphasized fear, would end up somewhere in the middle, or certainly away from the extremes. As defined in the introduction, two stages–fear outweighing coping and coping outweighing fear–characterized the school approach. It is not unimaginable that the panic of October 22 and 23 in Montgomery County might have been more characteristic of the entire period, but this simply did not transpire. It could have taken place had administrators concluded that the risk was so great that the schools could not assume it. Clearly, they took a more balanced approach.

As this narrative indicated, the divide between fearfulness and stoicism was not constant. Clearly, it had a chronology, with fear subsiding between the Tasker Middle School and the Conrad Johnson shootings. Essentially, as the shootings continued, systems became somewhat inured, unless they occurred locally. More importantly, the crisis was experienced differently at various times. It seems safe to say that, in general, most local schools carried on more normally, in far less of a crisis mode, than did the superintendents. In interviews, both Domenech and Weast expressed that anxieties were present throughout those days, even as they sought to deal with them. Weast put it this way: "Everyone was nervous." Everyone had to have a big knot in his or her stomach through this period. He or she was dealing with life-and-death decisions. The superintendents had a particularly big responsibility because they did not have the advantage of probability. Weast's explanation of his own actions, by focusing on probabilities, helps explain the topology of fear and normality. From his point of view, with well over 150,000 students and staff to be concerned about, it was always somewhat likely that someone would be shot. The principal of a small elementary school could reasonably calculate a far lower risk. The geographical difference was analogous. If someone were shot near you, probabilities rose; far away, statistics turned in your favor.

Although this was the general pattern, rules could be reversed in Montgomery County after the Conrad Johnson shooting. Passions were surely more heated in the schools in the vicinity of the shootings, with some evidence of total breakdown, than they were in the central administration, which kept a steady approach regardless of the internal concern of the top administrators.

Whatever position one held, one's geographical identity does seem to have really made a difference. While every school district reacted to the shooting at Benjamin Tasker, this proved to be an anomaly. Mostly, they were much more upset when they were close to areas where the sniper had struck. Montgomery County had loosened Code Blue even as shootings occurred across the Potomac. When the slaying of Conrad Johnson upset this momentum, colleagues in neighboring counties did not react as much.

Throughout these events, the school systems seem never to have articulated a particular vision of the sniper. They likely believed this to be the job of the police. However, in their actions, or calculations, they were imagining a resourceful and calculating killer. Yet rather than a demonic figure, they imagined an unseen figure of great skill and determination; but also a killer that sometimes could be managed. Indeed, over the course of the sniper rampage, school confidence seems to have advanced.

This vision of the unseen, capable sniper, and a system struggling between fear and hope and inclining toward the latter, surely is a social construction of importance. The school systems were mammoth in size and significance. How their image matched that presented by the news media in describing the shooters and their impact on society provides an analytic frame for a fair evaluation of the press's understandings. The following chapter will take up these issues to understand the framework of reporting.

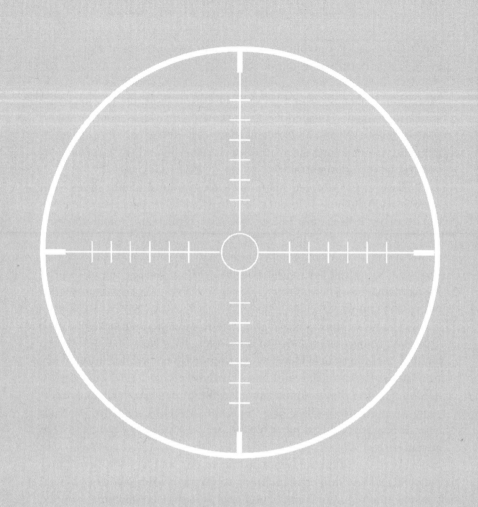

# CONCLUSION

A small army of journalists narrated the police chase and public response over that long October of 2002. These scribes produced millions of words that were avidly consumed by many millions of people. The citizens of the Washington region, unlike the politicians who usually dominate, occupied the world's stage.

Chronologically, what people witnessed was a story that seemingly came out of nowhere. Although Malvo and Muhammad had started their rampage long before October 2 and perhaps had targeted the Washington area from the very beginning, the event burst on the scene rather unexpectedly. At first, the press hesitated but then reacted strongly with much concern. The earliest images, sounds, and newspaper stories all communicated high anxiety. The police story added other aspects to create a narrative in which anxiety competed with the possible arrival of relief, through the capture of the snipers. Nonetheless, the shooting of Conrad Johnson on October 22 pitched the story in an entirely more negative direction. The equilibrium that could be found in the earlier reporting evaporated, and despair became much more dominant.

Then, suddenly, the press documented the denouement and early found the words to express relief. Although this study has concentrated on the press only until the capture of Malvo and Muhammad, it is worth noting the immense outpouring of relief and gratitude toward the police. Even Chief Moose experienced a brief honeymoon with the press that lasted until the resignation he handed in so that he could publish his autobiography. When the book appeared, reviewers and commentators were merciless.[1]

1. For criticism of Moose, see Letters to the Editor, June 20, 2003; an article by Marc Fisher, April 27, 2003; and an editorial on March 22, 2003, all in the *Wash-*

When considered overall, the coverage assumed every conceivable form, from questioning the reasons for Washington's fear to reports that could only encourage it. Of course, as readers of this book or residents in the area know, fear predominated. And for the most part, journalists produced many more pieces in which fear remained the major theme. This genre at one end included articles that encouraged some resistance and at the other end included those which conveyed a sense of panic. The panicky ones outweighed those that sought either to block or minimize the fear by calculating the odds or by providing strategies to minimize and lessen a sense of impending doom.

For many Washingtonians the actions of the press provided a clear window on the self-evident truth of the danger facing them. Indeed, the snipers meant to terrify the region, and even the nation. Why shouldn't residents be frightened? Already on the first day the sniper had killed five, and he had traveled and killed widely. A variety of ethnicities seemed to be targeted. As the press noted, the random nature of the attacks seemed to make them all-inclusive. Unavailable as rationales for personal safety were the common strategies of avoiding dangerous areas or a belief in certain groups being immune. Furthermore, had the snipers' full plans been known, as they came to be in trial testimony, even greater grounds for concern would have existed.

Yet based on the knowledge available at the time–such as the re-marks of Marjorie Williams and the reporting of the *CBS Evening News* and the *Washington Times*–a few contemporary journalists were able to look at the matter in an entirely different light. While not denying the relevance of fear, this reporting seemed to argue that the mainstream press had overemphasized it. After all, even some cable television opin-ion makers had suggested that the fear was overstated.

Thus, although all witnessed the same crisis, the schools did not fall into the same pattern as the press. While accepting fear for the most part, they sought to moderate it in most circumstances. Of course, they were reacting to a litany of fears; but by the end of the crisis they were attempting to go beyond the gloomy prospects to some kind of nor-mality. Even the shooting of Conrad Johnson only temporarily lurched the schools back; attendance and attitude both rebounded as the press's

*ington Post.* See also the *Washington Times,* May 15 and June 20, 2003. On Moose's book, see the *Washington Post,* September 14, 2003, and the compilation of re-views at www.amazon.com.

attitude tanked. This is all the more remarkable since school administrators and teachers read press coverage which presented matters otherwise. This pattern can best be comprehended through the concept of the limited effect of the media, which was initially advanced by scholars in the first half of the twentieth century. Although some of the methods of this approach have been repudiated as oversimplistic, its basic arguments seem quite relevant here. In essence, as Carl Hovland and Paul Lazersfeld have argued, a message is far more likely to be accepted if the reader/listener already believes its implicit values.[2] Perhaps school officials took a skeptical attitude toward the fear propagated in the media lest it undermine an essential commitment to keeping the schools open and children safe inside their walls.

Interestingly, a useful comparison might be to other places in the world–such as Northern Ireland, Iraq, and, at times, Israel–that have experienced unpredictable violence directed against certain populations. Evidently, these places develop a calculus of risk in which citizens accept fear but embrace some form of normalcy. Such comparisons might make clearer the reactions of the schools, students, and parents in the region affected by the snipers.

In my view, resolving this debate about who was correct is a hopeless cause. So little was actually known about the snipers that accurately assessing the justification for the fear was impossible. One reason Washingtonians could reach near pandemonium is that anything could be imagined, since nothing was known. Moreover, the experience of September 11 and the anthrax scare made the outer parameter of possible catastrophe far more extreme than it had been before. Thus, what was a reasonable response could not then be known. Assessing it now, with much more evidence, might be useful, but we still cannot determine what was then driving that state of knowledge, the proper understanding. Surely some fear was warranted, but how much can be endlessly debated.

Thus, the best question becomes why the press reported the level of fear that it did. To answer this, the schools offer a helpful beginning. Surely they were still experiencing anxiety from the events of September 11, yet they ended up adopting a pragmatic way of coping with the

2. For a summary of the arguments of Hovland and Lazersfeld, see Denis McQuail, *Towards a Sociology of Mass Communication* (London: Collier-Mac-Millan, 1969).

problem. Clearly, they chose this approach because of their belief that the safest place for children was school. Thus, schools accepted the reality of the fear and then sought to mitigate its significance and convince parents, students, and teachers and personnel to themselves remain firm.

What pushed the press well beyond the mood of the school system is much less clear and much more subject to speculation. However, many, many reasons can be given for why the press acted as it did. The attacks on Washington and New York on September 11, 2001, followed closely by the anthrax scare the following month, certainly produced a society-wide syndrome of panic. It is impossible to say whether these circumstances were more or less troubling than other past crises, but they were a part of many factors that led the press to write what it did.

In fact, recent scholarship, taken collectively, led to the conclusion that a society focused on fear had been emerging since the late 1970s, and that the events of September 11 only encouraged this development. These analyses suggested that the larger trend consisted of irrational fears. This literature also posited that some of the reaction to the attacks on New York and Washington likewise was exaggerated.[3] In any case, all these factors together contributed to the reporting of hysteria. Although this newer scholarship aligns with my analysis of the overweening fears expressed in the press, and contrasts completely with the widely held views that the fears were justified, my own work on the schools (and the variation in the reactions) suggests that these academic studies have overemphasized the pervasiveness of this fear.

3. For an excellent introduction to this scholarly literature, which draws the general conclusions I note, see Sasha Abramsky, "The New Fear," in *The Chronicle of Higher Education*, October 24, 2008, B6–B10. Individually, the studies take different tacks. Although all lead to the notion that there is too much fear in American society, they vary regarding its degree. The most relevant works for this study are Joel Best, *Random Violence: How We Talk about New Crimes and New Victims* (Berkeley: University of California Press, 1999); Barry Glassner, *The Culture of Fear: Why Americans Are Afraid of the Wrong Things* (New York: Basic Books, 1999); and Daniel Gardner, *The Science of Fear: Why We Fear the Things We Shouldn't—and Put Ourselves in Greater Danger* (New York: Dutton, 2008). But see also James Flynn, Paul Slovic, and Howard Kunreuther, eds., *Risk, Media, and Stigma: Understanding Public Challenges to Modern Science and Technology* (London: Earthscan Publications, 2001); Peter Knight, *Conspiracy Culture from Kennedy to the X Files* (London: Routledge, 2000); and David Murray, Joel Schwartz, and S. Robert Lichter, *It Ain't Necessarily So: How Media Make and Unmake the Scientific Picture of Reality* (Lanham, Md.: Rowman and Littlefield Publishers, 2001).

Nonetheless, these accounts are thought provoking. Furthermore, some assert (particularly Joel Best and Barry Glassner) that powerful social and political elites create structures that lead journalists to focus on threats. Such an argument adds a clear political motivation and suggests intentional fear mongering. But this last point remains unproven, and I did not find such behavior in any of the evidence examined for this book.

Indeed, another important factor to explain the position of the press was the work environment of the journalists. Unlike the schools, it was the press that had to cover these murders. And likewise, the journalists were forced to come into direct contact with the victims of the snipers. Among their number were those who stood in parking lots giving news reports in a situation where signs of the murder lay all around. Their own vulnerability must have been completely obvious to themselves. Likewise, they interviewed family members of the deceased and the wounded. The fear of some journalists documented in this account indicates that this conjecture is hardly hypothetical. That the readership also had encountered anxiety further encouraged the journalists. While the schools had a broad constituency, it was not as wide as that of the press. Perhaps not statistically but in perception, one could imagine how the violence could be kept outside the schools, but not outside the entire society. The purveyors of news were expecting serious coverage and were inclined to be afraid themselves.

Professional reasons also fed into the anxiety. From its very beginnings, the media had touted the product sold as news, meaning then as well as now, it was that which is new.[4] Its very existence was intertwined with the notion of novelty. But, as space was and is always limited, news also became defined as newsworthy, or that subgroup of news which was significant. The corollary of this packaging was that news would be significant, thus saddling the news with the need to prove its importance. Encased by its definition, the press defined its audience's expec-

4. For general studies in this vein, see Mitchell Stephens, *A History of News: From the Drum to the Satellite* (New York: Viking, 1988); and Robert W. Desmond, *The Information Process: World News Reporting to the Twentieth Century* (Iowa City: University of Iowa Press, 1978). For a specific example, see the excellent study by Jeremy D. Popkin, *Revolutionary News: The Press in France, 1789–1799* (Durham, N.C.: Duke University Press, 1990), and especially pp. 31–34. For an example of how repressive governments control media by undermining novelty and timeliness, see Carla Hesse, *Publishing and Cultural Politics in Revolutionary Paris, 1789–1810* (Berkeley: University of California, 1991), 205–39.

tations, and a bond was created that the press would achieve its worth by providing new pieces of information. Media that merely repeat themselves soon will have no watchers, listeners, or readers. Such a situation inclines the press to breathe as much life as possible into the information it purveys. While journalists constantly guard against the excesses of sensationalism, fear mongering, and falsification, they also spend their days on the slippery slope of providing stories relevant to their readers.[5] It is difficult to see how this situation can be remedied, fueled as it is by prizes and premier placement for the scoop. The extraordinary number of journalists competing for this particular story only intensified the desire to find new sources or new leaks. Analytical articles have displaced the scoop to some extent, but only somewhat. Alternatives to such a system, such as a state-run press in which the incentives might militate against accurate and timely reporting, seem worse than the problem.

Likewise, the perspective held by these journalists about their role may have influenced the news they produced. As we have seen from Jamie Stockwell and her colleagues, news reporters eschewed opinion but did embrace aggressive and questioning reporting. From the very beginning of American journalism, reporters espoused a role in which the fourth estate was acting as the eyes of the public. Visions of this role have ranged from quite passive to actively injecting the views and values of journalists. Clearly, the news men and women here stood at the end of a long historical change in which editorial writing had been separated from reporting. Those in charge of direct or straight reporting deemphasized reflection in favor of recounting the awful facts that kept flowing into their inboxes. More dispassion and the use of independent judgment might have reduced fearful reactions through adding a greater calculation of risk to how events were interpreted.[6]

Moreover, one should consider the genre of the crime story. Crime reporting forms a large part of modern media, increasing in the United

5. For an excellent general discussion of this subject, see Michael Schudson, *The Sociology of News* (New York: W. W. Norton and Sons, 2003), 90–133.

6. For interesting studies of the press and its definition of its role, see two important books on the origins of the press by Jeffery A. Smith: *Printers and Press Freedom: The Ideology of Early American Journalism* (New York: Oxford University Press, 1988); and *Franklin and Bache: Envisioning the Enlightened Republic* (New York: Oxford University Press, 1990). For a survey of the legal struggles on this issue, see Anthony Lewis, *Make No Law: The Sullivan Case and the First Amendment* (New York: Vintage, 1991). For an expansive definition of journalists' roles, see David Halberstam, *The Powers That Be* (New York: Dell, 1979).

States during the crime surge of the 1970s but not receding propor-
tionally to the decline in rates of crime in later decades. While the
coverage of crime has many facets, fear is an integral part of the media
treatment.[7] Crime can be portrayed as destructive to those who commit
it or as a response to poverty, but it almost always appears as predatory
of the innocent. This approach makes crime reporting a universal phenomenon worthy of significant attention, as it always considers either a
criminal or a potential target. Put in this way, stories of this ilk became
the staple of media wishing to find a substantial audience. Treated as
accounts of predator and prey, crime stories inevitably create fear. Of
course, the actions of the snipers could be easily fit into this mindset of
crime reporting.

Television contributed considerably to making fear a major trope
of the sniper story. As many have argued, images, much more than
print, communicate emotion of all sorts–in this case, those amplifying
fear. Media scholars have also asserted that television coverage of warfare produced a significant response in viewers, and the sniper tragedy
seems to have had a similar impact.[8]

Yet one type of television coverage–continuous coverage–increased
the tendency to emphasize fear. As chapter 2 showed, this was the
general message communicated by this broadcast media itself. Beyond
its own boundaries, continuous coverage set a standard against which
every other element of the media was forced to compete. Competing
meant an emphasis on emotionalism and immediacy, and this helped to
enhance the narrative of fear already operative. Although, in retrospect,
this coverage likely did not have a positive financial impact on any media
other than cable opinion shows, which ironically were less committed to
reporting the sniper, the others, for fear of losing their audience, had to
compete against the news potential of continuous coverage. More important, failing in this regard, at a time when most area residents were

7. See, e.g., Dan Schiller, *Objectivity and the News: The Public and the Rise of
Commercial Journalism* (Philadelphia: University of Pennsylvania Press, 1981).

8. For commentary on the impact of television, particularly on the news, see
Mitchell Stephens, "Television Transforms the News," in *Communication in His-
tory: Technology, Culture, Society,* ed. David Crowley and Paul Heyer, 3rd ed. (New
York: Longman, 1999), 276–82. See also Robin Andersen, *A Century of Media, A
Century of War* (New York: Peter Lang, 2006); and David Halberstam, *The Powers
That Be.* This is not to say that television in and of itself caused a particular reac-
tion; rather, its messages are apparently more poignant. Finally, continuous cover-
age proves to be an excellent example of the power of television.

genuinely concerned about the news, could have cost that part of the press their reputation for relevance. Competition was not optional.

The circumstances of October 2002 seemed to demand anxiety-producing stories. With all these factors, media inclinations, not surprisingly, lurched toward documenting and encouraging high levels of fear. This result was, it would seem, overdetermined. Accelerating the emphasis on fear was the treatment of the radical image of the sniper. Communications scholar David Hallin has divided public debate, including the press, into three different spheres: consensus, legitimate debate, and deviancy.[9] When a subject falls into this last category, it becomes possible to ridicule or exclude it from either concern or civil discussion. For example, those who would overthrow the U.S. government or undermine the U.S. Constitution would be met with scorn and disbelief. When faced with reporting the actions of a random sniper, journalists would be highly likely to be tempted to exclude such individuals from the social body. And, of course, as the above discussion described in the *Post,* this is precisely what occurred. Highly heated rhetoric in general created fears. Ironically, in the *Post* itself, this angry attack simultaneously seemed to strengthen community by excluding the snipers, but other media outlets left society aside and thus the specter of evil attackers remained frightening.

What this study thus indicates are the many factors, other than political bias and even direct attempts at a profitable bottom line, which compete in creating the news that appears at our doors, in our cars, and on our screens. But the snipers' actions and threats alone cannot explain the press's reporting, as the schools experienced the same circumstances and reacted differently. We need to consider the physical fear that journalists must face, the ambitions of the journalists themselves, the pressure of outlets to compete for present and future audiences, and the role of technology in the very presentation and selection of stories, as well as the emotions generated in audiences by television images. The logic of the coverage of the sniper likewise played a role. But most important is the very definition of "news" which requires novelty at every turn.

• • •

Like any other case study, this one justifies itself by the ability to produce a rich picture of details and nuances that would disappear were the

9. See David C. Hallin, *We Keep America on Top of the World: Television Journalism and the Public Sphere* (New York: Routledge, 1994), 53–54.

focus wider. Instead of a case study created by an embedded scholar whose arrival at a news outlet could not necessarily guarantee any particular significance for the next few weeks or months, this study took a historical perspective. Selecting twenty-three tumultuous days in the life of the media allowed a glimpse at a critically important group as its members navigated an experience that proved all-encompassing and had no necessary end. The tight focus and dramatic situation here, like that of biography, provided the materials to chart simultaneously both the journalists and the journalism. This approach attempted to satisfy the curiosity to understand better a time that gripped the nation and gained world attention and made the public extraordinarily dependent on and attentive to the work of the media. But this study can also cast light on debates in scholarly literature as well as recent history.

As noted in the introduction to this book, the stated purpose of this monograph was to illuminate the basic instinct of the press when politics, narrowly defined to mean bias or partisanship, is not an important factor. Through this account the non-political factors most sharply emerge. Because the sniper event created no evident political cleavages, it allows this sort of inquiry. So what did the approach here add to the literature regarding journalistic framing? The coverage of the story certainly backs up the notion that journalists did not rely on their political instincts in their reporting: they reacted much more as members of a community and as individuals in pursuit of a scoop. Moreover, new technologies played a particularly strong role in disseminating the story. In this way, this study validates both the scholarly findings regarding framing, as well as a plethora of autobiographies that emphasize the scoop as a primary factor.[10] Still, given my selection of an "apolitical" topic, this is somewhat to be expected.

Yet this study clearly does show politicization, if not political intentions, by the journalists. Indeed, the framing literature itself suggests the possibility of inadvertent political outcomes.[11] And some of those strongly committed to a belief that journalists are politicized will be able to fit these outcomes into their views. Those who see the press as driven by malevolent corporate interests will find some supporting evi-

10. For memoirs that emphasize the news scoop far more than any other factor in framing, see Katharine Graham, *Personal History* (New York: Knopf, 1997); Jack W. Germond, *Fat Man in a Middle Seat: Forty Years of Covering Politics* (New York: Random House, 1999); and Benjamin C. Bradlee, *A Good Life: Newspapering and Other Adventures* (New York: Simon and Schuster, 1995).
11. Schudson, *Sociology of News,* 33–63.

dence in a competitive situation where expensive electronic technology altered media coverage. Yet the relative indifference of the cable channels to the sniper story mitigates that interpretation. Perhaps the most compelling support for the existence of intentional political motivation comes from the same group of authors, noted previously, who argue the pervasiveness of fear in the recent past. In fact, this group avers that the dominant political and social class directly affects reporting.[12] But my own study perceived a political and economic context too variegated to overwhelm the more evident motives and behaviors of the press. The relative indifference of the cable channels to the sniper story undermines that sort of interpretation. No intentional political motivation could emerge. To be sure, the ultimate result has political implications; but the causes are a complex combination of unexpected factors, allowing career goals and other incentives to play important roles.

Nonetheless, those who wish to discover political bias in the predominance of the reporting on fear can note the power of inadvertent effects. Some on the right will be concerned about how fearful reporting dovetails with the doomsday approach by many concerned with climate change. This study also highlights this trouble with fear, because the focus on fright paralleled the Bush administration's own concerns and approach.[13] As such, the press became a handmaiden to the sitting government. Ironically though, most of those who focus on political bias believe the press to be left-wing. This study should unsettle that notion, as the unintended politics of the coverage did not go in that direction. Thus, this book supports framing as a good guide to understanding the press's handling of news, but not without amendment. Even in the most nonpartisan of stories, a strong political, even partisan, message unintentionally arrived. Such unintended consequences need to be considered more fully in the use of framing as a concept.

With so many factors that pushed the press to emphasize fear in its reporting, it is worth asking whether this presented a problem. The evidence in this book suggests that it is imperative not to overstate the

---

12. See Best, *Random Violence;* and Glassner, *Culture of Fear.*

13. For the Bush administration's effort to highlight fear, with direct emphasis on the media, see Michael Massing, *Now They Tell Us: The American Press in Iraq* (New York: New York Review of Books, 2004); and "Buying the War," an episode in the PBS series *Bill Moyers Journal.* Of course, there remains significant debate on the purposes, motives, and extent of the Bush administration's effort, many seeing them as fair and reasonable. Nonetheless, the existence of the effort is not in dispute.

problem, as the schools as well as some journalists clearly reveal the limits of a strongly shared view promoted in the press. Furthermore, the concern about fear may in itself be no problem. One of the most perspicacious readers of my manuscript suggested that journalists and their publishers see their role more benevolently, as erring on the side of warning the public about possible oncoming harm. Many times, the press may play this role, but clearly in these circumstances this view may be challenged. Even if the sniper case coverage was not an over-reaction, the analysis here shows that this type of reporting creates its own peril. In fact, those truly hostile to the media expect the press to remain a central feature of society. Consequently, here and elsewhere, it may be prone to emphasize fear. And certainly, a case can be made that in difficult times, resistance to fear is worth considering. Fear monger-ing by politicians to stampede the public has long been perceived as a political liability of democracies.[14] Likewise, when faced with an impla-cable foe, fear can cause societies to crumble from within. Although ignoring problems provides no solution, it seems worthwhile to under-take discussions, however tentative, of possible approaches to ensure that reporting closely matches the threat envisioned.

As noted previously, state intervention to cure what I perceive as the problem is, in my view, a remedy worse than the problem. Yet the media need to develop internal checks on their own.[15] In this account, the *Post* used a standard of proof; other periodicals relied on ombuds-men; and *Nightline* utilized rigorous procedures for developing stories. Newspapers need to formulate such policies to avoid overreactions that otherwise might occur. Internalization of these same values can also be a part of journalistic training and education. As Jamie Stockwell wrestled with how to report the sniper, some guidelines would have been useful.

Any good study should suggest future projects that can enhance understanding. This book has focused heavily on what was reported and what journalists did in 2002. One excellent way of enhancing this study could be comparing its findings to similar efforts in the press. The complexity and detail of this study explains why I myself did not under-take such analysis of the many comparable explosions in which fear

14. See Richard Hofstadter, *The Paranoid Style in American Politics* (New York: Vintage Books, 1967).

15. For a more detailed discussion of many of these issues, see Peter N. Stearns, *American Fear: The Causes and Consequences of High Anxiety* (New York: Routledge, 2006), 201–24.

dominated the journalistic realism. Recent occasions include the killings by David Berkowitz ("Son of Sam") in New York City in 1977, as well as the sniper attacks in Ohio by Charles A. McCoy in 2003. As Joel Best brilliantly points out, notions like "road rage" and "wilding," now largely forgotten, shook the nation's confidence about a decade ago.[16] While debunking this reality of a crime wave, Barry Glassner showed that such reporting could create shock among the populace.[17] Yellow journalists took a similar approach when considering the sinking of the *Maine* in Havana Harbor in 1898. Perhaps less well remembered than these and many others was the press scare that occurred after World War I and was best characterized by the anti-Communist Palmer raids initiated by the sitting attorney general. These fears also extended to the restlessness of black men who had returned to the United States after serving in the more racially enlightened environment of Europe. Battles erupted across the nation in 1919. For example, in the nation's capital, the *Post* and other newspapers whipped up enthusiasm for the riots that ensued after inflammatory articles about a crime surge in the city that was led by a "black fiend" who allegedly had attacked four white women.[18]

Although highly focused historical analyses of the press comparable to this one do not yet exist, clearly the potential is vast. Producing studies with a comparative dimension would help evaluate the variables that seem to influence the character of the reporting of the sniper. Likewise, the thesis advanced here, that though the reporters did not self-consciously embrace a politicized explanation but produced one just the same, could be reconsidered in light of its wider applicability. In a sense, the use of schools in this study serves as an important comparative point; so might other cases.

Yet another particularly relevant comparative point–post-sniper reporting–is omitted here but deserves at least some attention, even though a full-fledged study could accomplish much more. Even in this embryonic form, such a comparison can add to the value of this study. Studying the press during the sniper incident found an empirical point just as electronic media had begun to proliferate again through the arrival of cable television, especially twenty-four-hour news. Obviously,

16. See Best, *Random Violence*, 1–28.

17. See Glassner, *Culture of Fear*, 1–20.

18. See Robert Whitaker, *On the Laps of Gods: The Red Summer of 1919 and the Struggle for Justice that Remade America* (New York: Crown Publishers, 2008), passim, and especially p. 52.

the earlier inventions of radio and television had marked very important changes in direction. But the study here stands at the beginning of a new technological era–one preceded by a vast expansion of media through the growth of the Internet with its vastly speeded-up news day and the arrival of authors of independent voices through blogs, chat rooms, and personal websites. Moreover, the iPod heralds more rapid dissemination of news and images. By studying this more recent past, we can learn more clearly the precise impact of cable news when it largely stood alone on the innovative frontier. It does not seem too radical to say that much of what the first decade of the twenty-first century has been elaborating was pioneered in the heightened images, hyperbolic headlines, and intense coverage both from cable news and in competitive response from other, more-reserved media, including print and broadcast outlets.

The study also could have, and perhaps should have, considered framing more thoroughly. Partially, my focus here came to consider broadly not only what journalists did in this and other situations, but also what they did not do. I consciously abstained from setting abstract standards for judging the journalism that sprang from these shootings. As such, the response of the schools served as an alternative contemporary response.

To understand other possible courses of action open to journalists requires imagining both a hypothetical and potential situation, an action which makes the scholar a seer or diviner. Despite the risks of this approach, it possesses advantages that may outweigh the problems. In essence, constructing a theoretical realm of the possible permits a far better understanding of the overall frame for reporting.

More use of the notion of framing, developed by leading media analysts Todd Gitlin, Gaye Tuchman, Robert Entman, and Herbert Gans, among others, may be advantageous.[19] The notion of the frame can go beyond the effort here and consider the wide range of assump-

19. See Todd Gitlin, *The Whole World Is Watching* (Berkeley: University of California Press, 1979); Gaye Tuchman, *Making News: A Study in the Construction of Reality* (New York: Free Press, 1978); Robert Entman, "Modern Racism and the Image of Blacks in Local Television News," *Critical Studies in Mass Communication* 7 (December 1990): 332–45; Herbert J. Gans, *Deciding What's News* (New York: Pantheon, 1979); and Jim A. Kuypers, *Press Bias and Politics: How the Media Frame Controversial Issues* (Westport, Conn: Praeger Publishers, 2002). Schudson also describes and documents this viewpoint in his *Sociology of News;* see, especially, p. 216.

tions used and not used. The frame may contextualize the cultural, ethnic, class, racial, economic, and other categories at work. Akin to this comparison in this volume, which evaluated reporting in terms of the response of major public school systems, framing can achieve even more as it allows examination of the entire panoply of assumptions deployed in a story. For example, the entire notion of causality, or the meaning of race, may be tackled. One hopes that this more-complex model might be used on specific cases. Perhaps high-profile reporting, in which society has a stake in the findings, may not be the best place for this sort of analysis. Instead, obituaries, movie reviews, and classified advertisements can all provide fertile ground.

Another topic of consideration for further research concerns relationships within the media. To be certain, as *Washington Post* reporter Jamie Stockwell noted, journalists from different outlets fraternized, especially at Camp Rockville. And as her fellow *Post* reporter Serge Kovaleski and their *Richmond Times-Dispatch* colleagues Mark Holmberg and Andy Taylor observed, relationships included active assistance as well as open competition. Beyond these superficial interchanges were more important interactions in which actual coverage would be generated, either by mimesis or rejection of the approach of others. While some editors and managers interviewed for this study, including Jo-Ann Armao, Steve Hammel, and Rebecca Miller, recalled seeing, hearing, and reading the work of others, they did not remember how that other coverage influenced them. While professional independence may explain this erasure, I have found that the daily rush of putting out copy substantially obliterated this kind of detail. When I interviewed journalists only a year after the sniper incident, their answers could reveal little detail in response. Thus, to address this important subject will require much more proximate research into the reportage.[20] Perhaps the next scholar will be able to attack this problem.

This book has prolonged the life of the sniper case, which, after a long legal process, has likely come to an end with the execution of John Muhammad. Yet Lee Malvo is likely to live many years in prison, and to

20. For a historical example, see Robert Darnton, "An Early Information Society: News and the Media in Eighteenth-Century Paris," *American Historical Review* 105 (February 2000): 1–35. While this scholar could undertake such a study for a historical subject, the number of publications in the twenty-first century is so great that without direct guidance of editors and the like, these relationships will likely remain shrouded.

be the focus of retrospectives for a long time. He may be the focus of studies, totally unforeseen at present, by psychologists interested in child abuse as well as the effects of lifetime imprisonment.[21] Likely, societal fear, though, will not fade any time soon, if ever, and this case and the surrounding reportage will continue to be debated on many levels. If this book contributes to that debate, it will have done so by taking an essentially nonpolitical event and making it a window onto the fears which more than occasionally, for better or worse, plague our political system.

In fact, documenting this intense round of anxiety in October 2002 raises the significance of this book beyond the confines of the study of the press. While the focus here has mainly been to analyze, document, and compare the behavior of the media during an apolitical crisis in order to find the basic nonpolitical notions of the press, studying this particular episode can contribute to the general political history of the period. Fear is not new as a motivation and theme in American history, but its importance has evidently been episodic. In fact, the period following the dramatic attack on American soil on September 11, 2001, set off a cascade of worries, both public and personal. Stoking all this anxiety over the next several years were other attacks, to date mainly in other countries, as well as the efforts of authorities to describe and contain these threats. As many have pointed out, politicians sometimes have used these events to help justify their actions and secure political position. At times, analysts have suggested that such deliberate manipulation was the main factor in raising levels of fear.[22]

But this study, while not wishing to ignore cynical as well as wholly legitimate actions by authorities or to forget the limits on the impact of the press, points out that important apolitical and non-deliberative mechanisms exist in the press that encourage fear. Most important, this study shows how those who wish to engender fear in the American political arena had in the years immediately following September 11 a media that was only too willing to join that bandwagon. In other words, it is an incomplete story to show the fear permeating American society

21. Too recently to be incorporated into this book, Mildred Muhammad published her memoir, *Scared Silent* (Largo, Md.: Strebor Books, 2009). This book does not seem to further the specific purposes of my study, but will likely add to the issues raised as scholars and the public continue to consider the relationship between Muhammad and Malvo.

22. See, e.g., Clyde Haberman in the *New York Times,* July 13, 2007.

as generated only from governmental sources. Whether some of the press always acts in this way or is ineluctably inclined to do so, it did in the particular period at hand. We cannot understand the post-9/11 period without grasping the way that the media works. This study and others like it, make possible a better comprehension of the fear that has characterized American politics during the first decade of the twenty-first century.

# Primary Sources

INTERVIEWS

All interviews are by Jack Censer, unless otherwise noted. Media affiliation is that at the time of the interview. Interviews are in the author's possession.

Anonymous. Cable executive, April 2004.

Anonymous. Print executive, March 2004.

Ackland, Matt. FOX 5, January 2004.

Armao, Jo-Ann. *Washington Post,* December 2003.

Bettag, Tom. *Nightline* (ABC), December 2003 and March 2004.

Bradley, Paul. *Richmond Times-Dispatch,* January 2004.

Buchanan, Michael. WUSA, April 2004.

Bury, Chris. *Nightline* (ABC), March 2004.

Clarke, Ed. Montgomery County Public Schools, November 2003.

Clendaniel, William. Langley High School, October 2003.

Doane, Marty. WJLA, February 2004.

Domenech, Dan. Fairfax County Public Schools, October 2003.

Donvan, John. *Nightline* (ABC), March 2004.

Duggan, Paul. *Washington Post,* November 2003.

Eldridge, Steve. WTOP, March and April 2004.

Ellis, Fred. Fairfax County Public Schools, October 2003.

Farley, Jim. WTOP, March 2004.

Fox, James Alan. Northeastern University, January 2004.

Graham, Don. *Washington Post,* January 2004.

Green, Frank. *Richmond Times-Dispatch,* December 2003.

Hammel, Steve. KPHO (Phoenix television), March 2004.

Heigas, Jen. Marshall Road Elementary School, October 2003.

Holmberg, Mark. *Richmond Times-Dispatch,* December 2003.

Horwitz, Sari. *Washington Post,* January 2004.

Isaacson, Judith. Marshall Road Elementary School, October 2003.

Jabbur, Barbara. Marshall Road Elementary School, October 2003.

Kapsidelis, Tom. *Richmond Times-Dispatch,* December 2003.

King, Kristi. WTOP, April 2004.
Koenig, Lisa. *Nightline* (ABC), March 2004.
Kovaleski, Serge. *Washington Post,* January 2004.
Krishnamurthy, Kiran. *Richmond Times-Dispatch,* January 2004.
Langley High School Teachers. October 2003.
Lloyd, John. Benjamin Tasker Middle School, December 2003.
Mazzarelli, Tom. *Today Show* (NBC), December 2003.
McAllister, Keith. CNN, April 2004.
McMearty, Mike. WTOP, March 2004.
McNamara, Colin. Marshall Road Elementary School, October 2003.
Michael, Sara. *Montgomery (Md.) Journal,* July 2008 (by Lynn Price).
Miller, Rebecca. WJLA, March 2004.
Pennybacker, Gail. WJLA, February 2004.
Porter, Brian. Montgomery County Public Schools, January 2004.
Porterfield, Kitty. Fairfax County Public Schools, November 2003.
Qualls, Ellen. Governor's Office, State of Virginia, December 2003.
Redmon, Jeremy. *Richmond Times-Dispatch,* December 2003 (by Jack Censer) and July 2008 (by Lynn Price).
Robinson, Peggy. *The NewsHour* (PBS), April 2004.
Ruane, Michael. *Washington Post,* December 2003 (by Jack Censer) and July 2008 (by Lynn Price).
Rubin, Elissa. *Nightline* (ABC), March 2004.
Sesno, Frank. George Mason University, February 2004.
Sikka, Madhulika. *Nightline* (ABC), March 2004.
Stockwell, Jamie. *Washington Post,* December 2003.
Taylor, Andy. *Richmond Times-Dispatch,* December 2003 and January 2004.
Tedesco, Russ. Prince George's County Public Schools, November 2003.
Timberg, Craig. *Washington Post,* November 2003.
Van Zandt, Clint. self-employed, January 2004.
Weast, Jerry. Montgomery County Public Schools, December 2003.
Weiss, Eric M. *Washington Post,* July 2008 (by Lynn Price).
Zukas, Phyllis. Marshall Road Elementary School, October 2003.

PRINT MEDIA

*Chicago Sun-Times*
*Houston Chronicle*
*Indian Express* (Mumbai, India)
*Johannesburg Star* (South Africa)
*Le Monde* (Paris)
*Montgomery (Md.) Journal*
*New York Times*
*Richmond Times-Dispatch*
*San Francisco Chronicle*
*Sydney Morning Herald*
*The Australian*
*The Daily Mail* (London)
*The Guardian* (Manchester, U.K.)
*The Witness* (Pietermaritzburg, South Africa)
*Washington Post*
*Washington Times*
*Times of India* (Bangalore)

# ELECTRONIC MEDIA

RADIO
WTOP–1500AM

TELEVISION STATIONS/NETWORKS

| | |
|---|---|
| ABC | NBC |
| CBS | PBS |
| CNBC | WJLA (ABC 7) |
| CNN | WRC-TV (NBC 4) |
| FOX News Channel | WTTG (FOX 5) |
| MSNBC | WUSA9 (CBS) |

TELEVISION SHOWS

| | |
|---|---|
| *Aaron Brown* | *NewsHour* |
| *Abrams Report* | *Nightline* |
| *American Morning with Paula Zahn* | *On the Record with Greta Van* |
| *CBS Evening News* | *Susteren* |
| *Crossfire* | *O'Reilly Factor* |
| *Donohue* | *60 Minutes* |
| *Hannity & Colmes* | *Today* |
| *Hardball* | *20/20* |
| *Larry King Live* | *World News Tonight with Peter Jennings* |

# PUBLIC SCHOOL RECORDS
Fairfax County Public Schools (FCPS), October 2002
Montgomery County Public Schools (MCPS), October 2002

# Bibliographical Essay

The introduction to this book explains the approach, commonly labeled "framing," adopted in this study. Framing is designed to examine the assumptions in the press in a much broader perspective than that of politics. In this essay, I add to this work by providing a retrospective review of those studies, so prevalent and dominant outside universities, which characterize in a contrary way the press as politicized, either as partisan, ideological, or both. Further, that same literature proposes or assumes an unbiased press to replace the flawed one we have. The purpose here is to help the reader understand the context in which this study approaches the media.

To comprehend the literature that focuses on politics, we need to go back in time. Originally, the press existed to express political viewpoints, but the nineteenth and twentieth centuries witnessed a transformation of the public view toward a press free of politics. Indeed, Michael Schudson, in *Discovering the News* (New York: Basic Books, 1978), has pointed out the series of strategies used by the twentieth-century mainstream press to proclaim their objectivity with greater and greater credibility. These strategies have included the installation of higher walls between the reporting and the editorial functions of news operations; the labeling of analysis whenever it was included among news reports; and reporters' elevating almost to the level of a fetish the requirement to always present both sides of every story. The demise of competition in many cities throughout the course of the last one hundred years has contributed significantly to the increased efforts toward objective practices by the news media, especially among reporters and editors of the print media. In such circumstances, newspaper publishers wanted to offend as few readers as possible. They saw the opportunity to sell their products to an entire city, and perceptions of bias could have defeated that commercial objective. For broadcast outlets, which had to defend their reporting against government scrutiny, the process of review and examination also encouraged broad, uncontroversial stands. Moreover, contributing to this increased "objectivity" of the media was the increasing professionalization of the business of gathering and reporting the news, including the formal, and sometimes moral, education of many reporters in college journalism schools all across the country. Despite the embrace of news analysis after the turn of the twentieth century, then, the public seems to have accepted the notion of increasing unbiased news.

It was coverage of the Vietnam War and the fallout from the Watergate break-in that seem to have done the most to encourage the perception that objective approaches in the media were breaking down. Although newspapers in the United States neither returned to proclaiming their political allegiances, as in the early nineteenth century, nor embraced the sensationalism of "yellow journalism," the public nevertheless came to believe that the press had embraced a liberal agenda. This actually may not have been the case, as the critical reporting that observers saw, and themselves criticized, possibly sprang more from the actual failures in Vietnam and the actions of the administration of President Richard Nixon than they did from any bias among reporters and editors. Still, many observers believed that the media appeared to be following a liberal line. Many white Southerners saw this liberalism in the press confirmed by the media's strong support for civil rights, and nationally many came to see all media as liberal. And in fact, many Hollywood renditions of the press–from the general corruption and decadence pictured in *The Front Page* (Warner Brothers, 1931), *Citizen Kane* (RKO, 1941), and *His Girl Friday* (Columbia, 1939), to the liberalism celebrated in *All the President's Men* (Warner Brothers, 1976)–reinforced this view of an emergent liberal press.

Despite these developments in which the public saw the bias or inclinations of journalists as liberal, it was liberals themselves who were among the first to complain about media bias. David Halberstam's book *The Powers That Be* (New York: Alfred Knopf, 1979), probably the most widely read book ever in the history of the press, lauded the actions of the media in Vietnam and Watergate and in doing so began the most recent tendency toward a concern about political leanings. The book itself did not show, or even try to demonstrate, that journalists were political. Rather, Halberstam largely portrayed them as independent seekers of the truth hampered by government officials or conservative publishers. And though the writers Halberstam wrote about triumphed, in his telling, he closed his book with a lament that as these newspapers were transformed from family-owned-and-operated to publicly traded businesses, they would relapse to dutifully carrying an establishment message. Former *New York Times* journalist Ben Bagdikian sounded the same note, even more pessimistically, in *The Media Monopoly* (Boston: Beacon Press, 1983). Thus, the bias that concerned these journalists-turned-journalism-commentators was a conservative one.

These early books were followed by a tidal wave of studies that all shared an important characteristic with them. All the analysts either argued outright or at least implied that they were opposed to bias from any side and simply supported the objectivity of the press. Consequently, while most commentators have taken a left or right stance toward the press, self-descriptions are always presented as being honest, while identifying the other side as evidencing bias.

In fact, the greatest number of analyses of the press focus on political bias and attack its liberal leanings. For example, Jim A. Kuypers's *Press Bias and Politics: How the Media Frame Controversial Issues* (Westport, Conn.: Praeger Publishers, 2002) provides an excellent case study of the assaults emphasizing the press as a liberal fortress seldom penetrated by oppositional views. Kuypers's basic notion is that it is through the framing of stories, rather than direct commentary, that political bias enters in. He points particularly to "sandwiching," an approach in which liberal views encase and detract from conservative ones.

To highlight this tendency, Kuypers devotes separate chapters to media targets from the mid- to late-1990s. For example, Kuypers's second chapter addresses the 1996 remarks by Alabama state senator Charles Davidson regarding the Confederate flag. Starting with a synopsis of the senator's speech and his explanation of his intended content, Kuypers systematically describes the mainstream media's coverage which labeled Davidson a racist and called for his resignation. Kuypers argues that the press transformed the legislator's rather innocuous remarks into a defense of slavery. Kuypers uses the same format to address other controversies surrounding comments made by President Bill Clinton, Mississippi Senator Trent Lott, former NFL player Reggie White, and Nation of Islam leader Louis Farrakhan.

Kuypers's book illustrates well the emphasis on political leanings as a way of understanding the press. Because Kuypers employs the academic notion of "framing" (discussed in more detail in the introduction), one might expect a more-diffused analytical approach that includes non-political factors. But even though he deploys a schema developed by communications scholars, Kuypers primarily uses this approach to demonstrate how political factors predominate.

Bernard Goldberg's *Bias: A CBS Insider Exposes How the Media Distort the News* (Washington: Regnery Publishing, 2000) makes this point even more polemically. Goldberg argues that Dan Rather was a dictator who slanted the news. One of his examples concerns a report (February 8, 1996) in which Rather attacked presidential candidate Steve Forbes's flat-tax platform. Goldberg argues that CBS, by using unfairly selected experts, attacked Forbes. Goldberg makes his views very clear in his introduction:

> The bias I'm talking about, by the way, isn't so much political bias of the Democratic-versus-Republican sort. There is that, for sure, but I know that reporters would tear down their own liberal grandmothers if they thought it would make them look tough and further their careers. For me that isn't the real problem. The problem comes in the big social and cultural issues, where we often sound more like flacks for liberal causes than objective journalists. (22)

A final example of works seeking to document leftist political bias among the media is the interesting book by Stuart Taylor and K. C. Johnson, *Until Proven Innocent: Political Correctness and the Shameful Injustices of the Duke Lacrosse Rape Case* (New York: St. Martins, 2007), that studies the prosecution in 2006 of members of the Duke lacrosse team for rape. Although this book covers many issues, it focuses particular attention on the media role in the case. Like many of the other individuals and institutions involved, the book notes, the press rushed to judgment. While the authors do consider factors other than bias, and in particular discuss the general tendency in the news media to sensationalize coverage, their heaviest focus concerns political inclinations. Like Goldberg, Taylor and Johnson focus not on partisan politics but on social and cultural factors. In an interview on PBS (November 1, 2007), Taylor directly blamed political correctness for the press's siding with the accuser–an African American woman–against the Duke lacrosse players–white, athletic, sons of privilege. For other examples of the same approach, see another work by Jim Kuypers, *Bush's War: Media Bias and Justifications for War in a Terrorist Age* (Lanham, Md.: Rowman & Littlefield, 2006); also Brent Bozell, *Weapons of Mass Distortion: The Coming Meltdown of the Liberal Media* (New York: Crown Forum, 2004); and another book by Bernard Goldberg, *Arrogance: Rescuing America from the Media Elite* (New York: Warner Books, 2003); as well as Bob Kohn, *Journalistic Fraud: How the "New York Times" Distorts the News and Can No Longer Be Trusted* (Nashville: WND Books, 2003).

So well established is the scholarship that sees the media's political leaning as liberal that a number of scholars and analysts have undertaken to counter it. In fact, several commentators on MSNBC, but chiefly Keith Olbermann, position themselves as critics of the too-conservative press, and the radio network Air America largely exists just for that same purpose.

Equally interesting is the effort by Eric Alterman in *What Liberal Media? The Truth About Bias and the News* (New York: Basic Books, 2003). The book articulates the notion that the power of wealthy publishers and the fear of losing advertising from wealthy corporations led to the abandonment of liberal ideas in the press and even unbiased reporting, all to the advantage of conservative reporting. This point parallels that by Bagdikian and Halberstam. As Alterman notes, "The deeply intensified demand for profit places renewed pressure on almost all media outlets to appeal to the wealthiest possible consumer base, which pretty much rules out the poor and the oppressed as the topic of investigative entrepreneurship" (25).

The remainder of Alterman's book demonstrates the general absence of liberalism in the press. Several chapters point out the lack of this political inclination among pundits in every outlet of the media–print, television, radio, and the Internet. The next several chapters analyze reporting. While conceding that reporting on social issues is somewhat mixed, Alterman argues that the economic ideas communicated by the media favor globalism and the like over issues raised by poverty. Furthermore, regarding the "hot button" issues at the turn of the twenty-first century–the Clinton administration, the 2000 election, and George W. Bush and his administration–Alterman argues that conservative views prevailed. He closes his study with a chapter that reinforces the entire previous section on reporting: "the (really) conservative media" avers that even with the strong tilt in reporting, recent years have seen the arrival of a violently conservative and partisan press that allows for little or no variation in its pages, images, or sounds. Underlying much of this has been a ready supply of conservative funding, Alterman says.

Perhaps the sharpest attack on conservative bias emerges from Alexandra Kitty's *Outfoxed: Rupert Murdoch's War on Journalism* (New York: Disinformation Company, 2005). Partly sponsored by the liberal and highly partisan MoveOn.org, this book provides a polemic against FOX News. Kitty argues that from the very beginning, even when Rupert Murdoch had only one station, WTTG in Washington, he wanted to promote a conservative message. In the new network, FOX News Channel, launched in 1996, less effort was put into reporting than to ensuring that conservative ideals underlay all the reporting. Yet that conservative edge often was interpreted, or narrowed, to support Republican positions while excoriating the Democrats.

Oddly, this book, despite its polemical style against FOX's polemics, really does respect FOX News in its capability to drive home its points. In particular, Kitty is fascinated by Bill O'Reilly, the pundit and provocateur who has created both a fan base and a myriad of enemies–and even a spoof on the cable channel Comedy Central. Kitty, who detests O'Reilly and takes pleasure in his every blunder, also believes him to be an intelligent man who knows how to keep his guests totally off-message. As she notes, "Regardless of what his detractors may think of him, O'Reilly is brave, alert, ambitious, daring, capable, intelligent and persistent" (163). She even agrees with some of his stances. But in the end of the book, O'Reilly emerges as a bully who can never be wrong, epitomizing what Kitty wants her readers to believe about FOX.

For other books that see the press as a conservative bastion, consult Edward Hermann and Noam Chomsky, *Manufacturing Consent: The Political Economy of the Mass Media* (New York: Pantheon Books, 1988); Lawrence Lessig, *Free Culture: How Big Media Uses Technology and the Law to Lock Down Culture and Control Creativity* (New York: Penguin Press, 2004); Michael Parenti, *Inventing Reality: The Politics of News Media* (New York: St. Martin's Press, 1993); Sheldon Rampton and John Stauber, *Banana Republicans: How the Right Wing Is Turning America into a One-Party State* (New York: Jeremy P. Tarcher/Penguin, 2004); and James Wolcott, *Attack Poodles and Other Media Mutants: The Looting of the News in a Time of Terror* (New York: Miramax, 2004). See also R. W. Lance Bennett, Regina G. Lawrence, and Steven Livingston, *When the Press Fails: Political Power and the News Media from Iraq to Katrina* (Chicago: University of Chicago Press, 2007), which does not accuse the press of partisan politics, but of becoming conservative by simply accepting the views, without sufficient reflection, of the Bush administration's perspective.

And, finally, there are those who would define the media as sometimes liberal, sometimes conservative, and sometimes holding views not easily categorized by either end of the political spectrum. Indeed, the large wave of scholarship that seeks to characterize the media largely in terms of its political inclinations also includes some studies that view the press as taking a range of positions but never entirely without politics. Howard Kurtz (see his column in the *Washington Post*, November 5, 2007), one of the most influential news critics working today, often finds within the press that there are political biases of various stripes. Yet another study that shows bias, but not from the left or right, is Richard Campbell's *60 Minutes and the News: A Mythology for Middle America* (Urbana: University of Illinois Press, 1991). As the title suggests, this book argues that the show *60 Minutes* begins with a "commonsense" approach, which the author equates with accuracy, and so produces a comforting image of the middle class, which in turn appeals to its viewers in Middle America. From this perspective, *60 Minutes* is politicized, but only as a reaffirmation of a certain set of values that yield coverage from both ends of the spectrum. See also William David Sloan, *Media Bias: Finding It, Fixing It* (Jefferson, N.C.: McFarland, 2007) for an interesting perspective.

The literature summarized here, then, exists, and it currently prevails over a scholarly literature that seeks to transcend, or at least add nuance, to the concern with political bias. Many media scholars do believe that it may be possible to avoid focusing mainly on political issues, at least as defined by contemporary political debate, and in this book I add to that viewpoint. But the book goes further, showing that framing may still need to consider that, although inadvertently, contemporary political issues still play a part and need to be considered.

# Index

Page numbers in boldface indicate biographical notes; those in italics refer to illustrations.